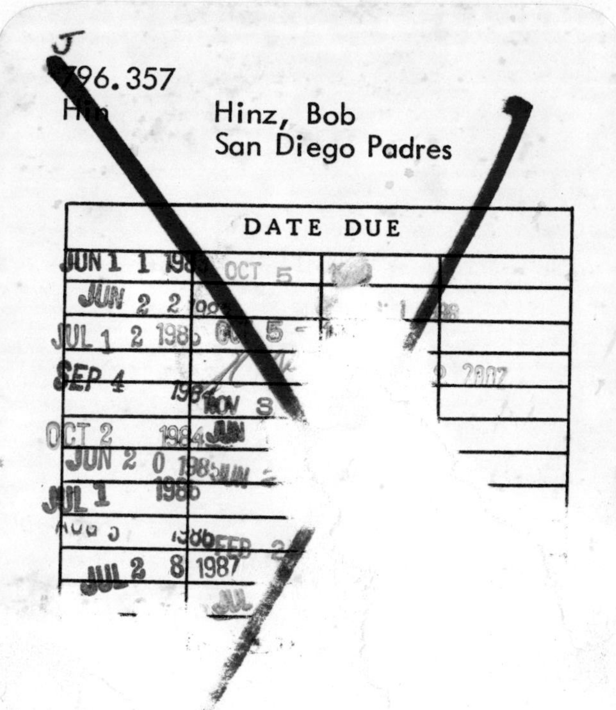

J
796.357
Hin

Hinz, Bob
San Diego Padres

DATE DUE

SAN DIEGO PADRES

BOB HINZ

CREATIVE EDUCATION

MORGAN
8

Big Dave Winfield hits the deck during 1979 action against the Reds. That's
little Joe Morgan going for the tag.

ISBN 0-87191-872-2

SAN DIEGO PADRES

A CLUB ON THE WAY UP

The San Diego Padres are a young ballclub. And an old one.

They're young because they officially entered the National League West in 1969. They're old because their roots go back to the 1930's when they played under the same name in the Pacific Coast League.

The city of San Diego, located at the southern border of sunny California, is a city rich in history and tradition. They named their baseball team after the brave Franciscan Padres — the missionary "fathers" who first settled this region 400 years ago.

As a rookie club in the always powerful N.L. West, the Padres weren't really much of a threat in the early 1970's. Fact is, they lived in the cellar the first six years.

Still, there were moments of sunshine for the Padres fans, even in the beginning. Like the double-header with Atlanta in 1972 when first baseman Nate Colbert blasted five home runs to tie Stan Musial's national league record. During those same two games Colbert got another piece of glory — a new major-league record for hitting 13 RBI.

Like a wild roller coaster ride, the Padres fans found themselves soaring to exciting peaks, followed by frightening dips and plunges. No plunge was worse than the

On this night in 1972, Nate Colbert (right) hit five homers. His 13 runs batted in broke the major league record of 11 for a doubleheader.

AN DIEGO

SF
WEST
420

'73 season when the club nearly left town for good. Here's what happened:

Attendance that year was sagging, so there really wasn't enough money coming in to pay the bills. It looked like the penniless Padres would be sold to buyers in Washington, D.C. Instead, they were rescued at the last minute by the owner of the famous McDonald's Corporation. Ray Kroc, the man who made the Golden Arches and Big Macs world famous, now purchased the Padres. Kroc's magic with fast-food hamburgers and milk shakes also worked at the Padres' box office. In '74, more than a million fans came to San Diego Stadium to see the club play ball.

Though his Padres finished last that first year, Kroc didn't really expect his team to become a championship contender overnight. His plan was for gradual improvement, and it seemed to work. The next year the Padres climbed out of the basement cellar. For the second year in a row, more than a million fans cheered the home club.

It was obvious to Kroc that the people of San Diego loved their baseball and their Padres. He made a commitment to them, then. And they have responded by

Ray Kroc surveys his ivy wall in center field. He also provided a non-smoking section, and special section for the handicapped who need wheelchairs.

supporting his team with a million-plus attendance in each year except the brief 1981 "year of the strike."

In many ways, the story of the modern-day Padres is the story of their gutsy, inspirational owner — Ray Kroc.

"JUST FOR FUN"
RAY KROC RESCUES PADRES

Ray Kroc fell in love with baseball in the Windy City of Chicago in the early 1900's. As a Cubs fan, he knew all the stats on such famous ballplayers as Hack Wilson, Gabby Hartnett, Rogers Hornsby, Stan Hack, Phil Cavarretta and Andy Pafko.

Baseball was important to young Kroc. But so was work. In fact, he dropped out of high school in his sophomore year to work full-time. During the day he sold paper cups. At night, he played the piano for a local radio station. In 1954, when Kroc was selling milkshake mixers, he met two brothers — Richard and Maurice McDonald — who immediately changed his life.

The McDonald's owned a tiny drive-in restaurant that attracted customers like clover attracts the bees. Kroc was amazed to see dozens of hungry people waiting for malteds and hamburgers, to go! Some even waited outside, lined up under two big golden arches.

Race to first. Padres pitcher Juan Eichelberger shows typical San Diego hustle in going after Lee Mazzilli of the Mets in 1981.

Ray Kroc liked what he saw. He asked the McDonald brothers for permission to start similar drive-ins nation-wide. The brothers agreed.

The rest is history. Golden Arches sprang up every-where. Soon, Ray Kroc — the man who had always loved baseball — was a multi-millionaire. What did he do with all that money? Well, in January, 1974, he bought his own professional baseball team — yeah, that's the one — the San Diego Padres!

"I just wanted a hobby," smiled Kroc. "It's an extrav-agant hobby, for sure. I could make more money out of one hamburger stand than I can out of baseball. But I love baseball and I have no interest in money. Never in all my life have I sought money; and yet I've never been poor. The only enjoyment I get out of making money is from the knowledge that people always say, 'If you're so smart, why aren't you rich?' Well, I'm rich, so I guess you could say I'm smart."

Kroc is also a generous man. On his 70th birthday, he gave $7.5 million to charity. Then handed another $9 million in stock to McDonald's employees. That's generosity!

But you still have to wonder. Why the Padres? Why

Padres catcher Gene Tenace closes the door on Houston Astros' Denny Walling. (1980)

buy one of the losingest baseball teams of the modern era? What would Ray Kroc — one of the winningest businessmen in the world — want with such a team?

"I'm in baseball so I can have fun," said Kroc. "Money doesn't have anything to do with it." Which, of course, was the right attitude in those first years as the Padres' new boss.

"I'm not going to be the type of owner who will tell the manager when to pull the pitcher, either," added Kroc. "I'm no Charlie Finley."

In the 1980's Ray Kroc — a spry old guy in his eighties — was still having fun with his Padres. Now, however, he was looking for that big winning season, that first pennant. And maybe, just maybe, a shot at a World Series.

WILLIE McCOVEY:
A LOVABLE LEGEND WITH A BIG BAT

Though the Padres haven't had many legends play for them yet, Willie McCovey is one man no true baseball fan will ever forget. He will be remembered, not so much for what he did for the ballclub. He came aboard in '74 and spent several seasons struggling with his bat. His

Record tieing homer. Willie McCovey is greeted at home plate in 1974 after hitting the 15th grand slam homer of his career. It tied him with Hank Aaron for the National League record.

.203 mark isn't memorable. But Willie's memorable, all by himself.

Willie grew up in Mobile, Alabama. No one's sure what it is about Mobile. The water. The food. The air. Nobody's sure. But Henry Aaron and Billy Williams also grew up in Mobile. And they all played baseball. Boy, did they!

Willie was one of 10 children. His father worked the railroad, while his mother ruled the house with a Bible firmly held in one hand. "We went to church every Sunday," he said, "and nobody ever smoked in front of my parents. Not even when we were all grown up. Of course, I never smoked anyway."

The largest of the McCovey clan, young Willie turned out to be the only sports-minded one in the bunch. He anchored the high school mile relay team, played center on the basketball team, and ran end in football.

Baseball? Central High didn't even have a team, so Willie developed his game on the sandlots with his friends.

Fortunately, a playground director named Jesse Thomas saw Willie in action. Thomas had connections with the San Francisco Giants. And in the winter of '55, the connection was made. The door opened for Willie

Fleet-footed Clarence Gaston roamed the outfield in the dog days of the '70s.

McCovey, and he rushed to a big-league baseball tryout camp.

After a few years of minor league ball, Willie was finally fitted with a Giants' uniform. On July 30, 1959, McCovey stepped to the plate against Robin Roberts, a future Hall-of-Famer. Not impressed, big Willie cracked out two singles and two triples. Never one to disappoint the fans, McCovey ended the year at .354, and was named the National League's Rookie of the Year.

Standing 6'4" and tipping the scale around 220, Willie was an imposing figure at the plate. There wasn't a pitcher in baseball who took Willie for granted more than once. "He's simply the most awesome hitter I've ever seen," said Gene Mauch, manager of the Minnesota Twins.

True enough, Willie's home runs were a thing of beauty, equal to the lost balls credited to such sluggers as Ruth, Foxx, Mantle, Howard, Stargell, Kingman or Luzinski.

Sadly, injuries to the neck, shoulder, arm, hip and leg plagued this lovable athlete. At San Diego, his statistics went up and down like an elevator. A few of the San Diego fans yelled for his retirement. But thousands of others stood loyally by him, lending encouragement to the aging warrior. It was these San Diego fans whom Willie McCovey says he'll never forget. They were the ones

Dave Kingman (bottom) bowls over Cubs second baseman Mick Kelleher to break up double play in 1977 battle.

who kept him going. He went right on rolling, starting his 20th major league season in 1977. Returning to his San Francisco roots, Willie recaptured some of his youthful magic.

That season included 28 homers, 86 RBI and a respectable .280 average. He also shattered Henry Aaron's record for grand-slam homers, belting out his 17th and 18th. Other totals were also mounting up including his 2,000th hit, and his 493rd home run (good for 11th place on the all-time list, tied with Lou Gehrig).

All in all, Willie McCovey had had an amazing season. It had earned for him the Player of the Year award. The old veteran was still loved and respected, especially by his loyal fans in San Diego.

As the '78 campaign opened, Willie and the Giants were to play the Padres. In the clubhouse before the game, a singing telegram was delivered by a kazoo-playing man, and a mechanical monkey, banging its cymbals. Singing to the tune, *Seventy-Six Trombones,* the lyric went:

> *"How d'ya do, Willie McCovey.*
> *The Riviera Rats have asked me here*
> *To express best wishes to you . . ."*

Breaking into laughter, Willie told his teammates

Flamethrower Butch Metzger took a rare break at 1977 Spring Training to pose for this team photo.

"That's from my fan club in San Diego. I used to live on Riviera Drive. The Riviera Rats were my neighbors."

But isn't it odd? Being celebrated by the day's opponents? "Oh no," smiled Willie with an emotional tremble in his voice."They're my friends. They root for me wherever I am." The fans in San Diego are like that.

NEVER SAY DIE!

While many had given up on the '74 Padres (they finished 33 games behind L.A.), the '75 Padres started the season with Ray Kroc's favorite saying on their minds. The sign in the clubhouse read:

"Press on — nothing in the world can take the place of persistence. Talent will not. Nothing is more common than unsuccessful men with talent. Persistence and determination alone are all-powerful."

Forgetting their past as the game's biggest losers over the last six seasons, the Padres jumped up to lead the N.L. West for 12 days in April. Said Manager John McNamara, "Last year we didn't have the talent to stop a losing streak. This year we do."

The "talent" consisted of some awesome young sluggers: Dave Winfield, 23, John Grugg, 26, and Mike Ivie,

With a chaw in his jaw, Dick Selma prepared to take the mound in '69.

22. Oh yes, and one wily veteran by the name of Willie McCovey, who at 37, was still one of baseball's most fearsome batters. Many pitchers would simply pass him to first with four very wide balls.

San Diego pitchers were doing their part, too. Youthful though they were, Dave Freisleben and Joe McIntosh, both 23, and Randy Jones, 25, were definitely handcuffing enemy batters.

Unfortunately the run didn't last. As the season wore on into the long, hot days of summer, the valiant young Padres watched the older, more experienced Cincinatti Reds — the Big Red Machine — run off with the pennant. "Press on," vowed the Padres. "Press on."

RANDY JONES MAKES THE SUN SHINE

One year later, the Padres' were riding the talented arm of an amazing sinkerball specialist who was beginning to shine like the Northern Star. A former Brea, Calif. Pee Wee Leaguer, Randy Jones, 26, had perfected a knee-high strike — the most difficult pitch to hit.

This low-speed sinker, which Jones waffled up to the plate about 70 percent of the time, produced many

Randy Jones, the stern-eyed lefty, shows the form that made him Cy Young Award winner in 1976.

ground balls for the Padres infielders — all easy outs. But throwing the sinker was far from easy.

Jones explained his unusual style: "I always try to release the ball over a bent front leg. On every delivery, I go through certain checkpoints. I have to let the ball go in front of me — not even with my head, but in front of my body. I also make sure I drop down on my back leg, the left leg that's on the rubber, so that I get a good push off the mound.

"Another thing I do is keep my right shoulder in, to get a little more arm speed. And I've got three other things I tell myself 90 times — *to relax, to concentrate and to react to the ball.*"

Jones did all that with amazing speed. In fact, the star pitcher hurried through games under two hours. Like the one he blazed through against the Pirates in '75. It took just one hour, 44 minutes. Randy threw just 68 pitches, including 44 strikes.

If you're wondering about his fastball, yes, he had one. It was clocked about 73-mph on radar, which was 10 mph slower than the average major league fastball, and a good 20-mph slower than Tom Seaver's.

As Padres third baseman Doug Rader joked, "It wouldn't

Gotcha! San Diego's Dave Cash is all smiles as he tags out Bobby Bonds of the Cardinals in 1980.

take Randy so long to pitch a game if his fastball got to
the plate a little quicker." But Jones knew what he was
doing.

"The thing is, if you throw a sinkerball too hard, it
doesn't sink," he said. "There's a perfect speed for the
pitch that will make the ball move best for you. So my
purpose actually is not to throw hard, because the har-
der I throw, the less effective the pitch."

No one argued with the young star, who was 20-12 in
'75, including a brilliant save in the annual All-Star
Game. Oh, yes, Jones also turned in the National League's
best ERA that year — a fine 2.24. Randy's performances
sparked the Padres, but they still finished 25 games
behind Cincinnati in '76, and 23 games off L.A.'s hot pace
in '77. Fortunately, the best was yet to come.

ROLLIE'S PICTURE WORTH A THOUSAND WORDS!

Rollie Fingers wasn't having his best year as a reliever
in '78, but the Padres were still fighting for a respectable
fourth in the N.L. West, with a 46-50 record. Still, it
looked like their 10th losing season was about to go on
the books, after 10 years in the league.

Then one night after a game, Rollie Fingers found

The one-and-only Rollie Fingers had a lot to smile about in 1979. Fingers is
one of baseball's all-time relief pitchers.

himself brooding alone in his trophy room at home. He happened to glance up at some old photographs taken when he was tossing fire for the Oakland A's. Suddenly, Rollie noticed something strange — like a clue in a mystery:

Rollie saw that his pitching hand was breaking out of his glove differently now than before. He looked closer, and found his glove was at his waist the moment he broke his hands apart.

"I realized my glove was higher up this season, around my chest," he said. By Finger's own estimate, that small mistake had been costing him about 10-mph in ball speed. Just what the hitters needed for an edge on the pitcher with the big mustache.

At 6'4" and 190 pounds, Rollie had become the premier reliever of the '70s. Those long, strong arms, when fully extended, served up a totally frustrating series of curves, sliders and fastballs. But he had begun to lose that magic, before the photo clue appeared.

Now, he went to work. For a solid month, Rollie pitched scoreless baseball. The fans were delighted. But no one was happier than Padres pitcher Gaylord Perry, the club's father-figure at age 39.

Gaylord Perry wins twentieth game of the 1978 season at the age of 40.

SD
AN DIEG
San Die

Acquired in an off-season trade from Texas, Perry had a fine '78 record, taking 15 of 21 decisions. But he had only three complete games. Eight of his wins came courtesy of Mr. Fingers.

"Never in my 16 seasons have I had the good fortune of having a pitcher like Fingers in my bullpen," said Perry.

Fingers, in turn, was grateful for 23-year-old Ozzie Smith, the Padres' second baseman. "One of the keys to my success over the years has been my shortstop," said Rollie. When he was with Oakland, Bert Campaneris picked up those ground balls. "Smith makes plays that Campy could never have made."

Signed before the '77 season to a $1.6 million Padres contract, Rollie wasted little time proving he was worth every quarter. He came on to save 35 games, and was named the National League's Fireman of the Year.

Consistency is his secret. "I learned how to preserve my arm by watching Mudcat Grant in Oakland," he said. "If the pitcher in the game gets out of a jam while I'm warming up, I sit down. If he gets in trouble again, I only soft-toss the ball in the bullpen, knowing I have eight pitches waiting for me on the mound. A lot of relievers burn themselves out in the bullpen."

A favorite with the fans, infielder Ron Slocum gave his all in 1970.

Well, it was a good year for Rollie and the Padres. They climbed the N.L. West ladder, coming within 14½ games of the powerful Dodgers. And, while there was still room for improvement, the fans appreciated what they saw.

THE PADRE WHO NEVER QUITE BLOOMED, BUT WALKED AWAY A MILLIONAIRE

Another popular attraction with the fans was Dave Winfield, a superb athlete who came to the club in '74 directly from the '73 College World Series, where he had pitched and played outfield for Minnesota. Even though they lost to USC, Dave got the MVP award.

"He was the best athlete I'd seen in all my life," said Padres coach Don Williams. Others thought so, too. Three other pro teams drafted him: the Minnesota Vikings of the National Football League; the Atlanta Hawks of the National Basketball Association; and the Utah Stars of the American Basketball Association.

When Dave and his mother, Arline, finally decided on the baseball career, the San Diego fans were delighted. Deep down inside, however, Dave knew he wasn't ready. Without any minor league play, he said, "I was seeing

In 1979 action, Kurt Bevacqua goes for another steal.

CKNER
2
padres
7

pitches I'd never seen before. I was playing in a ballpark the size of an airport. I was getting my legs all tangled up in the outfield. I was holding my hands too low on the bat — hitching my swing, overstriding, overswinging."

Dave Winfield learned professional baseball the hard way. "I became famous for my half-seasons," he said. In '75, his first-half stats read: .280, 9 homers, 43 RBI. In the second half: .255, 6 homers, 33 RBI. Both '76 and '77 looked like carbon copies.

Then in '78 he appeared to turn it around, going .302 with 15 homers and 59 RBI in the first half; and .315 with 9 homers, and 38 RBI in the second.

Dave said his secret was new-found concentration. To properly motivate himself, he'd been watching Pete Rose. "You watch a guy like Pete," laughed Dave, "and you realize his concentration lasts from April 1 to Oct. 1 and beyond. He's good all the time. So are Steve Garvey and Dave Parker. They are there constantly.

"It's a matter of telling yourself that, you, too, are there, that you are one of the best."

Dave Winfield never doubted that fact. Even when his 1980 stats dipped to .276, 20 homers and 87 RBI, he still believed in himself.

Ed Spiezio looks more like a choir boy than a fleet-footed Padres infielder. (1969)

Some of the fans continued to believe in Dave. But then the club fell 19½ games behind Houston, and disappointment set in. When it came time for San Diego management to negotiate a renewal of Winfield's contract, Dave wanted more money.

Management balked. And as the rules of the game say, "take your base." Winfield walked out as a free agent, and strolled right into a millionaire's contract with George Steinbrenner's New York Yankees. A San Diego superstar was gone, but the Padres were much too busy the following year to waste time looking back.

A WINNING MANAGER BRINGS NEW HOPE TO SAN DIEGO

One thing's certain about the Padres' baseball team: They'll never be the same after living with a winner named Dick Williams, the guy who became their manager in 1982.

"Mr. Williams," as some refer to him, is the fourth winningest active manager in major league baseball. With 14 years to his credit, Williams had tallied 1,045

At the '81 winter baseball meetings, San Diego Manager Dick Williams shakes hands with Expos Manager Jim Fanning.

victories going into 1982. The only men to better that mark are Gene Mauch (California Angels), Ralph Houk (Detroit Tigers) and Earl Weaver (Baltimore Orioles).

San Diego fans have to be happy about their new manager. Williams has been on a tear since '67, when his Boston Red Sox roared to a 92-70 record, taking the American League pennant. He literally lifted the Sox from cellar-dwellers to the top.

Williams is a tough man who believes in no-nonsense baseball. At Boston, he told the players he believed in stealing bases, proper execution of simple plays, bed checks and curfews! The players groaned. They also started winning.

There was more to come. In 1972 and '73, Williams finest single season took the Oakland A's to back-to-back world championships. His tour of duty with the A's also included a '71 pennant, as the team rolled to a 101-60 record, Williams finest single season mark.

He went on to make a solid contender of lowly little Montreal from '79 through '81.

"The situation in San Diego is very similar to what I found when I went to Montreal in '77," said Williams. Actually the Expos were digging their way toward China with 107 losses in '76. The Williams' effect produced 75

Gettin' home San Diego's Jerry Turner slides safely home despite a big effort by Mets' catcher John Stearns. (1979)

STEALING HOME
It isn't a trademark of the Padres ballclub, but Jerry Turner did it in '81 against the Cubs. Before that, home thievery had been ignored except for when Rich Morales did it against the Cubs on June 18, '74.

wins his first year; by the third year, the Expos had rallied to 95 wins, finishing a mere two games behind the league leader!

Dick Williams did his homework before accepting the Padres position. "This club has an abundance of good, young players that need to develop," he said. "I did some research on San Diego's minor league talent and I'm impressed by what I see. I know the organization is going in the right direction by developing our own talent. We'll start developing a winning habit the first day of spring training."

Believe it. That's the only way Dick Williams knows. His career as a manager proves that: .536 with American League teams; .519 with National League teams.

Before he turned manager, he enjoyed a fine playing career with stints at Brooklyn (the original Dodgers' home), Baltimore, Cleveland, Kansas City and Boston.

Now facing yet another career challenge, Williams believes (and the fans hope) he can produce yet another winner. Most agree that his arrival is the best thing that's happened to the Padres since Ray Kroc.

The Padres roared into the '82 season with guys like Rick Wise on the roster.

HIGH HOPES FOR THE '80s!

Things are looking up in San Diego. They improved their record in '81, coming within 14½ games of Houston. In '82, they were back for more.

Excitement continued to build as a number of Padres reached out for personal records in their major-league careers:
* John Curtis pursuing his 500th strikeout in the National League;
* Rupert Jones going for his 2,000th base;
* Gene Richards trying to steal his 200th putout;
* Rick Wise going for his 200th major league win;
* Gary Templeton driving in his 300th RBI.

"He's the best shortstop I've ever seen," said manager Dick Williams, watching Templeton scoop up balls in the infield. Replacing Ozzie Smith who went to the Cards, Templeton, a .305 career hitter, likes his new ballclub. "I'm doing more here than I did in St. Louis," he said, "I'm using all the talent I have, not just parts of it."

That's what Williams wants from his Padres. He wants 'em strong on fundamentals, and fast on the bases. Templeton will deliver, as will outfielders Billy North and

Ruppert Jones could well be a future Hall-of-Famer. (1982)

Gene Richards. What they need is more power hitting. Joe Lefebvre had eight of the nine Padres homers in the 55 home games played in '81. Management decided to cut the 17-foot-high outfield fence in half to help the hitters. But it helps the opponents, too!

"Pitching and defense are what wins games," says Williams. They've got a good starter in Juan Eichelberger, and an excellent lefty reliever in Gary Lucas, who was 7-7 in '81 with a 2.00 ERA and 13 saves in 57 appearances.

Experience seems to be the answer. It's something the San Diego Padres have been gaining lots of since they began back in '69. Their story is a bit like leftfielder Gene Richards' story. Since '77, Richards has started hitting like a pussycat in April. (.140, .234, .235, and 173); then when September rolls around, he turns into a tiger for the rest of the season (.350, .378, .333, and. 333.)

What Richards and his Padre teammates need to do is get that tiger personality into their performance from Opening Day to the Playoffs. With a man like Dick Williams managing the club, that's sure to happen soon.

Rangy infielder Rafael Robles bit his lip in concentration during 1969 Spring Training.

SD
PADRE

Padres infielder Gary Templeton helped anchor the determined San Diego squad in 1982.

DALLAS
A PHOTOGRAPHIC CHRONICLE
REDISCOVERED:
OF URBAN EXPANSION 1870–1925

WILLIAM L. MCDONALD

THE DALLAS HISTORICAL SOCIETY, DALLAS, TEXAS

PREFACE

The history of the city of Dallas has been, from its inception, an embodiment of the uniquely American ideals of nineteenth-century capitalism — those concepts of individual initiative, competition, the profit motive, and the right to private ownership of property, which were understood to be tempered by Christian charity and virtue. From the moment John Neely Bryan staked out his ten-block townsite, his overwhelming motivation was to make a profit on the small portion of the great American frontier he had claimed, thereby reaffirming not only the traditions of his Scottish and Irish forefathers but also his inalienable right to "life, liberty, and the pursuit of happiness."

The vast, unclaimed wilderness of the American West was in great part what nurtured the pioneer capitalists' aggressive self-interest; as Frederick Jackson Turner pointed out, as long as free land existed, there was opportunity for a man to acquire property and status — and thus economic and political power. Dallas, as a frontier town, was a microcosm of this evolutionary process of movement ever westward and of conquering a continent in the American experience. The city was founded, propelled, and sustained by a series of strongly independent, profit-seeking men who had few doubts about the moral rightness of capital advancement. These men, along with a few, powerful Eastern backers such as J.P. Morgan, Jay Gould, Adolphus Busch, and Pierre duPont, created Dallas out of open prairie as a monument to these nineteenth century ideals.

Yet by the 1890s, the frontier had essentially vanished. Most of the non-arid free lands were gone and the unrestrained, monopolistic actions of the robber barons, railroad lords, and land developers had begun to conflict sharply with the ideals of Karl Marx and his successors. Faced with the limitations of a vanishing frontier and spurred by the destructive potential of advancing technology, the reformers of the turn of the century confronted the real conflict between the welfare of the community and the freedom of the individual.

Like other American cities, Dallas considered and experimented with this philosophical turn away from unlimited individual freedom. The extremes of self-motivated developers and speculators like Bryan, McCoy, Marsalis, and Field began to be replaced by civic leaders and planners such as Gaston, Armstrong, and Kessler — men with a greater sense of community and social responsibility. But, inevitable and far-reaching as this process might have been, it had little more than a passing effect on Dallas. In most respects, the city has retained the older values of the American frontier even as it has leaped forward to embrace the twentieth century and all of its technological wonders. Today, Dallas stands as one of this country's last, relatively unrestrained centers of individualism and free enterprise.

The purpose of this book is to show, through the visual reference of hundreds of early photographs, the face of Dallas' urban environment as it was shaped by this frontier ideology during the critical years of formation and development between the arrival of the railroads and the mid-1920s. Dallas is explored through its architecture, its system of spatial growth and land utilization, and through the developers, land speculators, and urban designers who were so extremely important to the creation of the modern city.

The book focuses on the wealthy, the landed, and the influential members of the early Dallas community for two reasons. First, because of their economic positions, these people had the most far-reaching and long-range effect on the shaping of Dallas' physical environment. Secondly, the lack of photographic documentation of the less affluent districts made a detailed examination of these areas very difficult. *Dallas Rediscovered* is not intended as a definitive history of the city, but rather as a starting point for future urban scholars.

W. L. M.
Dallas, 1978

CONTENTS

INTRODUCTORY ESSAY

Land speculator, colonizer, real estate promoter, developer, agent: whatever you call him, he is an American folk figure who has had more influence on the way we live than all the mountain men, the cowboys, or the Civil War generals who have had ballads sung or books written about them.

Real estate promotion and development, as we know the process, is an American invention, brought about by the enormous subcontinent of free land that comprised the United States in the nineteenth century. The new nation wanted people to own land—citizen and immigrant alike—and made acquisition as easy as possible. In contrast, buying land in the Old World was a forbidding ritual, with royal approval implicit, and laws of entail which kept property in the same family, or same class, for hundreds of years, holding values at the same level because there was no market in lands. Thus, only in the United States did that ubiquitous symbol, the real estate agent, spring to life and so often guide our collective and individual history.

The way land changed hands — who gained possession of it and what they tried to do with it — has, from their beginnings, created the fate of virtually every American city west of the Mississippi — and a high percentage of those to the east, even the ones that derived their origins from royal grants and proprietary charters.

Nowhere in the United States has this been truer than in Texas. Stephen F. Austin, the so-called father of the Lone Star State, operated under a rather grand Spanish title, *empresario* (one who undertakes to do, on his own account, business of great importance), but was actually a land promoter, offering generous chunks of Mexican Texas to lure outsiders to come settle so that he, in turn, could profit from his undertaking.

When formed in 1836, the Republic of Texas's only capital asset was land, and its main business became not Indian fighting but land development; what Texas needed more than anything else was people: people in huge numbers to come pouring in and take over public land so that taxes, customs, and fees would build up the treasury. When the Republic joined the United States in 1846 it retained ownership of all its public land, making the State of Texas the nation's largest land promoter, aside from Uncle Sam himself.

And in Texas, no city was so conceived and created as a real estate promotion, and no city has been so controlled in its civic and municipal directions by land development, as has Dallas. The fact that there were no geographical features to arrange or confine city growth (only the Trinity River has had much effect) hastened the process. Houston, for example, began as a real estate project by the Allen brothers, but the natural features of the area led to its extensive port waterway and then to the type of industry that both blocked and redirected city growth. Real estate development, more than all physical factors or industrial locations combined, has guided the tide of Dallas. And the developer's control of life and lifestyle was even more absolute a century ago than it is today, because a century ago the municipal government offered no public transportation, no paved streets, no protection from the vagaries of nature or industry. It scarcely offered police or fire protection. If you wanted these amenities, it was the developer who offered them. So, the city went where the speculators and promoters forced, coaxed, or bargained it to go.

This is a facet of Dallas history which has been mainly overlooked by historians and other social chroniclers. Nearly all have noted various real estate developments: the Cedars, Oak Cliff, Munger Place, Highland Park — but none has inspected the why of movements and directions, the importance of such things as the location of streetcar lines, or public parks, and how it all made Dallas into the entity it has become — not just geographically, but politically and, to an even greater extent, philosophically. In Dallas, as in few cities, where you live can quite accurately express how you feel about all of the above.

So, let us go back to a historical beginning for the place which will someday be called *Dallas*; set the stage for this city which, some have claimed, had no reason to be where it is, much less thrive.

The area metropolitan Dallas embraces was late coming to history's attention. It had been known, in a general way, as Forks of the Trinity, or Three Forks, at least as early as the mid-1700s, but the nineteenth century was well under way before a few travelers made any notes concerning the lay of the land or its Indian inhabitants.

The most noticeable feature of the Three Forks country was, of course, the river. However, that stream was not notable for any particular landmark; it was not navigable, even by canoe; and the tribes that lived along its upper reaches were agricultural and non-nomadic, with little to barter to traders, who were primarily after furs, but also precious stones and metals. As for that, no legends of gold and silver, or even freshwater pearls, seem to have attached themselves to the fertile river bottoms where the Kadohadacho (Caddo) lived in conical grass-roofed huts.[1] Only in indirect ways did the Three Forks lie between important white settlements, and even as late as the 1830s it was far beyond the line of Texan settlement . . . so, the region lay undisturbed for decades at a time, so far as the rest of the Southwest was concerned.

The first Europeans who visited the site of Dallas were probably Luis Moscoso and the tattered remnant of Hernando De Soto's expedition, who wandered across the area in 1542 in an attempt to reach Mexico, after burying their dead leader in the Mississippi.[2] The Caddoes called the Trinity "Daycao" and warned Moscoso that on the western side the people spoke a different language, were of a rude culture, and lived in miserable hovels[3] (which sounds remarkably like a Dallas view, some 350 years later, of Fort Worth).

Alonso de Leon in 1689 named the Trinity — in Spanish, *La Santisima Trinidad,* after the Holy Trinity.[4] But he crossed the river near the coast, more than 200 miles below the Three Forks, and never knew his religious name coincided with the tri-branched upper formation.

The Dallas area saw more of the French than the Spanish during its mysterious past. By 1715 the French (who owned Louisiana — which included what is now Oklahoma and Arkansas) were pushing up the Red River, establishing posts and sending out far-ranging traders and explorers — all of which enraged Spanish authorities, who feared France was trying to take over Texas and New Mexico as well. Severe measures were taken to thwart French intrusion, and the Spanish began trying to settle the neglected province of Tejas. But Spanish laws and Spanish prisons failed to stop the French traders. One, Jean Baptiste Bénard de la Harpe, had the effrontery to offer the Spanish missionaries in Texas a five-percent commission on any business they sent him, and urged him "tell your friends." (More than one priest took him up on it.)[5]

The most colorful of the French traders (and one who undoubtedly visited the site of Dallas more than once) was Louis Juchereau de St. Denis. In 1714, this handsome young cavalier and a party of Louisiana French and Tejas Indians, made a 700-mile trading trek across Texas to San Juan Bautista, located in Mexico near Eagle pass and Mexico's grandest northern presidio (San Antonio, recall, hadn't been established).

St. Denis and his party were immediately made prisoner by Captain Diego Ramón, the presidio commander, but as one historian notes, "The Frenchmen did not find their incarceration irksome, for they were surrounded by persons of culture and breeding . . . linen . . . silver . . . and white women." Among whom was the captain's granddaughter, Mañuela (or Emanuelle; she was half French), said to be the most beautiful girl in all the northern provinces. Despite the fact he was an enemy and she was engaged to marry the governor of Coahuila, St. Denis eventually escaped from prison in Mexico City, married her, and stole her across Texas, back to Louisiana.[6]

Emanuelle lived with her trader husband out on the Texas prairies for months at a time. Another trader's account described what is believed to have been an encounter with St. Denis and Emanuelle: "He was a tall man (whose) only garment was a pair of trousers. I saw a woman, crouched to make fire . . . she was pretty and had a graceful smile (her) only garment, a corsage [bodice] and skirt . . . the corsage was so torn that her breasts were entirely visible. I saw two naked children . . . and was entertained at dinner with furniture and eating utensils most primitive." But the traveler said he observed a fine doublet and sword on the wall — and he sold St. Denis some red silk embroidered stockings for Emanuelle.[7] Every mention of Emanuelle points out her astonishing beauty, whether dressed for French society or like a savage. She bore St. Denis eight children. I think we should be allowed to place her and her cavalier at Three Forks from time to time as they moved across East and North Texas. Dallas, historically speaking, always seemed to attract pretty women.

The French traders eventually established a sort of headquarters at the Taovaya villages on the Red River in present-day Montague County. The Taovayas (or Wichitas) were at that time the "merchant" Indian tribe in the Texas-Oklahoma area. This post drew not only French traders, but Spanish soldiery to the Forks of the Trinity.[8]

When France turned Louisiana over to Spain in 1762, many of the French officials were retained, swearing allegiance to the Spanish king. One of the most valuable of these servants was Athanase de Mézières, French-born son-in-law of St. Denis. Despite internal opposition, he led Spanish policy toward the Indians and very probably camped somewhere near the same bluff above the Trinity that John Neely Bryan would stake out in 1841. De Mézières died just as he was appointed governor of Texas in 1779.[9]

But from about 1780 there is little regarding travel in Three Forks. A few Anglo-American adventurers began crossing, after the United States made the Louisiana Purchase in 1803, and in 1837 a group of Texas Indian fighters, who had been badly whipped near Decatur, waded up from the Trinity and camped for several days to recuperate at a spring where the Santa Fe building would someday stand (but nineteen feet below present-day ground level).[10]

The dark curtain of history was lifted, however, for the final time in 1841 when a Kentucky group carrying the name *The Texas Agricultural, Commercial and Manufacturing Company* was given the right, by the Republic, to settle non-Texan families within a grant which, by first contract (August 1841) didn't include Dallas, but by the fourth (January 1843) extended from the Red River south through Dallas County and westward for 160 miles.[11]

The cumbersome initial name was changed to *Texas Emigration and Land Co.,* but even this became known as, simply, *The Peters Colony* (for W.S. Peters and family, the prime investors). Heads of families were offered 640 acres of land (bachelors, 320) if they would come, build a cabin, fence fifteen acres, and stay for three years. The company was to be given specific amounts of premium land for each 100 families it brought to Texas, and it guaranteed to settle 600 families within three years.

The arrangement never worked well. In 1852 settlers staged a "war" (led by men from the non-Peters Colony town of Dallas) to drive out the company agent, ingrant — and the incorporators themselves made little, if any, profit.

But the Peters Colony did several things for Dallas: it brought a rush of settlement to the Three Forks, it opened the world's eyes to the potential of the region (the colony was widely advertised in the United States and Europe), it drew a number of names to the area which remain important today, and most consequential, it established a pattern of land development and control which, coupled with frontier attitudes toward commercial exploitation, contributed directly to the dimensions of Dallas leadership down to present times. The Peters Colony used land as bait, sheer numbers as its measure of success, and through its contracts with the Republic and the State, its agents had an authority that made them the equal of, or superior to, the elected local officials: the developer as benign monarch.

In its beginning, Dallas had only one prime commodity: land. Most of the people who came to the region came because of the ready availability of land (if not free, cheap) and not because of some natural resource or emerging major industry. Even agriculture, the biggest vocation, did not turn as many dollars per year as did land sales. To support this profitable structure, it was only a step to the beginnings of the second major economic factor in the growth of Dallas: high finance. Land sale and development naturally calls for fiscal stages of growth far beyond the simpler transactions of buy-and-sell. Lawyers, surveyors, title companies, must certify to the correctness of each step in a land sale. Interim financing has to be arranged when larger sections are developed, and the ultimate changing of hands of houses and lots adds costly intricacies to the process. The financing of new construction and the handling of mortgages can be an even larger financial undertaking. The Dallas insurance business began to be a major source of power for the commercial developers by the turn of the century, and the emergence of the Dallas banks — many forming the roots of the modern financial giants — had begun a decade or more earlier, offering the kind of support necessary for turning raw land into residential sections and industrial sites.

What this did was make the developer not only a citizen of means but a leader of immense proportions of control. He was looked on not as a promoter but as a provider, and no spot or acreage — be it farm, forest, or park — was beyond his reach. Dallas, until the beginning of World War II brought the aviation plants, had no industries of a size or scope to form automatic community leadership. Wholesale distribution and mercantiling, while involving enormous sums which made them increasingly important to the banks, faced internal competition which diluted unified aims for public direction. Besides, even the merchants seldom made the kind of direct effect on human life and environment that real estate did.

The developer, backed by banks and insurance companies, designed the destiny of Dallas — and by literal extension created the community atmosphere of most of most of the region now popularly described as "The Metroplex." One reason Dallas municipal government has not had two-party politics can probably be attributed to the fact that land development calls for a predictable, if not placid, city hall. Zoning decisions must not make wide swings over the years or be based on emotional or social issues. On the other hand, real estate development depends on mutual understanding and a certain level of trust and honesty (bribery and hidden influence upsets everybody) within municipal government, and abhors the sudden changes inherent in party politics.

Ultimately, no matter how much some of them may complain about "those damn developers," most property owners feel the same way — and Dallas, to this point at least, is still a city of property owners and would-be property owners. Local land investment is about as safe and productive a way as any to lay out capital. Dallas takes it for granted that a profit will be made, whether it is selling a one-family residence or putting together vast parcels of land for commercial purposes. And as long as this is true, its history will be written, in large part, by its developers.

A. C. GREENE

DALLAS REDISCOVERED

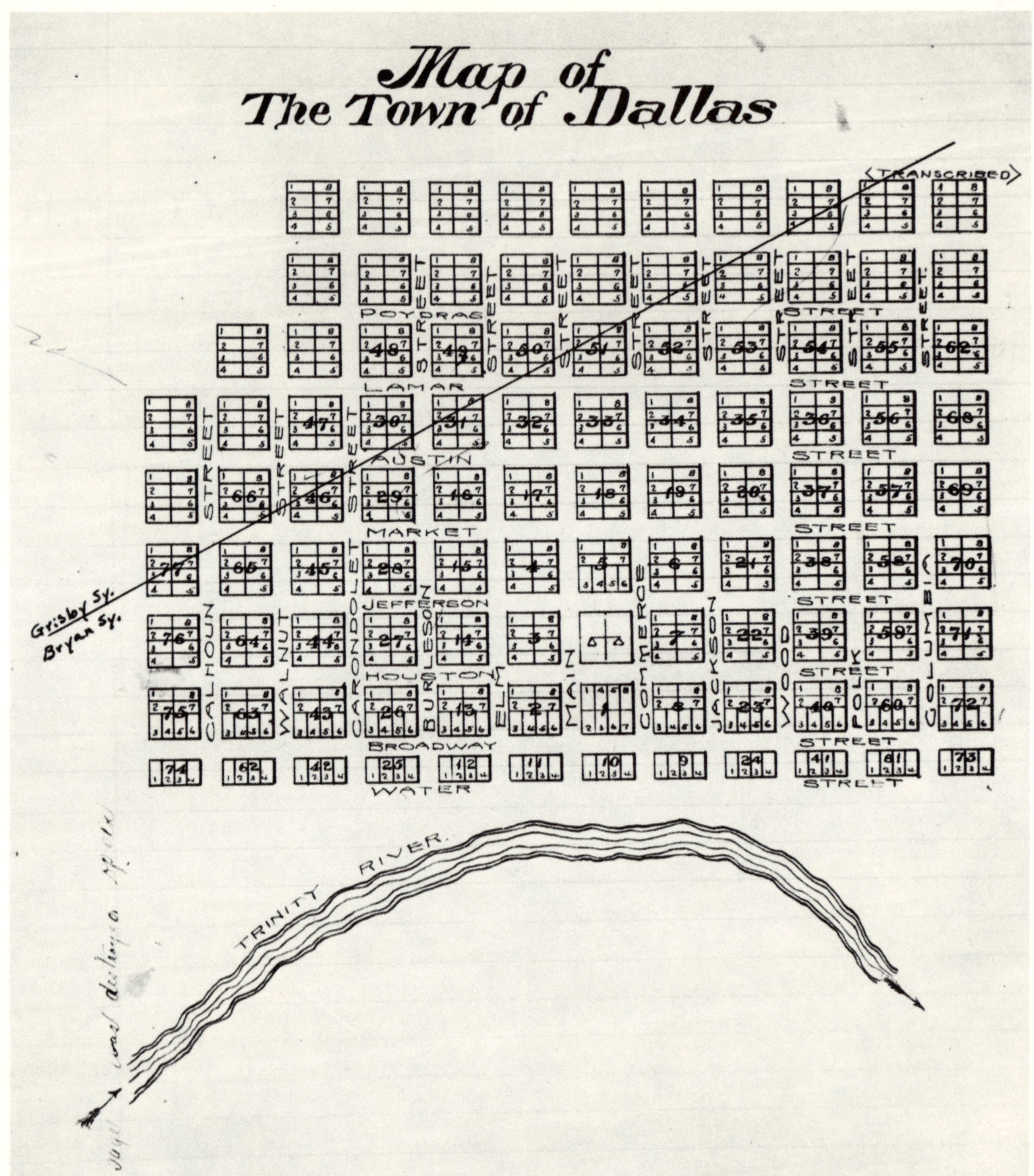

1. PLAT MAP OF BRYAN'S TOWNSHIP, c. 1850

1 EARLY YEARS 1839-1872

In the late fall of 1841, as the Peters Colony Company was securing its second charter with the new Republic and making preparations to begin luring thousands of new settlers into the wilds of North Texas, a restless adventurer named John Neely Bryan was making his way toward a bluff overlooking the Trinity River with the single-minded intention of starting a town.

Bryan, whom folklorist Frank Tolbert described as "a great-hearted frontier lawyer, wilderness scout, and close friend of Sam Houston as well as the wildest Indian," had originally wandered into Texas from Arkansas as early as 1839, drawn by the tantalizing tales of the lands to the south of the Red River and by a desire to establish a trading post to barter with the native Caddo Indians for hides and pelts. He immediately recognized that the area known as the Three Forks was a natural crossroads in the wilderness, one of the few sites for hundreds of miles with the potential for commercial and economic exploitation.

The present-day Dallas mythology, which maintains that the city came out of nowhere and had no real reason for being, simply ignores the inevitability of Bryan's choice. The land that drew his attention in the fall of 1839 was the crossroads of two major Indian traces, which carried hunting parties north and west into buffalo territory and linked the culturally related Caddo tribes to the south and east; an ideal site for Bryan's purposes.

Bryan, who shared Sam Houston's insight into the usefulness of Indian customs, must also have realized that these Caddo traces intersected at one of the few natural fords for hundreds of miles along the wide Trinity floodplain. At "Bryan's Bluff" the river,

which was an impassable barrier of mud and water between late fall and early spring, narrowed like an hourglass over a formation of Austin chalk, providing a hard rock ford suitable for commercial traffic as well as Indian crossings.

A similar wisdom was employed by Colonel William G. Cooke, who in 1840 officially surveyed the Preston Trail (commissioned by the Texas Congress in 1838) along the outline of the northern Caddo trace. Running from Fort Preston on the Red River, directly through Bryan's claim to South Texas, where it joined the Old Spanish Trail (Old San Antonio Road) at its crossing of the Nueces River, the Preston Trail formed the only link between North and South Texas. Bryan's luck was further enhanced in 1844 when the Congress of the Republic authorized construction of the National Central Road, another major frontier highway which tracked from a point on the Preston Trail one half-mile north of Bryan's crossing northeast toward Paris to the mouth of the Kiamichi River in Red River County. This highway created an overland connection between St. Louis and San Antonio, making Dallas' position at the fork of the National Road and the Preston Trail an important landmark for the great throng of immigrants and settlers who eventually converged at Bryan's ferry.

After marking his claim with a stick and some rocks, John Neely Bryan temporarily returned to Arkansas. Before he could return to the banks of the Trinity River to settle permanently, however, two important incidents changed the status of Bryan's claim. The first was the battle of Village Creek in May of 1841. In this, the last major armed skirmish with Indians in the Three Forks area, General Edward H. Tarrant and seventy Texas Rangers destroyed two Caddo encampments, forced the westward retreat of these natives, and established Bird's Fort to protect the new settlements to the east. This action terminated any ideas John Neely Bryan might have had about establishing an Indian trading post, and as a result his only concern when he returned to the area in 1841 was to lay the foundations of what would later become the city of Dallas.

The second incident was the signing of the Peters Colony Company's second contract on November 9, 1841. This contract granted the company control of over 16,000 square miles of rich, North Texas farmland for the purpose of colonizing and settling the vacant and unappropriated lands of the republic. Bryan, who had come to Texas independently and apparently without knowledge of the existence of the Peters Colony Company, quickly found himself without legal recognition for his claim; in effect, he had become a squatter on company lands.

To complicate matters further, the Republic of Texas had previously granted a headright of a "league and labor" of land (4,605 acres), to John Grigsby about 1837 for his service as a veteran of the War for Texas Independence and the Battle of San Jacinto. Grigsby's claim overlapped Bryan's, effectively reducing it from the usual 640 acres to 580. The conflict was not resolved until 1854 when the Peters Colony Company finally abandoned its claim to Bryan's narrow strip of riverfront property, allowing him to patent his claim. However, this did not resolve the problem of Grigsby's prior claim to the adjacent property to the east, which he surveyed and patented independently of the Peters Colony Company in 1842.

By 1874 this land was prime downtown

2. CRUTCHFIELD HOUSE, c. 1870
The Crutchfield House, Dallas' first hotel, was originally a log structure built c. 1852 which burned in the fire of 1860. Within a year, Tom Crutchfield had constructed a second, larger and more impressive inn at the northwest corner of Main and Houston. The plantation style hotel, shown in this rare photograph with the Crutchfields, their guests and staff standing just beyond the mud of Houston Street, burned in 1888 and is now the site of Dealey Plaza. *Dallas Historical Society Archives*

property and disputes raged over who actually owned, held title to, or controlled it. These battles finally culminated in a series of Texas Supreme Court decisions in a suit brought by the Grigsby heirs. John Henry Brown's explanation in his *History of Dallas County 1837 to 1887* stresses the complexity of the question:

> John Grigsby came to Texas with a second wife, by whom he had two children. By his first wife he had four or five children, all of whom came with him. The land was granted to him as the head of a family. By the laws of Texas, such land is community property, belonging equally to the husband and wife. Grigsby died [drowned in a rafting accident on the Trinity River]. His widow married Edens — by him had a child, and then died. Edens, father of the infant, afterwards married a daughter of Grigsby by his first wife, and became administrator of his estate, which was administered in the proper county and before the proper court. In the distribution of the land, in 1848, it was equally divided between all the children of Grigsby, by both marriages, and nothing set apart to the child of Mrs. Grigsby by her marriage with Edens. In 1874, the children by the second marriage and the Edens child, by then a married woman, brought the suit. The plea of the first was that on the death of the parent or parents, one-half the land descended equally to all of the children of Grigsby by both marriages — the other half equally to all the children of Mrs. Grigsby by her respective marriages with Grigsby and Edens. Hence the second Grigsby children had an equal share in the whole league, and the Edens child an equal share with them in the mother's half.[1]

Even the court decision caused considerable confusion, but most of the property owners capitulated and made financial settlements with the Grigsby heirs.

In the meantime, being only marginally concerned with the legality of the situation, Bryan pitched his tent beside the Trinity and began devising a way to subdivide, promote, and profit from his land. Born in 1810 to a Tennessee family of Scottish descent, Bryan grew up in an era when the near-religious fervor of that peculiar type of historical mysticism known as Manifest Destiny ruled the United States. Consequently, he was a product of those restless times, imbued with what Alexis de Tocqueville heard President Adams describe as "the discontent of American society." He was a complex, often contradictory, and always mysterious, uncommunicative man, whose psychological polarities led him to read law in Nashville, receive a license and practice in Memphis, only to abandon this course toward a prosperous life in civilized society in 1833 for a tribal lifestyle with the Quapaw Indians of Arkansas. After four years, for reasons known only to himself, Bryan left his primitive environment to again test his fortunes in white society and with the help of a partner in 1837, laid out the town of Van Buren, Arkansas, for development and sale. This early venture in urban design lasted only until Bryan heard rumors of the new fertile lands which lay to the south and west, and in 1839 he trekked down the faint Indian trail that would one day trace the Preston Road, to establish a trading post destined to become the city of Dallas.

Anxious as he might have been to lay out his new town, Bryan was forced to wait until the skills of a surveyor arrived in the person of J. P. Dumas in 1844. In the spring of that year, Dumas laid out a one-half-mile square pattern of blocks and streets bounded by Water Street (now the Triple Underpass), Young, Poydras, and Calhoun (now Munger). Though Bryan advertised his town widely and somehow managed to enlist the cooperation of the Peters Colony Company (the town appears on their early maps and promotions), the influx of people to purchase lots was painfully slow for many years. Those who did come usually reacted in the same way as John Billingsley, who arrived from Missouri in 1844 to record in this journal, "We soon reached the placed we had heard of so often: but the *town*, where was it? Two small log cabins — this was the town of Dallas, and two families of 10 or 12 souls was its population."[2] Dumas laid out his survey in a regular gridiron pattern, oriented to the river bluff, in an attempt to bring order to the irregular area claimed by Bryan along the meandering Trinity. As the city grew, this pattern prevailed only along the narrow strip of land between Pacific Avenue and Young Street. As the near North and South Dallas areas were developed, the street patterns took on an approximately 30-degree angle to the original town, conforming to Grigsby's claim instead of to Bryan's. Streets north of Pacific, such as Ross, Bryan, and Live Oak, were laid out southwest to northeast, perpendicular to Grigsby's survey line, and the pattern carried all the way to East Dallas. Similarly, the major streets south of town, like South Harwood, South Ervay and South Akard, were laid out northwest to southeast, parallel to the survey line, which as a division between the two claims ran from near the intersection of Woodall Rodgers Freeway and Lamar, through downtown to the Masonic Cemetery (now on the Convention Center grounds) and into South Dallas along Wall Street. This accounts for Dallas' mismatched streets and irregular grid pattern so unlike the typical midwestern surveyors' designs which Bryan originally tried to emulate.

The fledgling town's progress was indeed slow at first. The James Beeman family arrived in 1842, and the next year their daughter Margaret, aged eighteen, married the thirty-three-year-old founder of Dallas. Dr. John Cole and his three sons (who would later own thousands of acres of North Dallas land) settled at Cedar Springs in 1843, and in 1844 William Hord and his family named a high, pleasant hill across the river Hord's Ridge (which later evolved into the town of Oak Cliff). By 1856, when Dallas was at last officially incorporated, it counted a roaring population of about 350 people, almost all of whom were farmers.

The major exception was Colonel John C. McCoy, a lawyer who arrived as an agent of the Peters Colony Company in 1846, but remained to collaborate with Bryan in promoting the town. Like Bryan, McCoy had some experience in town promotion, having helped to start Kansas City only a few years earlier. Before McCoy's arrival, Dallas' only official recognition was the creation of a post office in 1844, but by the fall of 1846, Bryan and McCoy had persuaded the first Texas Legislature to establish Dallas County, with their town as its temporary seat. (Texas had been annexed as the twenty-eighth state in December, 1845.) In August of 1850, the new county residents voted on their choice of a permanent seat and Dallas received 191 votes against totals of 178 for Hord's Ridge and 101 for Cedar Springs. In a run-off election three weeks later, Dallas was victorious over Hord's Ridge (244 votes to 216) primarily because of Bryan's offer to donate land for a courthouse square. Bounded by Houston, Main, Jefferson (now Record), and Commerce Streets, Bryan had been using this plot as a corn patch even after the erection of the first log cabin courthouse in 1846 (located on the northeast corner so as not to disturb his field); after 1850, it became the heart of the new city and county. James W. Latimer had already located the city's first newspaper, the Dallas *Herald,* on the dusty street corner of Main and Houston adjacent to the courthouse square in 1849, and in 1852 the Crutchfield House (2), the city's earliest hostelry, was established across the street.

At 7 a.m. every Monday, Wednesday, and Friday, the Dallas & Houston Railroad Express Stage Line left from the courthouse, through streets that were often no more than mud bogs, for Houston or the thriving port of Jefferson, Texas. By the late 1850s, the little town could boast "five general merchandise stores, two hotels, two livery stables, two drugstores, two brick yards, two saddle shops, a steam sawmill, a carriage factory, a French tailor, a barber, a boot- and shoemaker, a tinner, a cabinetmaker, two mechanics, two blacksmiths, a milliner, a photographer, and an insurance agent"[3] — all clustered tightly, as in so many other western towns, in wood-frame stores and houses around the square.

In the pre-Civil War years, Dallas counted a large number of skilled craftsmen, artisans, and manufacturers as the result of one of those odd experiments in idealistic social organization that proliferated in the nineteenth century. The colony of La Reunion, founded on the west bank of the Trinity River in 1855

3. THE J.M. HARRY COMPANY BRICK MANUFACTURING YARD, c. 1883

Located "at Frenchtown, three miles west of Dallas on the Texas and Pacific Railway," the Harry Brick Company was the first industrial plant to locate at Clay Bank, known as Cement City by 1899. In the distance is a portion of the 2,000 acres purchased in 1852 by Victor Considerant for the establishment of the Fourierist Utopian colony of La Reunion. Over 200 French, Swiss, and Belgian immigrants settled there in 1855 near what is now the intersection of Westmoreland Road and Davis Boulevard, but by 1858 the colony had failed. Today, the French Colony Cemetery on Fish Trap Road is the only vestige of that idealistic European vision. *Dallas Historical Society Archives*

11

4. DELORD RUINS NEAR LA REUNION, c. 1950
The last remnant of the French Utopian colony of
La Reunion was the rock farmhouse of one of the
Reunion settlers, Emile Delord, who built it about a
mile northeast of the colony site in 1858 after the
dissolution of that socialist experiment. Texas was in
some respects a good location for an experimental
colony because of its almost limitless supply of land,
resources, and individual freedom, though the political and philosophical climate of the mid-1850s was
often less than friendly toward "foreign communism."
The *Texas State Gazette* in August, 1855, declared:

> We would rather see the State a howling desert
> than witness the spreading of waves of Socialism
> stretch itself [*sic*] over the Christian Churches and
> the Slave Institutions of Texas. To hold out
> inducements to these Socialists is to take steps
> to make every part of the State where they may
> inhabit, undesirable for settlement to Southern
> citizens of their States and as the Socialist
> increases, we must look forward to the repulsion
> and retirement of slaveholders...by Northern
> Aggressionists.

Dallas Historical Society Archives

5. MAIN STREET, c. 1873 *(Stereo View Card)*
This rare photograph, taken just after the arrival of
the Texas & Pacific Railroad, shows the muddy expanse of Main Street running east away from the
Trinity River. The Crutchfield House is behind the
trees to the left and the Courthouse is out of the
picture to the right. The long row of commercial
structures beyond the Crutchfield House — dry goods
stores, barber shops, saloons, and medical and law
offices — were built as a direct result of the enormous railroad boom that began in 1872. *Courtesy of
University of Texas, Barker Texas History Center*

6. DALLAS CITY HALL, c. 1873 *(Stereo View Card)*
Dallas' first City Hall was built c. 1872 at the corner of Main and Akard. The ground floor contained
market stalls for vegetable, meat, fish, and poultry
dealers. The top floor housed the city offices until a
new brick building was constructed c. 1880 on Commerce at Lamar. This frame structure was
demolished for its lumber in the 1890s. *Courtesy of
University of Texas, Barker Texas History Center*

7. DOWNTOWN, c. 1873 *(Stereo View Card)*
The row of commercial buildings on Main Street
across from the courthouse square, constructed in the
1870s in the dominant Victorian Italianate style,
were representative of Dallas' era as a western
cowtown, railroad terminus, and "den of gambling,
whoring, drinking and all manner of Godlessness."
*Courtesy of University of Texas, Barker History
Center*

by Socialist Victor Considerant, was a Utopian venture based on the writings of the French philosopher Charles Francois Fourier. The chosen site, purchased by Considerant through a Peters Colony agent, was a 2,080-acre tract three miles west of Dallas which today would be bounded by Hampton Road on the east, Westmoreland Road on the west, the south levee of the Trinity (the old river channel) on the north, and Davis Boulevard (the old Fort Worth Pike) on the south. Drawn by the glowing accounts of soil, climate, and unlimited possibility for socialist prosperity in Considerant's book *Au Texas* (published in 1854), almost 200 Swiss, Belgian, and French immigrants — some still wearing their wooden shoes — marched through Dallas toward their new colony in June of 1855.

Predictably, the colony was a failure before it even started. The poor land would have been difficult to cultivate even if the colonists had been farmers. However, most of them were artisans, musicians, tailors, watchmakers, stonemasons, or poets — people who would soon have a tremendous impact on the culture and commerce of Dallas, but who in 1855 were miserably inept at agricultural survival. To add to their problems, Considerant, their leader, was a better dreamer than administrator and spent most his time planning an empire of socialist phalansteries to be built throughout Texas and linked together by an elaborate network of trade and culture. Considerant's lack of self-confidence, growing doubts, and increasing absences from the colony eventually paralyzed the entire enterprise. By April of 1856, a small stone compound had been raised on the chalk escarpment south of the river, later described by the colony's physician, Dr. Savardan, in his book *Un Naufrage au Texas,* (Paris, 1858): ". . . a building for making soap and candles, a laundry, a building for offices, a cooperative kitchen, a grocery store, beehives, a chicken house, a forge, a cottage for the Executive Agent, and [the colonists] have begun the construction of two dormitories of eight apartments each."[4]

A large storehouse, a blacksmith shop, a hotel, and shops for a bootmaker, tailor, and mechanic were added, but by 1858, the combination of Considerant's mismanagement, relentless Canadian northers, and a plague of grasshoppers finally pushed the ambitious and courageous experiment to extinction. In 1919, a visitor to the site surveying the ruins saw only ". . . the remains of a store and concrete building about thirty feet or more square which had been the commissary for the colony; thick walls were still several feet high on the four sides. Between this ruin and the residence were outlines of old fence partitions preserved by indigenous shrubs, prickly pear, hoar hound, etc. with now and then a surviving plum tree."[5] After the breakup of the colony, some of the residents chose to stay and farm, some moved to New Orleans or took passage back to Europe, but many moved across the river to settle, adding to life in Dallas a dimension very unusual for frontier America — intellectual and artistic awareness.

There were other French settlers who made their way to Dallas independent of Considerant. Maxime Guillot arrived about 1850 and established the first manufacturing plant in North Texas: a wagon making yard on the site of what is now the infamous Texas Schoolbook Depository. Guillot later almost singlehandedly fostered the Catholic Church in Dallas, bringing the first circuit-riding priest to his house for Mass in 1859. He was commissioned by the Confederate Government to set up a munitions factory in Lancaster about 1862, and in 1872, he helped to establish the city's first parish, The Sacred Heart of Jesus. In 1852 Adolphe F. Gouhenant opened the first photographic studio in town, a daguerreotype establishment known as Gouhenant's Art Saloon on the courthouse square.

Just prior to the establishment of the La Reunion colony, Bryan entered what can most kindly be described as an unsettled period in his life. He began to fear that the cholera he had contracted as a young man was driving him mad. In 1849, having sold only eighty-six Dallas lots in seven years, he left for the California gold fields and dreams of instant riches, but returned in 1851 with nothing to show for his adventure but a consuming taste for whiskey. In 1852, Bryan sold his townsite real estate to Alexander Cockrell for $7,000; at the age of forty-two, feeling too old for further pioneering and unable to cope with a town rapidly becoming too structured and too civilized, he resigned himself to a life of drink. In February, 1877, Bryan was committed to the State Lunatic Asylum in Austin, where he died and was buried in an unmarked grave in September of the same year.

The man who bought Bryan's town, Alex Cockrell, was well qualified to be called Dallas' pioneer capitalist. He was the first of a legendary line of men who achieved power, influence, and leadership in the city, creating their own local version of the Texas myth. "Dallas was a place where a man was measured by his individual entrepreneurship and ingenuity. The town existed because of that spirit among the men of her earliest generations. Making your mark was not simply one of the options in Dallas; it was a required rite of every young man."[6] Between 1855 and April, 1858, when he was shot and killed in a dispute over money, Cockrell replaced Bryan's decrepit ferryboat with a wooden toll bridge over the Trinity, established the town's first steam sawmill on Commerce Street near the river, built a large Greek Revival home at the foot of Commerce,[8] sold and developed several choice townsites, and began construction of a three-story luxury hotel which his widow, Sarah, completed in 1859.

Cockrell's Dallas Bridge and Causeway Company built the first toll bridge at the end of Commerce Street in 1855. This red cedar wooden span was destroyed in the flood of 1858, but Sarah Cockrell maintained the crossing by assigning her most trusted slave, Barry Derritt, to reopen the ferry. In 1872, she erected a new "Wrought Iron Arch Girder Bridge," purchased from the Moseley Iron Company of St. Louis, at the site of the old wooden structure. The expense and trouble involved in shipping this mail-order bridge down the Mississippi and across the Gulf to Galveston, then overland by rail and wagon to Dallas, illustrated the importance it held, both as a real economic resource for the town and as a symbol of Dallas' determination to maintain its position as a major crossroads of trade. In 1882 Dallas County purchased the bridge from the Cockrell family for $37,500 and opened it for free public access.

On a hot July day in 1860, with the temperature standing at 104 degrees in the shade, Dallas experienced its own version of the great fire that was to sweep Chicago in 1871. Though much smaller in magnitude, the blaze proved just as devastating in its effect on the morale, and property of the townspeople. Losses included "the *Herald* office and printing plant, the Crutchfield House, [Sarah Cockrell's] St. Nicholas Hotel, the brick store of Smith and Murphy, the large storehouse of Herman Hirsch, nearly all the law, dental, and medical offices around the square, the Stackpole warehouse, Lynch and Son's saddle shop, Caruth and Simon's warehouse, the R. R. Fletcher and Company storehouse, [and] Darnell's stable,"[7] as well as scores of saloons, frame houses, and a small section of the new courthouse, just completed in 1856.

Damage was estimated at $250,000 to $300,000 and what amounted to a vigilante committee appointed itself to determine the cause. Although the *Herald* explained that "the fire originated in some boxes (loaded with sawdust) in front of W. W. Peak Bros. Drugstore,"[8] probably ignited by a careless workman's match, rumors and accusations nevertheless spread faster than the fire had. The intense emotional climate of the South on the eve of the Civil War inflamed the mass hysteria of the crowd and a "jury" of 52 men quickly uncovered a "nefarious plot" by Negro slaves and Northern abolitionists to put the town to the torch. Three black men, Uncle Cato, "a notorious Negro," Pat Jennings, and Sam Smith, were hanged on a gallows erected at the river end of Commerce Street and two Iowa preachers were arrested, whipped, and run out of town. An order was also issued demanding that every slave in the county be whipped as an example, but the value of these people and the close family ties that usually developed between the small land

8. COCKRELL HOME, c. 1880
The Greek Revival home of Alexander and Sarah Cockrell was built in 1858 on the original site of John Neely Bryan's third log cabin. In 1852 the Cockrell family purchased this lot, along with Bryan's unsold townsite property. The house, which stood at the southwest corner of Commerce and Broadway (now the Triple Underpass) was looked upon as a shrine to Dallas' pioneer past until 1911 when it was demolished because of damage sustained in the flood of 1908. The Post Office Annex now occupies the site. *Dallas Historical Society Archives*

holder and his one or two slaves probably prohibited its execution.

In spite of its horrifying consequences, there was a positive aspect to the fire: it destroyed most of the primitive wood-frame buildings that flagrantly announced the little town's provinciality. As in Chicago after the fire, Dallas' citizens and new arrivals began to dream of the emergence of a well built, vibrant city on the open prairie — a great transportation and commercial center for the entire Mid-South. People envisioned more substantial stone or brick (preferably fireproof) buildings, and into this atmosphere stepped the city's first architects to supply the demand.

T. B. Borst and John Ryan probably arrived in Dallas sometime during Reconstruction, bringing with them the genesis of the hundreds of two-story Italianate commercial structures built between 1860 and 1890 (most of which remained well into the twentieth century and some of which can still be found today in obscure corners of downtown). Not much is known about these first architects. They were part of an itinerant breed of skilled builders, usually without formal training, who provided their services along the frontier in boom towns, mining camps, and railroad terminals. The Italianate style was the dominant architectural form used by these men in business and commercial construction until Henry Hobson Richardson's Romanesque designs began to be widely copied during the late 1880s and early 1890s. One of the best Italianate examples in Dallas was Louis Wagner's grocery and liquor store (9), built on the square at the southeast corner of Main and Jefferson streets about 1868. Widely used in the western states, this style often employed a brick or stone false front covering a tent or a frame building, but its most popular and versatile form was the cast-iron facade, first erected in New York in 1848. The use of cast iron quickly spread across the country because it was strong, light, durable, economic, and noncombustible. Unaffected by rapid oxidation, decay, or extreme temperatures, it could be designed to resemble the already-present wood and stone

fronts, prepared and fitted at the factory, transported to the site, and rapidly erected. Much of the architectural ironwork used in Dallas and throughout the Southwest was supplied by the Mosher Manufacturing Company of Dallas, begun about 1885 by Theodore Mosher of Peoria, Illinois, or by the Trinity Iron Works, established in 1874.

Of course, the city's real construction boom occurred after the cessation of the Civil War in 1865. Though it sent several volunteer batteries to the battlefields, Dallas was never directly involved in the hostilities. It did serve as a Confederate administrative center with quartermaster, commissary, transportation and recruiting headquarters located in town, but the most enduring impact of the war came with emancipation of the slaves and the subsequent creation of several freedmantowns in and around the city. Black refugees, along with huge numbers of white emigrants, flooded North Texas in apparent response to Horace Greeley's advice to "go West."

The freedmantowns that evolved in Dallas County just after the war included one along Alpha and Noel roads in far North Dallas, the Little Egypt community near Northwest Highway and Abrams Road, a settlement along Ten Mile Creek and Bonnie View Road in South Dallas, the Jones community near Grapevine, the Thomas Hill community in Oak Cliff, Elm Thicket near what is now Love Field, Freedmantown in North Dallas near Hall Street and the Houston & Texas Central tracks (now Central Expressway), and the Deep Ellum district, which reached its "zenith" in the 1920s and 1930s (only to be almost totally obliterated by the construction of Central Expressway in the early 1950s). These Negro settlements were not only products of white intolerance and the need among blacks to unite for protection, but also of a newfound sense of pride in a long-awaited freedom.

The city's population grew steadily from about 600 in 1860 to nearly 3,000 by 1872, when the *Texas Almanac* referred to Dallas as one of three North Texas towns "already beginning to put on the airs of a city."[9] As Henry Coit wrote in a letter to his cousin in

1871, "Dallas is improving very fast. The census gave us over 2,700 inhabitants to the corporation. People anticipate its becoming another Atlanta and fortunes have been made in buying town property."[10] Three banks had been established and two cotton gins and a flour mill were in operation; Dallas was the world center of the leather and buffalo hide trade, initiated in 1867 with the opening of John Tenison's saddlery shop and expanded in 1869 by G. H. Schoellkopf. More importantly, Dallas in 1872 stood on the brink of an event that would permanently alter the destiny of the city. Within two years, Dallas would become a railroad crossroads, embracing the future and deliberately setting itself apart from every other hamlet in North Texas. The city's horizons were on the verge of expanding, and opportunities were limitless for those both willing to exploit them and able to evade or overcome those particular restraints and constrictions of society which usually stood in the way of wealth.

9. WAGNER'S GROCERY AND LIQUORS, c. 1915
After the disastrous fire of 1860, hundreds of durable, brick, cast-iron-facaded, Victorian Italianate commercial structures began to replace the log cabins and wood frame buildings of Dallas' pioneer days. Typical of this architectural mode, Louis Wagner's grocery and liquor store was built c. 1868 at the southeast corner of Main and Jefferson streets on the courthouse square. After their arrival in Dallas in 1870, the Wagner family lived over the store just as they had in Europe, but by 1883, the family had joined the American rush to the suburbs and moved to Bryan Street. The store was demolished in 1967 to erect the John F. Kennedy Memorial. *Courtesy of Mr. Charles Coldwell*

2 DOWNTOWN 1873-1890

Dallas realized very early that as a town with no natural waterways for shipping, a rail connection was an absolute necessity for urban growth and prosperity on the isolated North Texas prairie. Consequently, the entire populace was constantly alert to any means, fair or foul, by which the railroad companies might be induced to build through Dallas. As early as August of 1866, a public meeting was held, presided over by John Neely Bryan, in which "the necessity of a railroad connection with the sea coast was strongly enunciated, and delegates appointed to a railroad convention to be held at Tyler on September 11th. Disappointment was expressed at the tardiness of the Houston & Texas Central Railway in building its road, and the Southern Pacific Railway [Texas & Pacific] heartily commended for its energy and enterprise."[11]

In 1871, the H&TC intended to build its line eight miles east of the courthouse — a plan which would have left a catastrophic gap between the struggling town and the much-needed tracks. To entice the railroad nearer to the courthouse, several of the town's leading businessmen, led by Captain William H. Gaston, donated $5,000 and a right-of-way through Gaston's property to the H&TC.

On July 16, 1872, the first wood-burning locomotive, pulling eight freight cars, steamed into town after its fifteen-hour trip from Houston, and was met by a jubilant, cheering crowd of over 5,000 citizens. In anticipation of this day, the city had extended its geographical limit over a mile eastward to insure the railroad a large enough target, and had raised over $10,000 in gold, primarily by sale of stock through Gaston's bank, to build the Dallas City Railway Company, a mule-drawn streetcar line, from the H&TC tracks down Main Street to the courthouse.

Six months later, the city again faced the problem of needing to change a planned route; the T&P tracks were pressing westward from Shreveport along the 32nd parallel — a path which would bypass Dallas by over fifty miles to the south. Once more, Gaston and his business partners manipulated the fate of the city by persuading their state representative, John Lane, to attach a rider to the bill granting right-of-way lands to the railroads. The rider required the T&P to pass within a mile of Browder Springs (in what is now Old City Park), and since no one knew where Browder Springs was, the bill passed and the Texas Legislature adjourned for two years before the T&P engineers discovered they had been duped. When they did, the company threatened to run the tracks one mile *south* of the springs but were quickly appeased after $200,000 in bonds and $5,000 in cash were subscribed for the railroad's use. The city also granted the use of Burleson Street (now Pacific Avenue) as right-of-way from the eastern city limits to the river; Captain Gaston donated 142 acres for another right-of-way through his East Dallas property near the present State Fairgrounds, as well as ten acres for a depot at the intersection of the H&TC and T&P tracks (Central Expressway at Pacific). On February 22, 1873, the T&P obligingly made the city a rail transportation crossroads when its first locomotive pulled up near the courthouse, and the era of the railroad boom in Dallas began.

Within a few months after the arrival of the railroads, Dallas had been transformed from a largely agrarian village of less than 2,000 people into a bustling commercial and industrial center with a population of over 7,000.

TODD MILLS.
FULL CENTRIFUGAL SYSTEM.

The year 1873 saw the construction of 725 new buildings and residences at a cost of over $1,377,000, and by 1875, the city was already beginning to develop urban sprawl. The Dallas *Herald* lamented on January 29, 1875, "With the exception of a few old residents, the great body of our people are strangers to one another." By then, the town had built seven churches, ten or twelve private schools (but no public ones), two foundries, fifteen to twenty lumber yards, three planing mills, a sash and door factory, five large brick yards, two soap factories and five steam-powered flouring mills.

The Todd Flour Mills at the corner of Pacific and Broadway (10) were the largest and most important of these enterprises. The natural successor to the dozens of small leather-and-grindstone operations that had dotted the county since 1845, this concern, founded in 1874 by Sarah Cockrell and her son Frank, was the first mercantile mill in Dallas, buying the raw wheat from local farmers and marketing the flour by railroad transport. The industry grew so rapidly that by 1877 Dallas County-milled flour earned $2,750,000, exceeding by $300,000 the value of the entire state output only seven years earlier.[12]

Also flourishing in the city were a brewery maintained by former members of the Reunion colony; a second streetcar line begun by W. J. Keller, the Dallas Street Railway Company, which operated two miles of track in the newly opened sections of North Dallas along Ross and San Jacinto; a cotton mill and a wool carding plant; a magnificent fairground situated where Baylor Hospital now stands; a new two-story courthouse; wooden water and gas lines laid under the unpaved streets; a daily paper, the *Herald*, which received Associated Press service; and several large agricultural implement businesses and warehouses.

The all-important rail connection established in 1873 helped to make Dallas one of the largest inland cotton exchanges in the country. With the completion of its line to Denison in 1873, the Missouri, Kansas & Texas Railroad (through its connection with the H&TC) provided Dallas with a marketing link to St. Louis, which was just establishing itself as a major cotton market and beginning to compete strongly with the Gulf ports of Galveston and New Orleans. In 1874 a group of St. Louis and New York investors extended the St. Louis, Iron Mountain & Southern Railway into Texarkana where it joined with the east-west T&P to give Dallas a second outlet to the Midwest.

With such a lucrative combination of industry and transportation on the horizon, Dallas was quick to invest an estimated $3 million in the cotton and grain industries, which employed 4,000 of its citizens.[13] Instrumental in this development were R. V. Tompkins and J. C. O'Connor, who in 1874 organized the Dallas Compress Company at Lamar and Wood with capital of $34,000 (11), and in 1876 built the Dallas Elevator and Compress Company, a massive cotton compress with the state's first adjoining grain elevator, at Houston Street adjacent to the T&P tracks (12). The powerful, efficient compresses could reduce the cotton bales to about half their original size, enabling each railroad car to load nearly 25,000 pounds.

10. TODD MILLS, c. 1890
The milling of flour and meal was Dallas County's single most important industry between 1845, when the first mule powered, rawhide belt mill was established, and the arrival of the railroads in 1872. The Todd Flour Mills, the first mercantile mills in Dallas, were part of a large production and marketing system which by 1877 was shipping almost $3 million worth of flour by rail to St. Louis and Kansas City. The original steam powered mill, built by Sarah Cockrell in 1874 at the intersection of the Texas & Pacific Railway and the Trinity River, remained in operation with a few improvements until it was damaged by the flood of 1908. *Dallas Historical Society Archives*

11. DALLAS COTTON COMPRESS, c. 1874 *(Stereo View Card)*
The construction of the Dallas Compress Company at the corner of Lamar and Wood in 1874 marked the beginning of the city's role as capital of the North Texas cotton industry. Almost half of Texas' 4 million acres of cotton-producing land was located within a 100-mile radius of Dallas, and the city's rail connections to Chicago and St. Louis made it an important and prosperous distribution center. *Dallas Historical Society Archives*

12. DALLAS ELEVATOR COMPANY, c. 1908

The Dallas Elevator Company, built about 1885 by Frank Cockrell, was a major part of the grain, cotton, and lumber industries that comprised Dallas' economy in the 19th century. This photograph was made during the flood of 1908 which cost the city millions of dollars in damages, and undermined the foundation of the elevator, prompting its demolition. The site is currently occupied by the Hyatt Regency Hotel, which sits just off what was the old river channel, before its course was altered by the construction of the levee system in the 1930s. *Dallas Historical Society Archives*

When this mechanical efficiency was coupled with the rail accessibility to midwestern and eastern cities, the long overland shipments of cotton from Dallas became economically feasible. Galveston and New Orleans, having shunned the railroads in favor of their natural river and port advantages, suddenly faced the railroads' constant price cutting on "through car lots," which made the inland routes much more attractive to most shippers than the water routes. This revolution in trade practice happened so quickly that the southern ports could not match the economic strength of the northern and eastern cities in competing for Texas cotton. As the Dallas *Daily Herald* commented in 1874, "Galveston's monopoly in cotton presses was broken ... and henceforth, the cotton business will be conducted with more satisfaction to all parties concerned than ever heretofore."[14]

In addition to cotton, there was a large eastern market for Texas livestock and hides; in return, the St. Louis merchants sent shipments of breadstuffs, dry goods, clothing, boots, shoes, saddlery, agricultural implements and all kinds of general merchandise. Furthermore, the MK&T and the Iron Mountain encouraged immigration to Texas, which in turn contributed to increased cotton activity.[15] As railroad mileage increased from 591 miles in 1870 to 9,867 in 1900, cotton shipments grew proportionately from 431,463 bales worth $23,730,465 in 1860, to 3,526,649 bales worth $177,714,544 by 1900.[16] Almost half of Texas' 4 million cotton acres was located in the rich blacklands of Northeast Texas within a hundred-mile radius of Dallas, and most of that production was either warehoused, traded, or shipped through the city, clogging lower Elm Street in season with hundreds of wagons crammed to the sideboards with bales, and transforming the street into a sea of white cotton. Thus, Dallas developed stronger economic ties to St. Louis and Chicago than it did to Houston or Galveston, a phenomenon reflected in Dallas' cultural and architectural orientation as early as the 1890s, and which still exists to a degree today.

By virtue of its rail connections to the manufacturing centers of Kansas City, St. Louis, and Chicago, the city had become a major distribution point for mule- and horse-drawn farm machinery by the late 1870s. The agricultural implement business had begun in Dallas in 1852 with the opening of a McCormick Harvesting Machine Company agency on the courthouse square. McCormick was followed by the Aultman Miller Company of Akron, Ohio; the Parlin and Orendorff Company of Canton, Illinois; the Mansur and Tebbetts Implement Company of St. Louis; and the Keating Implement and Machinery Company of Dallas (13 and 14). By 1891 Dallas surpassed Kansas City as the largest distribution center for farm machinery in the country.

The city was growing, but it remained, in many ways, a frontier town; until about 1900, Dallas was still very much a part of the wild west. A terminus for cattle drives bound for G. W. Rose and Company's Butchers and Drovers Stockyards (near Elm and Murphy streets), it was a stomping ground for all sorts of infamous desperadoes. When the financial Panic of 1873 hit Dallas, the T&P had to stop its westward construction at Eagle Ford, a small town six miles to the west (located approximately where the T&P tracks cross Chalk Hill Road today). Overnight Eagle Ford became a roaring, wide-open railroad terminus, competing with Dallas for the title of most disorderly, reckless, and outrageous frontier town in Texas. The outlaw Sam Bass contributed to the general aura of lawlessness by holding up the T&P four times near Dallas in the spring of 1878, infuriating the Dallas populace to such a degree that a posse relentlessly pursued and killed him in July of that year at Round Rock, Texas. Gamblers in Dallas operated openly and flagrantly to the point that they became a major industry. When the law tried to clean them out in 1883, a delegation of businessmen informed the district attorney that the gamblers' arrest would be a severe blow to the economy of the town and that Fort Worth was waiting in the wings with offers of free rents and money for them if Dallas proved inhospitable.

13. LOOKING NORTH, c. 1901
The view is from the Courthouse across Pacific Avenue, toward the MK&T switching yards and repair shops. The round tanks to the left are the Dallas Gas and Fuel Company's coal-to-methane gasification plant and storage facilities, built in the 1880s; beyond them is the Dallas Brewery and Bottling Works, built in the 1890s; the tall stacks in the distance belong to the stone generating plant of the Dallas Electric Light and Power Company, now the site of the DP&L plant. *Dallas Historical Society Archives*

14. LOOKING NORTHEAST, c. 1901
About 1900, several farm implement dealers began to build warehouses and showrooms north of the Courthouse. The area, shown in this photograph of the intersection of Elm and N. Jefferson, is known today as the West End Historical District. Beyond the warehouses are the MK&T depot and Dallas' notorious red-light district known as Frogtown. *Dallas Historical Society Archives*

15. LOOKING SOUTH, c. 1901
From the Courthouse towers, the Farmers' Alliance Exchange warehouse, built in 1888 at the southwest corner of Market and Wood streets, dominated the view. The dilapidated wood-frame houses surrounding the Alliance Building are the cribs and sporting houses of the red-light area known as Boggy Bayou which sprang up with the arrival of the railroads in the early 1870s. According to legend, Boggy Bayou had a secret, underground connection to the Courthouse for the convenience of Dallas' dignitaries. *Dallas Historical Society Archives*

CARTER'S WILD CHERRY
CANTON CLIPPER PLOWS
PARLIN & ORENDORFF CO.
MANSUR & TEBBETTS IMPCT CO.
CARRIAGE REPOSITORY
HEATING IMPLEMENT & MACHINE CO.
IMPLEMENTS
MACHINERY.
BUGGIES
WAGONS &C.
AULTMAN, MILLER & CO.
BINDERS.
REAPERS.
MOWERS.
CORN
HARVESTERS

PLOWS
J.I. CASE & SONS

The railroads may have brought economic prosperity, but they also trailed behind them the hangers-on, the camp followers (to whom General Joseph Hooker inadvertently lent his name during the Civil War), the gamblers, rowdies, hustlers, drunks, pimps, demimonde floaters and other assorted "undesirables" who flocked to the edges of town, threw up their shanty saloons and cribs, and were in business.

There were three main "red-light" districts in the city where respectable people were never seen (unless by accident). The oldest, predating the railroad, was a black "Freedman's Town" established soon after the Civil War. The "chock beer" houses and juke joints which grew into the notorious Deep Ellum of the 1920s were located along Main, Commerce, and Elm streets, directly east of the point where the T&P and H&TC railroads met in 1873. The area was rough. Cribbies plied their trade out of boxcars and tents, violence and murder were commonplace, and the law — when it even bothered or dared to enter — was enforced callously and capriciously.

Yet in this community a rich, native music form was born and flourished. Derived from Negro spirituals, it grew into the blues and jazz produced by such men as Blind Lemon Jefferson and Huddie Ledbetter (Leadbelly). Jefferson, the son of a sharecropper and ex-slave, was born blind near Wortham, Texas, in 1897 and began singing at age twelve or thirteen just to survive. He lived in Dallas off and on from about 1917 until the mid-1920s when Paramount Records discovered him and sent him to Chicago, where he became a major recording figure. Leadbelly, who spent most of his life in prisons and on chain gangs, sang with Blind Lemon in several Deep Ellum brothels, along with other Dallas bluesmen such as Bobby Cadillac, Perry Dixon, Willy Day, Coley Jones, and Alex Moore, developing a musical expression which has had tremendous impact on contemporary American music. In addition to the sporting houses, many black-owned and operated businesses had developed in Deep Ellum by the 1920s, including several Negro hotels, secondhand stores, the Airdome Theater, and The Harlem

vaudeville house. As A. C. Greene so aptly summarized, "Deep Ellum became a haven, a black sanctuary in a white world where conditions of existence were often miserable, but where a black could be left alone. And out of it rose a whole culture of black passion, loneliness, and eventually, independence."[17]

The second district ran north of the courthouse along the river, and became known as Frogtown for the thousands of bullfrogs that climbed out of the Trinity at night to serenade the revelers. Frogtown was a racially mixed neighborhood which occupied a run-down housing development begun by William Caruth in 1854. By the late 1870s, the original residents had moved out to Thomas Street and Ross Avenue, leaving their rapidly decaying frame homes (located in what is now the West End Historical District) to the girls who catered to the working men.

The third red-light district was south of the courthouse, stretching from near Young and Lamar streets southward into a small Negro area near the river called Boggy Bayou. This district, with streets lined by gambling halls, sporting houses, and saloons, was the most fashionable "amusement area" and was rumored to be the frisking grounds for many of the city's most prominent men. Until 1872, the back of John Neely Bryan's cabin was one of the few saloons in town, but by 1880, Dallas had over forty, mostly located on the north side of Main (ladies always walked on the south side as a result) between Houston and Lamar streets and along Houston, Lamar and Austin, south toward Wood Street. By

16. SANTA FE DEPOT, c. 1890
The Gulf, Colorado & Santa Fe Railroad, chartered in 1873 by the citizens of Galveston as an outlet to the Texas interior, reached Dallas in 1884 and built its first wooden depot near the intersection of Young and Poydras streets. *Dallas Historical Society Archives*

17. SANTA FE-COTTON BELT TERMINAL, c. 1898
In 1896, the Santa Fe Railroad and the St. Louis & Southwestern Railway (commonly known as the Cotton Belt) replaced the original wooden depot with a stone structure at the corner of Commerce and Murphy streets. This Richardsonian Romanesque terminal was demolished in 1926 to build the present Santa Fe Building. *Dallas Historical Society Archives*

18. OLD UNION DEPOT, c. 1890

The arrival of the Houston & Texas Central Railroad in 1872 marked Dallas' rite of passage from frontier hamlet to glistening metropolis on the blackland prairie. The H&TC built a permanent station, called Union Depot, about 1885 where their north-south line crossed the east-west tracks of the Texas & Pacific Railroad. Today that intersection is Pacific Avenue (the T&P tracks were removed about 1922) at Central Expressway (H&TC tracks removed about 1947). The massive fortress-like structure was demolished in 1935.

Dallas Historical Society Archives

1891, the number had peaked out at 189.

Trail drivers fresh from weeks of eating Longhorn dust were eager to frequent even the most notorious of these establishments, including Miss Lillie Cain's Red Light Saloon at the corner of Austin and Columbia, The Two Johns Saloon across the street, the opium den of Charlie Chunn, and the Black Elephant, a notoriously wicked Negro dive that the *Herald* pronounced, "a disgrace to civilization." The ladies employed in these quarters were supposedly the finest and most beautiful west of New Orleans' fabled Storyville, and legend has it that when the fifth county courthouse (21) was built in 1881, it included a series of secret underground passages leading from hidden antechambers in the courthouse, down and through the caverns used by the Santa Fe Railroad, to emerge in the lairs of the "Grande Horizontals" a block or two away.

Dallas developed an elaborate display of dissolute entertainments, such as cockfights, dogfights, and horse racing at the fairgrounds (with many of the best thoroughbreds coming from Colonel Henry Exall's farm in what is now Highland Park). Six pool halls and sixteen gambling houses, as well as numerous saloons and bawdy-houses offered hours of drinking and dalliance, despite the city's location deep in the heartland of the Bible Belt. Although the evangelical cries of "hallelujah" and "amen" streaming out of a revival tent or the rhythmic cadence of the Baptists thumping their Bibles on Sunday night might temporarily drown out the shrieks of all-night revelry from Frogtown and Boggy Bayou, tales of the city's rare delights constantly beckoned the farm boys from Cleburne, Tyler, or Waxahachie by the thousands, just as the sirens of the rocks beckoned Ulysses' men, moving one Dallas visitor to record in the late 1870s: "There are many temptations here to invite young men to throw their money away."[18]

There were, however, a few voices crying in the wilderness, among them the Reverend J. Frank Smith, a Presbyterian preacher. Step-

19. MISSOURI, KANSAS & TEXAS STATION, c. 1900
In 1892 the Missouri, Kansas & Texas Railroad built
a permanent passenger depot at the northwest corner of
Pacific and Market streets to replace the wooden structure erected in 1887 when the MK&T completed its spur
line into Dallas from Greenville. The depot's Second
Empire detailing, typified by the projecting central
pavilion and the modified mansard roof, presented a
dignified and stately first impression to the thousands
of new settlers arriving daily in the city. The depot was
demolished in 1924 to build the Interstate-Trinity
Warehouse.
Dallas Historical Society Archives

ping off the train in 1896, he noted "something about the whole scene, the little church
and its need, the fact that the city had no
YMCA building, no public library, no great
regard for moral law, with saloons wide open
on Sundays. These things seemed to call to
me."[19] Nevertheless, years would pass before
the outraged forces of morality and justice
would prevail.

Aside from the back-street attractions of
the red-light districts, Dallas offered a few
more innocuous public amusements such as a
roller skating rink, a shooting gallery, several
indoor and outdoor dancing pavilions, the
rides and exhibits at the fairgrounds, and the
German beer gardens like Meisterhans' on
Bryan Street or Simon Mayer's on Elm,
where outdoor orchestras and polka festivals
were held.

Dallas also boasted fine regional theater,
employing both local and New York talent,
and in the 1920s, the electric-arc dazzle of
the Elm Street vaudeville and movie houses
created a Broadway aura which the city has
never regained. The Dallas Opera House
(22), opened in 1883 on the southwest corner
of Commerce and Austin streets, delivered to
clamoring audiences anything from light
comedy to Shakespeare. The three-story theater was built, by public subscription, of rusticated cream sandstone with two galleries
and a seating capacity of 1,200. Two other
opera houses had been built previously: Tom
Field had opened the first in 1873 on the
south side of Main Street, across from the
Sanger Brothers Dry Goods Store, and in
1879, Lemuel Craddock opened another over
his wholesale liquor emporium across the
street from Fields', but these were crackerbox
provincial theaters by comparison. Dallas'
Opera House was part of the theatrical circuit which included Austin, Houston, San
Antonio, and (after Henry Greenwall took
over its management) Galveston, Fort Worth,
and New Orleans. It brought in well known
touring companies with stars like Edwin
Booth in *Hamlet*, Lily Langtry, Maurice
Barrymore, and the "Divine" Sarah Bernhardt.

20. TEXAS & PACIFIC DEPOT, c. 1916
The Texas & Pacific Railroad's second passenger depot
was built in 1901 on Pacific Avenue between Lamar and
Griffin streets, the site of an earlier brick station which
had been built in 1885 and burned in 1900. The second
depot was designed by Otto Lang, head of the T&P
architectural division until 1905 when he left to form
the prestigious and prolific Dallas firm of Lang and
Witchell. Like all of Dallas' independent stations, the
T&P Depot was abandoned in 1916 when the city's rail
traffic was consolidated at the present Union Terminal.
The T&P Depot was demolished in 1921. *Courtesy of
Missouri Pacific Railroad*

By 1880, Dallas' population had reached
10,385, and its industries were beginning to
increase in size and number. The Howard Oil
Company built a huge cottonseed oil mill on
the H&TC tracks at Polk Street about 1879,
and several other factories and mills were
constructed including two more steam flouring mills and two steam-driven corn mills,
several broom-making plants, a barrel manufacturer, a barbed wire factory, and several
cement plants and brick kilns.

The development of an industrial base in
Dallas in the 1880s and 1890s was a direct
consequence of the city's new rail connections
and the growing industrialization of the
South in general. Like most other southern
cities, Dallas' economy before Reconstruction
was primarily dependent on the agricultural
production and natural resources of the surrounding area. When the railroads arrived in
1872 and 1873, Dallas, like Atlanta, found itself in a strategic geographical location for
the trade and transportation of its abundant
regional products to northern and eastern
manufacturing plants. Commerce and transportation therefore were the resources that
gave life to the city of Dallas.

But by the late 1870s, most southern busi-

nessmen realized that the South could not
sustain itself on its traditional agrarian economy alone, as it had before the Civil War.
They resolved to release themselves from de-
pendence on the industrialized North and began to build their own manufacturing plants
in towns with far-reaching rail connections.
Dallas, Atlanta, Birmingham, Nashville,
Louisville, and Memphis were the primary
beneficiaries of this expanding urban view-
point and by the early twentieth century had
become not only major trade and transportation centers, but significant manufacturing
centers as well (23).

As its commerce and industry grew, Dallas
began to regard itself in more cosmopolitan
terms, and decided finally in 1881 to do
something about its streets. That was the year
Thomas Marsalis got tired of slogging
through the mud on Elm Street to get to his
wholesale grocery business, near the corner of
Murphy. The merchants on Main and Commerce streets had streetcar lines to help bring
in customers, and something had to be done
to promote Elm Street. Marsalis hired William Johnson, former engineer in charge of
track construction for the T&P and at that
time serving as city engineer, to lay bois d'arc

21. THE FIFTH DALLAS COUNTY COURTHOUSE, c. 1885
The French-inspired, Second Empire style Courthouse was completed in 1881 by James Flanders. Using limestone quarried at White Rock Creek, it was built at a cost of $100,000, and was widely believed to be the first fireproof courthouse in the city's fire-plagued history until it burned in August of 1890. *Dallas Historical Society Archives*

blocks in the street as paving. The process was not perfected until 1884 but by the end of that year, most of the downtown streets had been done. Macadam paving (rolled, crushed stone and gravel) was first used by Johnson in 1885 on Ross Avenue between Ervay Street and the H&TC tracks, and by 1910, the city had taken over maintenance of the streets and begun to apply the new bitulithic (asphalt) process.

The Dallas Gas and Fuel Company (13), with its plant on the corner of Houston and Carondalet (now Ross) had been supplying methane gas, artificially extracted from coal, through underground wooden pipelines since 1874. In 1882, the company's president, Jules E. Schneider, along with Alex Sanger and W. C. Connor, secured a charter from the city to also begin supplying electricity. Service began in 1883 from a small wooden building on Carondalet between Austin and Market streets — four years after Thomas Edison announced the invention of the incandescent lamp and just one year after he installed the dynamos to begin operation of New York City's Pearl Street Station, the first electric light plant in the world.

The company's first customers were the Main Street saloons and the Sanger Brothers Dry Goods Store but within a year, most major businesses had fixtures for both gas and electric lighting (in case one or the other failed as they frequently did), and the city began installing electric street lights. The 1883 city directory commented that the new technology "beautifully illuminates the streets in the heart of town with its pale, ghostly and weird rays." Over the next thirty-four years, eleven different power companies vied for control of the city, and it was not until 1917 that Colonel J. F. Strickland managed to call a halt to the whole confusing, inefficient mess by buying out and consolidating the largest competitors. The old Dallas Electric Company plant which had stood at the MK&T tracks and Sumpter Street since 1890 was replaced by the present Dallas Power and Light plant, and a city-wide distribution network was constructed.

The evolution of the Dallas City Gaslight Company was much less complex. Schneider retained possession of the company, changed its name in 1890 to Dallas Gas and Fuel Company, and erected an auxilliary plant on Ross at Akard Street near the palatial mansion he built about 1879 (185) from the enormous profits of his monopoly. In 1909, he was finally forced out of business by the newly chartered Lone Star Gas Company which had been laboring for several months to construct a nearly 150-mile long, sixteen-inch natural gas pipeline from the Petrolia field in northern Clay County (near Wichita Falls) through Fort Worth into Dallas. Thousands of people gathered on May 7, a balmy Saturday night, to watch the ignition of a gas torch atop the Cotton Belt Terminal Building at Commerce and Lamar streets that shot flames forty feet into the air, celebrating the inauguration of natural gas service to the city.

Another important milestone in the city's growth occurred in 1885 with the arrival of Alfred Horatio Belo and the Dallas *Morning News*. Originally the Dallas *News* served as the North Texas branch of the Galveston *News*, the oldest publishing institution in the state. The Galveston paper began printing in the embryonic days of the Texas Republic on April 11, 1842, then was taken over and reorganized by Colonel Belo in 1876. The Dallas branch of the news was a pioneering effort, not only in the fact that it was the first "chain" newspaper established in the United States, but also because it sprang from the radically innovative idea of telegraphing the news from Galveston to Dallas — the first time in Texas it had ever been done. The

22. DALLAS OPERA HOUSE, c. 1883
The Dallas Opera House (southwest corner of Commerce and Austin streets) was typical of the Victorian Italianate style as it was adapted in the American West. This architectural mode represented the ideals of pragmatism and commerce, virtues which endeared it to the democratic consciousness of the American frontier. Hundreds of similar structures were built in Dallas between 1870 and 1900, few of which still survive. The Opera House burned in 1901. *Dallas Historical Society Archives.*

23. TRINITY COTTON OIL COMPANY, c. 1895
Dallas Historical Society Archives.

DALLAS OPERA HOUSE
CARDWELL
THRESHERS
BOSS C
TEX. COT.
CASCARINE
TRINITY COTTON OIL CO

**24. THE INTERSECTION OF COMMERCE AND
S. LAMAR STREETS, c. 1890**

From the far left stand the Windsor Hotel, built in
1879; the original Dallas *News* Building, constructed
in 1885; and the two-story City Hall and fire station
built c. 1880. Both the *News* and the City Hall
buildings were demolished in 1900 to build the newspaper's new plant. The Gaston and T&P buildings
dominate the center of the photograph. To the right
can be seen the top story of the Blankenship and
Blake warehouse, built c. 1884 by the architect A. B
Bristol, which still stands today at the southeast
corner of Commerce and Lamar. *Dallas Historical
Society Archives.*

34

News Building (24), near the corner of Commerce and Lamar streets, was completed about the time the first issue hit the streets, October 1, 1885, and within two months the *News* had eliminated its competition by buying out and absorbing James Latimer's *Herald*. In 1887, the *News* began running a special train to McKinney, Sherman, and Denison to deliver its papers in an attempt to meet the threat of the St. Louis newspapers, which in 1885 had a larger circulation in North Texas than any state paper. With the founding of the paper, Colonel Belo moved his family to Dallas and built a splendid Colonial Revival mansion on Ross Avenue, a showplace which stands to this day.

In those early days, the Dallas *News* ranged far ahead of the city's other institutions in promoting and drawing national attention to Dallas — a claim substantiated by the *New York Times'* Adolph Ochs, who said in 1924, "I received my ideas and ideals from the Galveston *Daily News* and the Dallas *Morning News.*"[20] The single exception to the *News'* pervasive influence was the Sanger Brothers Dry Goods Company, which by the 1890s had become the South and Southwest's equivalent of Marshall Field's in Chicago and was widely renowned and respected for its innovative approaches to retailing, merchandising, advertising, employee relations, and public service. Philip and Alex Sanger, who ran the Dallas operation, readily adapted to the Gilded Age's romanticized vision of the merchant princes, dispensing exotic finery from their temple emporiums. Accordingly, they built not only the landmark complex of buildings on Elm between Lamar and Austin streets (30), but also palatial residences (99 and 101) in the southern part of the city known as The Cedars.

As Dallas prospered, its growing self-esteem found visual expression in the buildings, both public and private, that its citizens commissioned. James E. Flanders was Dallas' most important nineteenth century arhcitect, not only because of the large number of buildings he constructed in the city and all over the state, but also because of the tremendous variety of styles — ranging from the eclectic High Victorian Gothic and Spanish Colonial Revival modes to the emerging Chicago School style — that he was willing and able to use. He was so flexible and adaptable that some critics have accused him of being an architectural hustler, a draftsman willing to do anything for anybody with the money.

Born in Chicago in 1849, Flanders was educated in the public schools there. It is possible that he met and was influenced by Daniel Burnham, a contemporary who graduated from Chicago's single central high school in 1865, and went on to found the famous firm of Burnham and Root. No record exists indicating that Flanders ever received formal architectural training, and it is more likely that he gained his knowledge of carpentry, drafting, and engineering through apprenticeship to a firm of established masters and journeymen, as Burnham and even Frank Lloyd Wright did. In 1871, he was employed as a draftsman in the minor firm of Schmid and Zucker, where he remained until moving to Minneapolis in 1874.

He arrived in Dallas in August of 1876, drawn by the glowing tales of a promising boomtown, but found what he described as almost a shantytown. The people had reverted to building temporary, wood-frame buildings because of the tremendous, immediate demand for new construction brought by the arrival of the railroads. As Flanders recalled the situation in 1925:

When I arrived [in 1876] the outlook for a man of my profession was gloomy in the extreme. The town undoubtedly was doing a rushing business and in it all lines were prospering. But the buildings were of the flimsiest and most temporary kind. Nobody expected to remain here permanently. People seemed to regard development of the property as incident to the coming of the two railroads and destined to vanish in a short time, and their idea was to make all the money they could while the town lasted. I was the only exclusive architect in town but the fact that the ones here before me had departed did not augur well for me.[21]

Flanders got his first contract in 1877 for the Binkley Hotel at Sherman; in 1884, three years before Thomas Marsalis began his real estate venture called Oak Cliff, he opened the first residential development west of the Trinity River. He called the area, naturally enough, Flanders Heights and built his home there. However, the development, situated approximately at Sylvan and what is now the Dallas-Fort Worth Turnpike, was not in the line of Dallas' growth and proved to be a disaster. Flanders fled to California but returned four years later, reestablished his practice, and remained in Dallas for over twenty-two years.

During this period, he constructed an incredible number of buildings throughout the North Texas region. He was responsible for 15 county courthouses, including Dallas' fifth, and 125 churches including his masterpiece, the Trinity Methodist Church (212). His commissions in Dallas included the residence of Dr. L. W. Locke, who was the first man in the city to seek the aid of an architect in building his home; of Jules E. Schneider (186); of W. H. Flippen (185), as well as his bank building; of John Bookhout (192), Charles Ott (180), C. A. Keating, and George Atkins. He also built many commercial buildings and schools including Oliver and Grigg's Bank, the Cockrell Building (41), the first T&P offices (29), the original State Fair Exposition buildings of 1887 (251), the Alamo School (119), the Columbian School (115), the San Jacinto School (169), and the Grand-Windsor Hotel and Annex (27). In 1913 Flanders returned to the West Coast where he built another Flanders Heights development in Hollywood, emphasizing the California Bungalow style. He died there in 1928.

His Grand-Windsor Hotel was by far Dallas' most pretentious and opulent, and for a decade after its construction would house the city's most noted visitors. The first of the hotel's three stages was the LeGrande, built in 1875 on the southwest corner of Commerce and Austin and followed in 1879 by the Windsor on the northeast corner of Main and Austin streets. In 1882, Colonel William

25. LOOKING EAST FROM THE COURTHOUSE TOWER, c. 1895

Many of Dallas' lost architectural landmarks can be seen in this view looking east along Commerce Street. From the left foreground can be seen the four-story Windsor Hotel, the top of the Gaston Building, the dome of the Dallas Club, the 1889 City Hall, and the tower of the Post Office Building. Across Commerce from the Post Office tower is the spire of the First Methodist Church, and the Oriental Hotel looms to the right. The mercantile warehouse of Blankenship and Blake (shown here as the Texas Drug Company) stands in the center of the photograph and to the right one sees Ben Cabell's Livery Stable, Ben E. Wolfe and Company, the Dallas Opera House, the mansard roof of Boren and Stewart's wholesale grocery warehouse, and in the distance, the residential area known as The Cedars.

Dallas Historical Society Archives.

GRAND-WINDSOR

HOTEL

CORNER MAIN, AUSTIN AND COMMERCE STREETS.

DALLAS. : : : TEXAS.

THE ONLY FIRST-CLASS HOUSE IN THE CITY.

RATES, $2, $2.50 AND $3 PER DAY; ROOMS AND ACCOMMODATIONS GOVERN PRICES.

FINEST SAMPLE ROOMS IN THE STATE

THE House recently has undergone changes, which in appointments and furnishing, none surpasses it. The Cuisine is now under the care of Col. John W. Ross. His superior in this department is not in the State. Capacity of House, 300 persons.

W. H. WHITLA, Manager.

E. Hughes purchased the two independent hotels, joined them by a diagonal, second-story bridge across Austin Street, and merged them as the Grand-Windsor. Flanders then built a new, four-story addition in 1884-85 on the northeast corner of Commerce and Austin streets, across from the Dallas Opera House. The Grand-Windsor (26) was acclaimed by the actors, drummers, and businessmen who stayed there for its elaborate menus featuring venison, prairie chicken, and oysters, and for its luxurious accommodations including a well-publicized $1,100 chandelier in the lobby.

Though vaguely Italianate, the Annex, with its rough stone walls and heavy arches, was very reminiscent of the similar Rhineland-inspired buildings of Chicago, built by German immigrant architects such as Edward Baumann, Cord Gottig, August Bauer, and Otto Matz. The Windsor section was demolished in 1900 by the *Morning News* to expand its plant. The LeGrand section was converted into the Windsor Auto Storage and Repair Shop in the 1920s, which left only the outer shell of the original building to be demolished about 1952.

A block down from the Grand-Windsor, on the northeast corner of Commerce and Lamar streets, Flanders pioneered the use of pressed brick in Dallas with the construction of two of the finest commercial buildings in the city. The Merchants Exchange Building (28), was a magnificent blending of the High Victorian Romanesque and Italianate styles. Built in 1884 at an enormous cost of $50,000, the building housed the 200-member Merchants Exchange, a consolidation of the old produce and cotton exchanges whose primary purpose was to promote the mercantile and manufacturing interests of the city. As part of the Exchange's inaugural celebration in October of 1884, a recently organized gentlemen's ballroom dancing club known as the Idlewild held its first Grand Ball in the newly constructed "palazzo." The horse drawn phaetons, driven by white-gloved black servants, drew up by the dozens to the entrance, allowing the debutantes of Dallas' finest society families to enter and perform their coming out ritual before what is today recognized as the oldest social club in Texas.

Directly east of the Merchants Exchange was the Gould Building (29), housing the executive offices of the T&P Railway. This structure, named after the railroad's owner Jay Gould, was also designed by Flanders in the High Victorian Italianate mode, complete with screaming eagle atop its central gable. Built in 1885, it stood witness to Gould's triumphant march into Dallas in January of 1887 when he predicted, "Dallas is the finest city in the Southwest, destined to have a population of over 250,000 in my lifetime."[22] Ironically, Gould, who rose from the position of country store clerk in upstate New York to the presidency of four of the nation's most important rail lines, New York City's elevated railways, and Western Union Telegraph Company (while wresting control of the Erie-Lackawanna Railroad from Cornelius Vanderbilt), died in 1892 when Dallas' population had reached just under 43,000, two years after his Commerce Street headquarters burned to the ground.

The architectural styles used by Flanders — the High Victorian Romanesque, Gothic and Italianate, were a post-bellum phenomenon in the United States that achieved distinctive appearance through the use of polychromatic contrasts. John Ruskin first advocated the High Victorian principles of "constructional coloration" and "permanent polychrome," in his book *The Seven*

26. GRAND-WINDSOR HOTEL, c. 1886
Dallas' most luxurious hotel in the 1880s was the Grand-Windsor where visitors such as John L. Sullivan and Admiral Winfield Scott Schley dined on buffalo tongue, venison steak, quail, sea turtle, oysters, and wine jelly. Created by the merger of the LeGrande and Windsor hotels in 1882, it was the pride of the city until it was eclipsed by the construction of the Oriental Hotel in 1893. The last remnants of the Grand-Windsor were destroyed in 1952. *Dallas Historical Society Archives*

27. GRAND-WINDSOR HOTEL, c. 1890
James Flanders' 1885 addition to the hotel. The sheets in the foreground were erected as construction barricades. *Dallas Historical Society Archives*

28. GASTON BUILDING, c. 1895 *(Above left)*
The Gaston Building, constructed in 1884 as the Merchants Exchange at the northeast corner of Commerce and S. Lamar streets, was purchased by Dallas civic leader Capt. W. H. Gaston in 1889. In 1928 the building's intricately detailed facade was stuccoed, a prelude to its destruction in 1969 for a parking lot. *Courtesy of Dallas Public Library.*

29. GOULD BUILDING, c. 1885 *(Left)*
The home office of Jay Gould's Texas & Pacific Railroad was festooned with patriotic banners and bunting when it was opened in 1885 on Commerce Street adjacent to the Gaston Building. Both structures were designed by Dallas' most flamboyant and enigmatic 19th-century architect, James Flanders. Built in the exuberance of the Italianate style, the **T&P Building** burned in 1890. *Dallas Historical Society Archives.*

30. SANGER BROTHERS BLOCK, c. 1892 *(Above)*
Established in 1872, the dry goods emporium of Alex and Philip Sanger dominated Dallas' commercial life for years. When the Romanesque structure was completed adjacent to the original polychromatic Italianate building (left) in 1890, Sanger Brothers was acknowledged as the finest and most progressive retail department store in the South. The Sanger block was demolished in 1977. *Dallas Historical Society Archives.*

31. SECURITY MORTGAGE AND TRUST BUILDING, c. 1895
Constructed in 1888 at the northeast corner of Main and Austin streets, the Trust Building was a rare, classic example of Richardsonian Romanesque architecture in Dallas. Purchased in 1922 by the Sanger Brothers and incorporated into their operation until the mid-1960s, this splendid building was demolished along with the rest of the complex. *Courtesy of Dallas Public Library.*

32. DOWNTOWN, c. 1900
This photograph of Dallas' commercial district, illustrates the effect of only a few decades on the city's transformation from its overwhelmingly rural and agricultural origins toward a goal of urban and industrial prosperity. A reporter for *Frank Leslie's Illustrated Newspaper* of New York reviewed the transition in 1888: "As I walked Dallas' streets and saw on every hand so many evidences of prosperity and wealth, I could not but stand in awe at the scenes presented. Colossal buildings were all around, the sidewalks were full of goods, and the streets were jammed with vehicles, while thousands of people were rushing up and down, business bent."
Dallas Historical Society Archives.

Lamps of Architecture, published in London in 1849. His proposals were embraced enthusiastically by later architects, who emblazoned a marvelous array of bands, crisscross patterns, and stripes across the width and breadth of their buildings.

As exemplified by the Merchants Exchange and the Gould Building, the High Victorian stylists reveled in their disdain for "classical" beauty, for this quality was tainted by its association with the Greek Revival. Instead, these architects sought to achieve "truth," "reality," and "character" — terms easy to use but difficult to define. "Character," however, was easily understood by the Victorians. It was that quality in a man which expressed strength of will, forcefulness, determination, and fierce individuality, and which had forged not only a British colonial empire, but also an American empire from the Atlantic Ocean to the Pacific. The dictum of Louis Sullivan and Frank Lloyd Wright that "form follows function" stands appallingly pale in comparison. Part of the importance of Victorian architecture is that it stands as one of the last monuments to that uniquely American ideal of what the individual can be, an ideal which is quickly disappearing in the twentieth century. It is symbolic of a time when a man at least had the opportunity to try to freely direct his own destiny with little fear of control, manipulation, and constraint by corrupt unions, government bureaucracy, or monolithic, multinational conglomerates.

Among Dallas' early civic leaders, perhaps the Sanger Brothers best grasped the potential that this era proferred. Partly from their parents' desire that they better themselves and partly from a desire to avoid the rigors of Prussian military service, each of the five Sanger brothers — Philip, Alex, Lehmen, Samuel, and Isaac — immigrated to the United States from the tiny town of Obernbreit, in German Bavaria, at two-year intervals beginning in 1852. Each brother, independent of the others, hustled around New York and Connecticut, and all eventually settled into jobs in retail merchandising, one of the few professions readily open to Jews at that time. In 1857, Isaac was offered a partnership in a wholesale clothing firm in McKinney, Texas, by Jacob Brown, and in 1858 Lehmen joined the firm; but in 1860 they moved the business to Weatherford because of some religious and anti-abolitionist sentiments aimed against them. When the Civil War broke out, Lehmen, Philip, and Isaac judiciously enlisted in the Southern cause, fighting sporadically until the crushing defeat of the Confederacy prompted them to once again consider the dry goods market in Texas. In 1865, Lehmen established a store in Millican, about seventy-five miles northwest of Houston and at that time the northern terminus of the H&TC. A few months later, Philip and Isaac joined him and they began their careers as terminal merchants; gradually expanding northward as the H&TC laid tracks, the brothers opened stores at each consecutive terminus. These stores were no more than wood-frame crackerboxes, typical of the buildings being thrown up overnight everywhere along the frontier, but the Sanger brothers used them to great advantage, establishing themselves successively at Bryan, Hearne, Calvert, Bremond, Kosse, Grosbeck, Corsicana, Waco, and in 1872, Dallas.

Operating first in a two-story brick building on the courthouse square, the Sangers recognized that this crossroads town was at last the place to stop chasing the railroads and settle in permanently. At this point the dedication to make the store and the town the finest in the South began. The business was departmentalized: Isaac became the buyer for the firm, first in Galveston and later in New York; Lehmen and Samuel managed the store in Waco; and Alex took over operations in the Dallas store with Philip assisting in advertising and public relations. Thus was born the mammoth enterprise "which began on nothing, but by fair dealings, clear judgments, and patient labors, along with great taste and symmetry in arrangement and display, attained the very summit of ambition and the most liberal patronage enjoyed by any house in the city."[23] By the mid 1890s, they were doing over $3 million in business annually, a phenomenal amount for the time and place.

The Sanger Brothers Buildings (until they

33. NORTH TEXAS NATIONAL BANK BUILDING, c. 1895
Among the city's most outstanding architectural examples of the Western tradition was the massive North Texas National Bank, built 1888-95 on the north side of Main Street between Lamar and Poydras. Its impregnable, Romanesque stone-fortress appearance echoed the banks of Colorado and California gold rush towns which relied on the overt display of strength and security to assure depositors they were bandit-proof. Continuously occupied by financial institutions until the 1940s when it was converted into the Maurice Hotel, the building was demolished in 1967 for the proposed Two Main Place. *Courtesy of Dallas Public Library*.

34. ALLIANCE BUILDING, c. 1895 *(Left)*
The Texas Farmer's Alliance Exchange Building, built in 1887 at the southwest corner of Market and Wood streets, was the national headquarters and central warehouse of the Farmers' Alliance, the rural progenitor of the American Populist Movement. This enormous structure with its elaborate Queen Anne brickwork and roofline, designed and constructed by Albert Ullrich at a cost of $52,000, was an expression of the tremendous pride and independence these Southern farmers felt in their "agrarian revolt." As Populism slowly died in the early years of the 20th century, the Exchange Building was sold to a succession of agricultural implement dealers and finally demolished for a parking lot in 1922. *Courtesy of Dallas Public Library*

35. KNEPFLY AND SONS, JEWELERS, c. 1892 *(Above)*
Kneply and Sons jewelry store, completed c. 1888 at the southwest corner of Main and Poydras, presented a fine example of Victorian splendor in Dallas' commercial architecture. Designed by Albert Ullrich, this quietly Byzantine structure with its intricately detailed stone carving and pressed-metal facade (accented by the picturesque cast-iron sidewalk clock) burned in the early 1920s. *Dallas Historical Society Archives*

were demolished in 1977 by the Dallas County Community College District) occupied the entire block bounded by Elm, Austin, Main, and Lamar streets (30), and for decades stood solidly and defiantly proclaiming Dallas as a city of note. The first, built in 1884, evoked the High Victorian Italianate style and featured a partial cast-iron facade manufactured by the MacMurray-Judge Company of St. Louis.

The second, built in 1889-90, facing the corner of Elm and Austin streets, was a magnificent structure very similar to the 1888 Security Mortgage and Trust Company Building (31), located behind it on the corner of Main and Austin streets. Sanger Brothers was occupying the Trust Building by 1922 and remained at that location until the mid-1960s, when the building was sold to the DCCCD for the first of its campuses, El Centro. Both of these red sandstone edifices, with their ponderous pillars, sweeping, arched entrances, and rusticated ground floors, were florid examples of the Richardsonian Romanesque style which was at the time astonishing the country. The originator of the style, the brilliant architect Henry Hobson Richardson, startled the public in 1874 with the completion of his Trinity Church in Boston, and went on to singlehandedly change the American concept of the Romanesque by his use of rock-faced masonry, and by the power, simplicity, and dignity with which he disposed a sense of weight and massiveness in his works.

However, as much as these two buildings depend on the influence of Richardson, they retain, quite by chance, a uniqueness and vitality which he never suggested. The second Sanger building, with its dwarfish Norman battlement, and the Trust Building, with its extended bays and elaborate decorative detailing (especially in the scrollwork of the protruding oriel and in the carved sandstone portraits of a woman, said to be the mistress of the Trust Company's president, J. T. Trezevant) reveal the added influence of the Chicago commercial style which was evolving contemporaneously with Richardson. This Chicago style focused exclusively on the needs of merchants and businessmen, and as a result, emphasis was placed on wider windows and bays to allow for increased sunlight, airiness, and storage room. Features of both styles were incorporated into these buildings, primarily because of the architect's lack of formal, structured training. Yet this same flaw — the fact that the architects practicing in Dallas never studied at the Massachusetts Institute of Technology or the Ecole des Beaux-Arts in Paris — gave the city's buildings a unique flair, exuberance, and distinctiveness. Because Dallas' architects were too unschooled to make sophisticated copies, they instead evolved a very freewheeling architecture: a lyrical composite of all the prevailing styles, the knowledge of which had been garnered from pattern books, popular literature, visits East, and by comparing notes with other local architects.

Both Sanger Brothers buildings, and probably the Trust Company Building as well, were designed and executed by A. B. Bristol, a Cleveland-trained architect who had been practicing for nearly twenty-five years when he moved to Dallas in 1884. He began his practice in Cleveland in 1859 and moved to Houston eighteen years later, where he developed a keen sense of the local market, the aesthetic climate, and the available materials necessary for obtaining prestige contracts. His work in Dallas included the mercantile house of Blankenship and Blake (25), the 1888 City Hall (37), the twin school buildings of Cumberland Hill and Oak Grove (191 and 50), St. Mary's College (148), and several residences including those of Thomas Jefferson Word (138) and Mrs. M. A. Morrill (188).

Bristol's use of the Romanesque, as in the Security Mortgage and Trust Company Building, was far from innovative, especially when applied to banking or financial establishments. The impregnable appearance of the rough stone in that style made it extremely popular with bankers and it appeared in hundreds of towns, primarily west of the Mississippi — places where people like Butch Cassidy or Cole Younger might make their presence felt in a somewhat antisocial manner.

Bartholomew Blankenship and Colonel Henry Exall were very sensitive to this possibility when they commissioned the J. B. Legg Archi-

36. FIRST BAPTIST CHURCH, c. 1895

In 1890, Colonel C.C. Slaughter donated $60,000 to the First Baptist Church for the construction of a monumental house of worship. The congregation hired the Cincinnati-trained Albert Ullrich as architect, and by 1891 he had finished this polychromatic, brick and stone masterpiece. Designed originally to face Patterson Street, the church was remodeled in 1928 by C.W. Bulger to open on Ervay. This magnificent church, brilliantly mixing elements of the High Victorian Gothic and Romanesque styles, is one of Dallas' few remaining 19th century structures.
Dallas Historical Society Archives

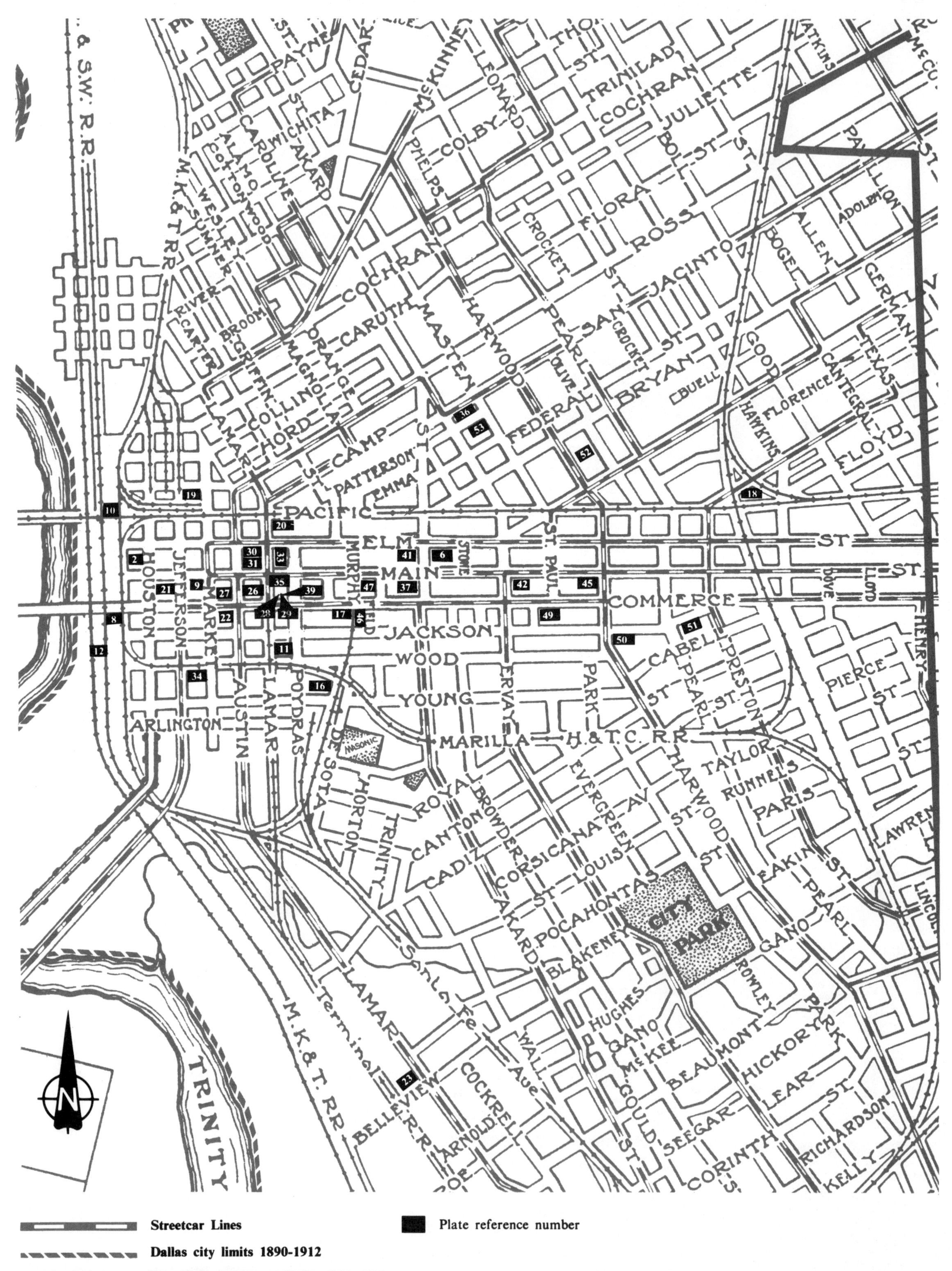

Streetcar Lines
Plate reference number
Dallas city limits 1890-1912
East Dallas corporate limits 1883-1890

37. CITY HALL, c. 1895

A.B. Bristol's unusual design for Dallas' third City Hall was one of the city's first attempts at architectural innovation and originality. At first hesitant, the public response was later enthusiastic; the Dallas *News* called the design "very modern, mainly, with a slight leaning toward the Gothic ... but mostly un-like anything ever built here before." This ponderous, ungainly structure, with its potted-plant roof finials, was built in 1888-89 at the northwest corner of Akard and Commerce streets at a cost of $80,000 in public bonds.
Dallas Historical Society Archives

tectural Company of St. Louis to design the North Texas Building (33) in 1888. Located on Main Street between Lamar and Poydras, this massive, fortresslike structure, complete with Norman battlement, also carried traces of the influence of H. H. Richardson. It was originally the home of the North Texas National Bank, which failed in the Panic of 1893. The North Texas Building was, of course, no monument to organic genius like Adler and Sullivan's Chicago Stock Exchange Building or Richardson's Trinity Church, but it was an accurate reflection of the mind and spirit of Dallas; it embodied those qualities of raw power, determination, strength, and even a little blind recklessness that made the city what it is today.

This spirit of fierce pride in the individual found its strongest wellspring in Texas, not only in the mercantile, robber-baron mentality of the Gilded Age but also in its opposing movement — that manifestation of the agrarian revolt known as the Farmers' Alliance, which reached its full flowering in Dallas in 1887 with the opening of the huge statewide marketing and purchasing warehouse called the Texas Alliance Exchange (34). This revolt, and the Farmers' Alliance which fostered it, grew out of the harsh, humiliating economic conditions that Southern farmers,

38. COMMERCE STREET, c. 1906
Looking west on Commerce Street from the corner of Akard, part of the third City Hall can be seen to the far right. Next door are the ornately detailed Police Station-Fire House and the offices of the Dallas *Dispatch*. These two florid buildings, reminiscent of the Victorian Italianate splendor of the gold rush era in San Francisco and Denver, were constructed in 1888 and demolished along with the City Hall in 1911. In the background is the Hotel Southland, still under construction. *Courtesy of Mr. Charles Coldwell*

39. DALLAS CLUB BUILDING, c. 1910
The Dallas Club, a prestigious gentlemen's organization which restricted membership to the business, civic, and professional leaders of the city, was a direct result of the great economic surge of the 1880s. Designed by the architectural firm of Stewart and Fuller, the Dallas Club Building was built in 1888 at the northwest corner of Commerce and Poydras streets. At a cost of $45,000, they created a distinguished, eclectic structure which included a bar, restaurant, and apartment rooms for members of this august body. The building was demolished in 1920 for a parking lot. *Courtesy of Dallas Public Library*

40. INTERIOR, DALLAS CLUB, c. 1910
With the influx of new wealth and its attendant class consciousness, the Dallas club's charter proposed "the encouragement of social intercourse among its members, the support of literary undertakings, the study and cultivation of literature, the maintenance of a library and reading room and the promotion of the fine arts." *Dallas Historical Society Archives*

THE
COTTAGE

41. COCKRELL BUILDING, c. 1890
The Cockrell Building, built c. 1885 near the northeast corner of Main and Field streets, was an early office structure commissioned by the Cockrell family, Dallas' celebrated pioneer capitalists and entrepreneurs. Designed by James Flanders, the building served from 1922 to 1926 as headquarters for the fledgling Republic National Bank. It was demolished in 1930 to make room for a wing of the Republic's new structure, now called the Davis Building. *Dallas Historical Society Archives.*

42. DALLAS FEDERAL BUILDING, c. 1895
The Dallas Federal Building, housing the Post Office and U.S. Circuit Court for the North Texas District, was the city's only notable example of civic architecture, other than the County Courthouse. It was built in 1884 at the northeast corner of Commerce and Ervay — when that section of mid-downtown was only a sea of mud. *Dallas Historical Society Archives.*

43. DALLAS FEDERAL BUILDING, c. 1910
By the time the Annex facing Main Street was completed in 1904, the Dallas Federal Building had superseded the Courthouse as the center of town. This symbol of Dallas' growing self-assurance was razed in 1939 and the site served as a parking lot until construction of the present Mercantile Bank Building began in 1941. *Dallas Historical Society Archives.*

44. DOWNTOWN, c. 1895

Henry Stark of St. Louis visited Texas in the winter of 1895 and took this photograph of mid-downtown Dallas, looking east along Commerce Street from the Oriental Hotel. From left to right are the Middleton Building, the Federal Building, and the spire of the First Methodist Church. The residential structures seen in the foreground were common to the downtown area as late as World War I.

Dallas Historical Society Archives.

both white and black, faced at the end of the Civil War. This radicalization of the farmers was an attempt to break the stranglehold of the crop lien system, the two-tiered pricing of the furnishing merchant, and the abusive currency contractions caused by the bankers' and financiers' resumption of specie payments on the gold standard. It was a revolt against the emerging corporate state which the farmers believed would erode completely the democratic promise of America and suppress any reorganization of the country's exploitive monetary system seeking to bring a measure of economic fairness to the little man. The Farmers' Alliance was far from Marxist, however, and was socialist only to the degree that they banded together in a cooperative marketing of their cotton crop for the common good.

The Alliance was born in Lampasas County, Texas, in 1877 and reached its height in 1892, when it mobilized nearly 500,000 southern farmers in a cooperative effort to end the burden of poverty. The strongly pro-Alliance Dallas *Mercury* stated it this way: "The Alliance is growing in a most wonderful way and in a little while the farmers' community will be united solidly against these few dictatorial speculators and it is plain which side our merchants will be compelled to take."[24]

The chief target of the movement was the crop lien system which allowed the furnishing merchant to grudgingly dole out a miserly supply of foodstuffs and implements to the farmer at an enormously inflated credit price during the growing season, in return for a mortgage on the crop. This meant that at harvest time, the furnishing merchant col-

45. SIMPSON-McCOY HOUSE, c. 1890
Colonel James B. Simpson, an early Dallas lawyer and editor of the *Herald*, built this residence on the southwest corner of Main and S. Harwood streets in 1878. It was purchased in 1885 by Colonel John C. McCoy, who arrived in Dallas in 1845 as a Peters Colony Company agent and stayed to help John Neely Bryan organize the county and the town. The home remained in the McCoy family until 1906 when it was razed for commercial construction.
Dallas Historical Society Archives

lected not only his principal but also an exorbitant 100- to 200-percent rate of interest out of the farmer's crop, in effect confiscating his entire production and invariably leaving him still in debt as the cycle began all over again the next year. The desperate, cashless farmer, unable to obtain credit elsewhere, remained in bondage to the merchant as long as he failed to meet the outrageous required payments.

This system, which had driven millions out of the ruined, ramshackle South toward the West in the 1870s, was by the 1880s forcing additional thousands of farmers into foreclosure and the realm of landless tenantry. So great was the exploitation that the furnishing merchants, and the corporations that manipulated them, soon held title to nearly half of the workable farmland of the South. The Alliance and its warehouse gave the farmer an outlet to other, more distant markets, where he and all the other co-op members could get the best possible price for their crop. It also gave the organized farmers tremendous buying power to obtain discount prices on agricultural implements as well as their daily household and food supplies.

One of the major reasons the Alliance decided to locate its warehouse in Dallas was the freight rates on cotton and other commodities charged by the Missouri, Kansas & Texas Railway between Dallas and St. Louis. The railroad's discount freight structure, described by the Texas Railroad Commission as "the lowest local class rates as a whole of any of the railroads of the state," was allegedly made possible by an elaborate kickback scheme involving the St. Louis merchants, and

46. THE FIRST TEMPLE EMANU-EL, c. 1905
Temple Emanu-el, Hebrew for "God with us," was
an outgrowth of the Hebrew Benevolent Association
founded in 1872 by Alexander Sanger. From the beginning, the congregation practiced "enlightened, liberal Judaism," reflecting their perception of Texas as
a land of new beginnings and new ways. The first
Temple was built in 1876 at the southwest corner of
Church Street (now Field) and Commerce. Probably
designed by James Flanders, its Moorish Revival
style was a bit of Victorian exotica evocative of the
beautiful Mudejar synagogues of 14th-century Spain.
The building had been converted to the University of
Dallas Medical Department just prior to its demolition in 1906. *Dallas Historical Society Archives.*

allowed the MK&T to charge only 52 cents
per 100 pounds on cotton from Dallas to St.
Louis, as opposed to the H&TC rate of 65
cents per 100 pounds from Dallas to Galveston;[25] this made the St. Louis connection
much more desirable to Dallas merchants
than the Gulf Coast ports. The lower fee
schedules were also a direct factor in Dallas'
tremendous growth in this period, attracting
not only merchants and businessmen from the
surrounding towns, eager to relocate and take
advantage of the shipping rates, but also organizations like the Farmers' Alliance, which
received an added discount from the MK&T
for shipping their cotton by the carload
rather than by the bale.

The Alliance's revolutionary attempt at res-
tructuring such an entrenched economic system did not occur peacefully. Hostility to the
movement on the part of the merchants and
a misguided press and public increased in

proportion to the growing size of the coopera-
tives. The Dallas *News* was one such paper
which never fully understood the extent of the
farmers' alienation:

> The discontented classes are told, and are
> only too ready to believe, that the remedy
> is more class legislation, more government,
> more paternalism, and more state socialism.
> The current gospel of discontent as a rule
> is sordid and groveling. Its talk is too much
> about regulating capital and labor . . . and
> too little about freeing capital and labor
> from all needless restraints and so promot-
> ing the development and diffusion of a high
> order of hardy manhood.[26]

Violence erupted sporadically during the
Great Southwest Strike of 1886, especially in
Fort Worth where Alliance men were supporting the Knights of Labor in their struggle
against Jay Gould and his railroads.

47. ST. MATTHEW'S CATHEDRAL, c. 1885
The second St. Matthew's Episcopal Cathedral was built in 1874 at the northeast corner of Commerce and Church streets, across from the Temple Emanuel. Built in the simple, primarily monochromatic early Gothic Revival style popular in New England c. 1800-1850, the cathedral exemplified the architectural style lag that was characteristic of the expanding westward frontier. This structure was never fully completed nor even consecrated because the rapid growth of the congregation and the noise from the nearby Santa Fe Railroad yards made worship services nearly impossible, forcing a relocation by 1888. The cathedral was demolished about 1900. *Dallas Historical Society Archives.*

48. INTERIOR ST. MATTHEW'S EPISCOPAL CATHEDRAL, c. 1885 *Dallas Historical Society Archives.*

The beginning of the end for the Alliance came in 1889 with the bankruptcy of the Dallas warehouse. The Alliance leaders had overextended their debt in an attempt to put together an enormous and elaborate marketing plan which they believed would break the backs of the furnishing merchants and of the crop lien system. They found instead that the bankers, either through conspiracy or out of fear of business reprisals, refused to advance enough financing to cover the Alliance commitments, and so after twenty months of operation the Dallas charter failed.

The movement struggled along, beleaguered on every side by politicians, capitalists, and the press, with only the agricultural poor fighting to sustain it. Its political arm, the Populist Party, continued to draw concessions from the brokers of power, wresting from Governor James Hogg in 1891 a state railroad regulatory commission. By 1896, however, it was apparent that "there was no way a political institution, a mere party — could continue to sustain the day-to-day democratic ethos at the heart of the Alliance cooperative. In the absence of the kind of hope and momentum engendered by the cooperation vision, the driving democratic energy that was the essence of the agrarian revolt gradually began to wear out."[27]

The Alliance's Dallas warehouse, which had been built in 1887 on the southwest corner of Market and Wood streets, was sold in 1893 to B.F. Avery and Son and later served as warehouse space for a number of agricultural implement companies. The building's architect, Albert Ullrich, used an elaborate pattern of Queen Anne brickwork and stark, jutting walls in this monument to the strong-willed American farmer.

Ullrich was a graduate of the Ohio Mechanic's Institute and served his apprenticeship under several professional Cincinnati architects before coming to Texas in the early 1880s. He worked as a circuit builder for several years, constructing a number of courthouses, jails, and school buildings throughout the state before arriving in Dallas to take over J.E. Flanders' firm about 1887. Flanders was making his first trip to California that year, after the failure of his West Dallas develop-

49. FIRST METHODIST CHURCH, c. 1895
Established in 1868 in a small, wood-frame chapel on Commerce Street at Lamar, the First Methodist Church began construction of this imposing, Gothic Revival brick church at the southeast corner of Commerce and Prather in 1886. In what was probably the earliest organized, mass flight to the suburbs in Dallas history, the church fathers decided in 1895 that the concept of a strong central church was anachronistic and that several suburban churches would best serve the interests of the congregation. Accordingly, the Trinity Church at McKinney and Pearl streets was dedicated as the First Church and the Grace Methodist Church was established at Junius and Haskell streets, leaving the downtown building abandoned by 1916. Within a few years, the church reversed its philosophy and attempted to reunite its congregation in a central church, built on Ross Avenue in 1924, but by then the damage was irreversible. The Prather Street church was demolished in 1920 to build a parking garage.
Courtesy of Dallas Public Library

58

50. OAK GROVE SCHOOL, c. 1890
The Oak Grove School, the identical twin of the Cumberland Hill School, was built in 1889 at the southeast corner of S. Harwood and Jackson. The work of architect A.B. Bristol, this eclectic Victorian structure was demolished in 1915 for commercial usage of the property. *Dallas Historical Society Archives*

ment, and apparently Ullrich took over his office at 709 Main Street and possibly some of his contracts. During Ullrich's first years in Dallas, he furnished the plans and superintended the construction of many prominent structures, including the Farmers Alliance Building at a cost of $52,000; the East Dallas School Building (156), $18,000; Knepfly and Son's Building (35), $20,000; the First Baptist Church (36), $60,000; and numerous other residences, warehouses, and mercantile buildings. By 1890, he had become the city's preeminent architect, handling contracts totaling over a quarter of a million dollars.

If Dallas was a little freewheeling about its architecture, it was even more so about its urban planning. A definite attitude of laissez-faire prevailed in terms of building codes, street design, regulation of housing development, or any sort of municipal planning. With the arrival of the railroads came an instantaneous influx of thousands of people, and predictably, the railroads also governed the growth pattern. With the H&TC situated a mile east of the courthouse, fully eighty percent of the population diffused itself in a narrow band between these two poles almost in the shape of a bell; the flange ran along the river with its two short, lateral extensions into Frogtown and Boggy Bayou, and the two sides

were bounded by the tracks of the T&P on the north and the H&TC switching yard (Marilla Street) on the south. The large-scale population shift north and south was not well established until the 1880s, leaving most of the population to congregate either around the courthouse or the East Dallas depot. The section in the middle, between Akard and Harwood streets, remained a muddy wasteland until 1884, when the federal government began an enormous, $150,000 Federal Building

51. TEMPLE SHAARITH ISRAEL, c. 1895
Because the terminal merchants who organized the Temple Emanu-el were almost exclusively Reform Jews, Dallas did not form an Orthodox church until Rabbi Louis Rathner created the congregation Sharis (later Shaarith) Israel over a feed store on Elm Street in 1887. The first temple was built near the corner of Jackson and Pearl streets in 1892. It was demolished in the 1920s when a new temple was built in The Cedars on Park Avenue across from the City Park. *Courtesy of Dallas Public Library*

52. CENTRAL CHRISTIAN CHURCH, c. 1895
The Victorian Gothic formalism of the Central Christian Church represented one of the rare, secluded enclaves of quiet dignity in the boisterous ferment of 19th-century Dallas. The church was built in 1891 at the southwest corner of Masten (now St. Paul) and Patterson streets by an unknown St. Louis architect who designed several remarkable features, including a unique, offset spire and a dazzling array of stained glass. The congregation, which formed in 1863 and in 1867 built the first church structure of any denomination in Dallas at Carondalet and Austin, began to dissolve about 1903 into several smaller, suburban "mission" churches; the building they abandoned was demolished in 1951 for a parking garage annex to the First Baptist Church. *Courtesy of Dallas Public Library*

53. MCCOY HOUSE, c. 1900
When Captain John M. McCoy, the nephew of John C. McCoy and a partner in his law firm for several years, built his home on N. Harwood Street near the corner of Live Oak c. 1895, the near North Dallas section had reached its zenith as an affluent, upper-middle-class suburb. Soon the city's virulent expansion farther north into Highland Park and Oak Lawn relegated the N. Harwood Street area to commercial development, and by 1928 the McCoy home was demolished for a parking lot. *Dallas Historical Society Archives*

to house the Post Office and United States Circuit Court for the North Texas District (42) at the northeast corner of Commerce and Ervay streets. At the time, the local citizenry scoffed at a location so far from the courthouse, but by 1890, the city's swelling 38,000-plus population had proved the federal government right as the Post Office surpassed the courthouse as the business center of town.

W. J. Edbrooke, special architect for the United States Treasury Department, was commissioned to design the building, and he constructed a beautifully articulate expression of Dallas' attitude toward itself. The building was derived from the grand Second Empire style of the French Second Republic, yet it vividly projected the stark, no-nonsense reality of the Texas frontier rather than the lavish, baroque quality of Napoleon III's Paris.

The greatness of Dallas' nineteenth-century, transitional era architecture lay in its relative honesty. There was very little attempt to promote a well-mannered imitation of any style, be it European or Chicago. Instead, the city's eclectic, audacious, wild-cattish individualism took over, freely adapting good taste and refinement to reflect the social system that existed on the frontier. The influence of Chicago and St. Louis was there, but instead of being a simple imitation of those cities, Dallas was an unrestrained eruption on the face of the prairie, built by men like Faulkner's Colonel Sutpen, "who came out of nowhere and without warning upon the land, with a band of wild negroes, tore violently a plantation from virgin swamp."[28]

Like the architect Albert Ullrich, the entire city was prospering. The rival city of East Dallas was incorporated in 1890, adding its population of 5,000 in that census year and making Dallas, with 38,067 people, the largest city in the state. Manufacturing was expanding, bringing new markets in furniture, tin, and steel; the leather industry had become the largest in the South; but disaster lurked in the shadows, waiting to cripple the country with the depression of 1893.

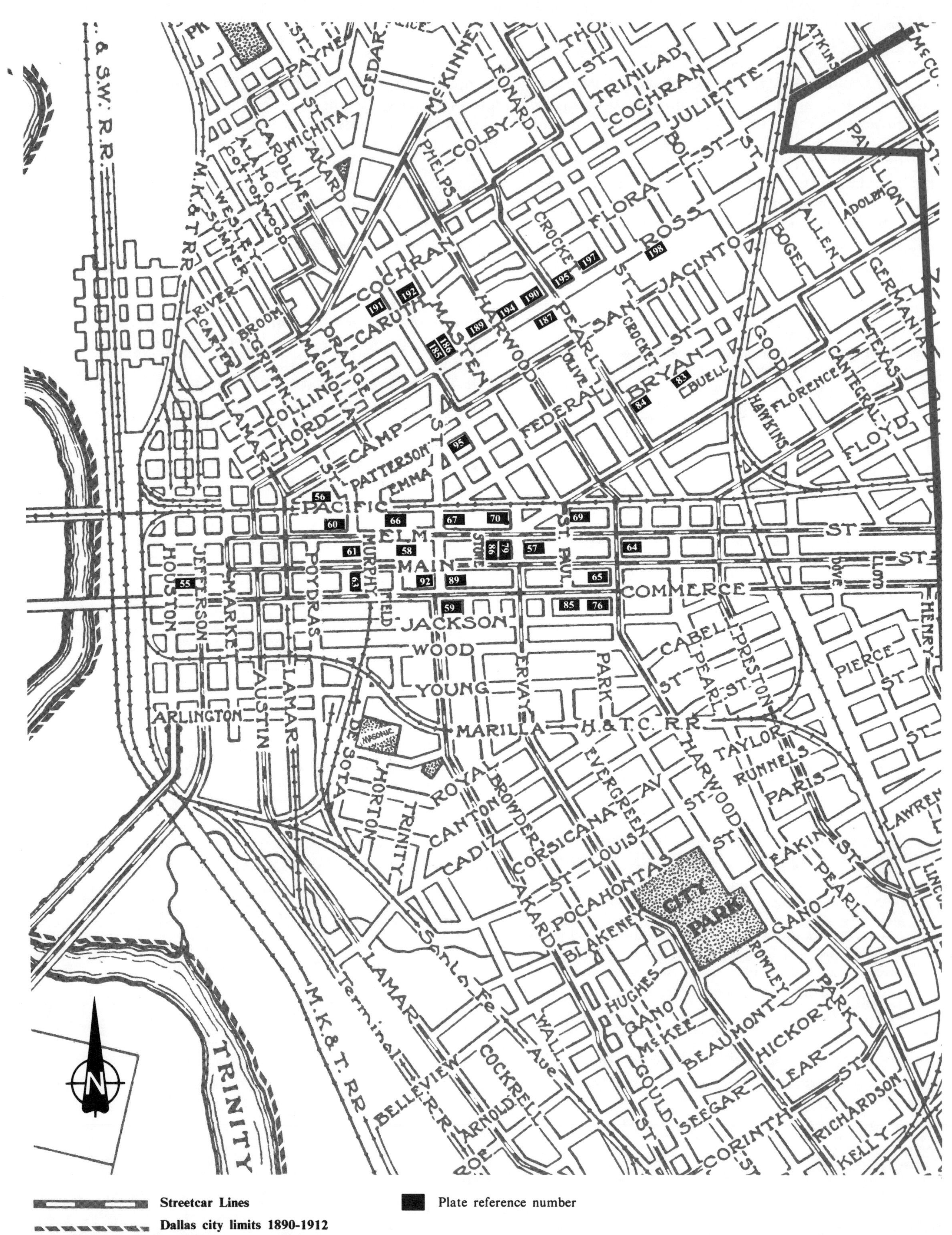

N
& S.W. R.R.
M.K.& T. R.R.
TRINITY
PAYNE
CEDAR
SKINNER
LEONARD
TRINILAD
COCHRAN
JULIETTE
ADOLEM
GERMANIA
WICHITA
AKARD
COLBY
PHELPS
FLORA
ROSS
JACINTO
TEXAS
CANTEGRAL
ALLEN
CAROLINE
ALAMO
COTTONWOOD
WESLEY
SUMNER
RIVER
CARTER
GRIFFIN
BROOM
COCHRAN
CARUTH
MASTEN
HARWOOD
CROCKE
PEARL
SAN
BRYAN
CROCKET
OLIVE
BUELL
GOOD
FLORENCE
HAWKINS
FLOY
191 192 189 194 190 195 197 198
186 185 187 84 83
MAGNOLA
ORANGE
COLLIN
HORD
CAMP
PATTERSON
EMMA
FEDERAL
95
PACIFIC
ELM
MAIN
STONE
PAUL
ST
DOVE
LLOYD
HENRY
56 60 66 67 70 69
61 58 86 79 57 64
63 92 89 65
59 85 76
COMMERCE
55 JACKSON
HOUSTON
JEFFERSON
MARKE
AUSTIN
LAMAR
POYDRAS
MURPHY
FIELD
WOOD
YOUNG
ERVAY
PARK
CABEL
PRESTON
PEARL
PIERCE
ST
ARLINGTON
DE SOTA
MASONIC
MARILLA
H. & T. C. R.R.
TAYLOR
RUNNELS
HARWOOD
PARIS
HORTON
TRINITY
ROYAL
BROWDER
CANTON
CADIZ
CORSICANA AV
EVERGREEN
LOUIS
AKARD
POCAHONTAS
BLAKENEY
HUGHES
GANO
McKEE
WALL
GOULD
SEEGAR
CITY PARK
BEAUMONT
HICKORY
PEARL
GANO
PARK
ROWLEY
EAKIN
LEAR
LAWREN
LINC
RICHARDSON
KELLY
CORINTH
LAMAR
Terminal
Santa Fe
BELLEVIEW
M.K.& T. R.R.
COCKREL
ARNOLD
ROE
Streetcar Lines
Dallas city limits 1890-1912
East Dallas corporate limits 1883-1890
Plate reference number

3 DOWNTOWN 1890-1925

The early 1890s marked a transition period for the city. Dallas had accumulated the largest urban population in the state and its business enterprises were thriving, but there was still an insecurity about its humble frontier origins and a particular disdain for its cowtown image. Dallas began a conscious effort to cast off its backwoods ties and become a sophisticated trading center, St. Louis being the specific model most officials and businessmen wanted to imitate. During this time civic boosters turned their focus away from frontier enterprises toward a more "Eastern" cosmopolitanism, a change exemplified by the business community's increasing reliance on New England banking and financial houses, by the increasing trade with Chicago, St. Louis, and New York, and by the conspicuous growth of large, Newport- and Long Island-inspired mansion residences.

Thus, while the city was ripe for transition, "clean" industry — banking, finance, and insurance — began to ascend into the public eye, pushing the cattle interests ever westward with the railroads. Beginning with Trezevant and Cochran in 1883, through the Praetorians in 1899 and Southwestern Life in 1903, the number of insurance companies establishing home offices in Dallas grew, reaching forty-three by 1939 and making Dallas the fourth largest insurance center in the country. Similarly, banking houses and deposits multiplied rapidly; bank clearings for 1890 stood at \$96,371,000, over seven times what they had been only three years before, and in 1914 the Federal Reserve Bank for the Eleventh District was established in Dallas, securing the city's role as a regional financial center.

Much of this change of focus was directly attributable to Dallas' peculiar brand of civic "boosterism," a phenomenon scoffed at by some urban scholars, but which was nonetheless an unashamed and powerful factor in the city's growth. Dallas in fact was founded only through the persistence of John Neely Bryan's boisterous boosterism, motivated partially by self-interest and partially by true civic pride and benevolence. Dallas, like William Faulkner's mythical Jefferson, Mississippi, "awoke from its communal slumbers into a rash of Rotary and Lions Clubs and Chambers of Commerce and City Beautifuls," following the archetypal pattern of the Southern American small town, "dubbing itself city as Napoleon dubbed himself emperor and defending the expedient by padding its census rolls — a fever, a delirium in which it would confound forever seething with motion and motion with progress."[29] This self-inspired momentum produced results for Dallas which otherwise would never have occurred.

A good example of this useful self-delusion was Dallas' quixotic dream of navigating the Trinity River, and the influence this scheme had on local rail freight rates. Dallas' civic leaders, especially those with large manufacturing or retailing interests, had for many years tried to promote development of the river as an alternate freight route to the Gulf. Part of the noise they made was genuine and part of it was a bluff to convince the railroads to lower their freight schedules, and thereby stall commercial Trinity River development and competition. Apparently, the ruse worked and the people of Dallas successfully used the "snagboat" *Dallas*, which arrived from Galveston in 1892, and the *H. A. Harvey Jr.*, a steam paddlewheeler which ran excursion trips from its Commerce Street tie-up to a

54. THE HARVEY, c. 1893
In 1893 the Trinity River Navigation Co. purchased
the steam paddlewheeler *H. A. Harvey, Jr.* (shown
here at its Commerce Street mooring), and brought
it from New Orleans up the Trinity to Dallas. Its
67-day trip fired the public imagination over the
possibility of commercial river development and
enhanced the local effort to threaten the railroads
into lowering freight rates. By 1897, the immediate
prospect for Trinity navigation had died, but Dallas
had succeeded in intimidating the railroads. Within a
year, the Harvey was sold and returned to Louisiana.
Dallas Historical Society Archives

dam thirteen miles downstream in 1893, as
persuasive levers against the railroads to
lower their rates. In 1895, the Texas Railroad
Commission commented on the tremendous
pressure from cities like Dallas: "The efforts
of rival cities, and of different localities, each
to obtain advantages over the others gives us
much labor and anxiety in endeavoring to al-
lay their jealousies ... Some of our cities
have sought to have us arrange rates as to
make them jobbing centers for large parts of
the state. And we are often requested to
make special low rates for some particular
company or person." Later in the same report, the commission acknowledged that a re-
duction of from one to six cents per 100
pounds had occurred on the shipment of commodities such as cotton, grain, cotton seed
products, lignite and wool. On cotton alone
the commission noted savings of over
$825,000 to shippers, who that year freighted
a record 3.3 million bales out of the state.[30]

The city expanded its limits in 1890 — almost trebling its size — and the suburban
land boom began in earnest, creating fashionable developments like Colonial Hill in South
Dallas and Maple Avenue to the north. Real
estate transfers rose from just under $6 mil-
lion in 1888 to nearly $15 million by 1890, a
year in which 769 new buildings were erected
with a value of $40,710,000.[31]

The most celebrated of the new structures
was the towering Dallas County Courthouse
(55), a stately and dignified Victorian edifice
well suited to the city's emerging image of
solid mercantilism. Its cornerstone was laid in
1890 on the same property that John Neely
Bryan had donated in 1850, and it was completed late in 1892. The architects, Orlopp
and Kusener of Little Rock, built this graceful Romanesque structure of red sandstone,
quarried near Pecos in West Texas, and blue
granite from Arkansas. It cost nearly
$350,000, an immense sum for the 1890s, but
unlike the majority of its predecessors, it has
yet to burn down. (Flander's 1880 courthouse, the first "fireproof" courthouse ever
built in the city, burned to the ground in
1890. The previous one, built in 1871 for
$100,000 — possibly by J. Reilly Gordon of
New York, a notorious Texas courthouse
hustler — burned in 1880.)

55. THE SIXTH DALLAS COUNTY COURTHOUSE, c. 1895

The magnificent Victorian Romanesque structure built 1890-92 on John Neely Bryan's original courthouse square is the last survivor of a long series of ill-fated 19th-century county buildings. The first courthouse, a 10-by-10-foot log cabin erected by Bryan in 1846, burned in 1848; the second, a double log cabin built in 1850 when Dallas officially became the county seat, was dismantled in 1857 to construct the third courthouse, a square, red brick building. On the verge of collapse, it was replaced in 1871 by a sophisticated, gray stone building with a bell tower which partially burned in 1880. The fifth county courthouse was built by James Flanders in 1881 out of the remaining walls of the previous building, but it too burned in 1890. Fortunately, the only damage the surviving "Old Red" Courthouse has sustained in its near ninety years was the removal of its clock tower in 1919 along with one of its two griffins, christened "Hindsight" and "Foresight." In spite of being labeled in the 1940s as "unsafe, unsightly . . . a decayed monument to the grandiose and ornate taste of the 1890s . . . and an architectural monstrosity," Old Red has survived her critics and is now protected by a listing in the National Historic Register.
Courtesy of Dallas Public Library

56. THE SECOND GOULD BUILDING, c. 1895
Built in 1891 at the corner of Griffin Street and
Pacific Avenue, the General Office Building of the
Texas & Pacific Railroad was the first and only
Dallas example of the geometrically regular Chicago
School commercial design until construction of the
Praetorian Building sixteen years later. Designed by
Otto Lang, at that time chief of the T&P
architectural division, this small office structure was
amazingly similar in principle to the great mercantile
edifices constructed in Chicago in the late
19th-century by the firms of William LeBaron
Jenney, Burnham and Root, and Louis Henry
Sullivan. The structure was demolished in 1954 for a
parking lot. *Courtesy of Dallas Public Library*

57. MIDDLETON BROTHERS BUILDING, c. 1895
The exuberant eclecticism of the Middleton Brothers
Building was a direct reflection of the growing
wealth and boomtown spirit of Dallas, which by the
1890 census had become the largest metropolitan
area in Texas. Prosperity in the city seemed
boundless when the Middleton brothers, who made
fortunes as real estate brokers and gravestone
makers, built their offices at the northeast corner of
Main and Ervay streets in 1892, but within a year,
Dallas felt the devastating effects of the financial
Panic of 1893. Built on the eve of one depression,
the Middleton Brothers Building survived until the
brink of another, the Great Depression of 1929,
before it was demolished for new construction.
Courtesy of Dallas Public Library

The designer, Maximilian A Orlopp, Jr., was born in Brooklyn, New York, in 1859. In 1881 he graduated from the U.S. Naval Academy at Annapolis as a civil engineer specializing in railroad surveys, but he began to practice architecture in 1885, apparently without formal training. Orlopp moved to Fort Worth after the construction of the Dallas Courthouse, entered the firm of Sanguinet and Staats, and built several courthouses around the state.

Orlopp's son Donald followed his father to Sanguinet and Staats as an office boy at age thirteen in 1904, rose to the position of chief designer by 1914, and left to establish his own practice in Dallas. Among the most notable structures built by his firm were the Cedar Crest Country Club, the Queen Theater (67), the Crystal Theater, Galveston's Crystal Palace, and many residences, schools, and ice plants in North Texas and Oklahoma.

While Dallas and the rest of the country were obliviously engaged in the innocent architectural fantasies of the High Victorian post-Civil War era, a revolution had been going on in Chicago. In 1882, two brash young architects named Daniel Burnham and John Wellborn Root constructed the ten-story Montauk Building, which most architectural historians acknowledge as the world's first skyscraper. Though Winston Weisman has shown that the Montauk had roots in William LeBaron Jenney's First Leiter Building (Chicago, 1879) which in turn was probably derived from James McLaughlin's Shillito Store (Cincinnati, 1877), most historians note the fully developed conceptualization of the Montauk as a straightforward structure of brick, relieved only by thin string courses of

58. SCOLLARD BUILDING, c. 1895
In the two decades following construction of the Texas & Pacific General Office Building, Dallas saw little more of the Chicago influence. Like the aboriginally austere Scollard Building, most of the city's commercial structures retained their Western Victorian characteristics. Designed by M. A. Orlopp, Jr., architect of the 1892 Courthouse, this rough stone Romanesque structure was leveled in 1923 to build the original Republic National Bank (now called the Davis Building). *Courtesy of Dallas Public Library*

59. ORIENTAL HOTEL, c. 1893
Adolphus Busch's $500,000 Oriental Hotel, completed in 1893 on the corner of Commerce and Akard streets, was touted as the most luxurious hotel in the South. When President Roosevelt visited Dallas in 1905, he was greeted by 75,000 people, the Fourth Regimental Band, a twenty-one gun salute by the Dallas Artillery Company, and a parade down Elm and Akard streets to the Oriental's plush Presidential Suite. Although it was unrivaled in its interior splendor, the hotel's exterior was relatively unadorned. The squat, Arabesque dome and an exotic Turkish bath were its sole "Oriental" features. The hotel was demolished in 1924 to build the present Baker Hotel. *Dallas Historical Society Archives*

60. SHELL BUILDING, c. 1895
James Bogardus, America's first "Architect in Iron," invented the popular 19th-century system of cast-iron construction, using prefabricated piers, columns, beams, and wall panels, in his Eccentric Mill Works in New York City (1848). Although this system of total cast-iron construction was never employed in Dallas, elements of it appeared in the wonderfully elegant cast-iron facade of John F. Zang's Shell Building (1894) on Elm near the corner of Griffin Street. The structure, probably designed by Albert Ullrich, was vacated by Zang in 1906 when he sold his Texas Installment Company furniture store to open the "Crystal Hill" housing development in Oak Cliff. The Shell Building was destroyed in 1919 for a parking garage. *Courtesy of Old City Park, A Museum of Cultural History, Dallas, Texas*

61. NATIONAL EXCHANGE BANK BUILDING, c. 1894
The fortress-like National Exchange Bank on Main
Street was one of the most powerful and influential
Dallas financial institutions during the determinate
decades of the eighties and nineties. Chartered in
1875, the bank gained prominence in 1881 by
merging with the private banking firm of Gaston and
Thomas. In 1905, the National Exchange
consolidated with the American National to form the
mighty American Exchange National Bank, business
home of such civic titans as Royal Ferris, W. H.
Gaston, J. B. Wilson, C. C. Slaughter, and Nathan
Adams. In 1930, the American Exchange National
merged with the City National to form the present
First National Bank of Dallas. The old National
Exchange Bank Building was leveled in 1940 and is
now the site of One Main Place. *Courtesy of Dallas
Times Herald*

62. NATIONAL EXCHANGE BANK BUILDING, c. 1906
Courtesy of Dallas Public Library

terra cotta and completely devoid of Greek columns or Victorian furbelows, and agree with Thomas Tallmadge's assertion that "what Chartres was to the Gothic Cathedral, the Montauk Block was to the high commercial building."[32]

Then in 1884, William LeBaron Jenney, an engineering graduate of the Ecole Centrale des Arts et Manufactures in Paris who had built bridges for the Union Army during the war, added a revolution in construction methods to Burnham and Root's revolution in design when he built the world's first steel-framed, internal-skeleton structure, the Home Insurance Building of Chicago. Jenney's steel skeleton, coupled with Elisha Otis' 1857 invention of the passenger elevator, gave buildings the potential to reach almost any height and allowed thick masonry walls to be replaced by thin curtain walls with larger windows and more light, air, and space than ever before.

Aesthetically, the new skyscraper looked awkward and ungainly until Louis Henry Sullivan brought to the problem of unity in elevations a classically symmetrical solution in the Wainwright Building (St. Louis, 1890), a solution which later also led to the classical discipline of the Second Renaissance Revival. At the heart of this revolution in style was the belief that architecture must celebrate its own time, not look to the examples of the past, and accordingly the Chicago architects believed the primary expression of the 1890s should be the period's deference to technology, industry, and democracy. The Chicago School skyscraper represented the country's first independently American, democratic architecture — one which was not provincial, not colonial, and which, as Sullivan wrote, "would soon become a fine art in the true, the best sense of the word, an art that will live because it will be of the people, for the people and by the people."[33] The modern era in the history of the American city had begun.

Even though it was not of the skyscraper class, Dallas' first experience with the design forms of the Chicago style occurred in 1891 with the construction of the second Gould Building (56) by the T&P Railroad. Although only five stories tall and not a steel skeleton building, it reflected exactly the Chicago School tenets of straight fronts, flat roofs and level skylines, regular patterns of windows, and subordination of ornament. However, the financial Panic of 1893 and other forces combined to isolate the Gould Building as an aberration, rather than the norm in Dallas building.

In the 1890s, Dallas architects were primarily concerned with designing extravagant and unrestrained structures like the Middleton Brothers Building (57) or starkly primitive structures like the Scollard Building (58), until the crisis and depression of 1893 called a virtual moratorium on construction.

The reasons for this financial panic were many and complicated, but in general it began with the failure of the Philadelphia & Reading Railroad in February, 1893, which caused widespread alarm among bank depositors because of the country's overextended monetary position. Depositors began demanding their cash and hoarding gold; later, European countries began to withdraw gold reserves from the U.S. Treasury through their balance of payment notes, partly because of the Baring Brothers Bank failure in England in 1890, but also because they feared the recently enacted Sherman Silver Purchase Act to be an indication that the United States planned to abandon the gold standard. The Treasury's gold supply dropped to less than $20 million and an overproduction of paper money was allowed to fill the gap. By June, business activity was severely depressed due to the prevailing doubt in the government's ability to maintain gold payment on all the paper money, and by July, the banks had begun to fail. Before the year was out, 158 national banks and 415 state and private banks and trust companies went under.[34]

Dallas saw five of its banks fail, and business and agriculture were badly hurt. The price of cotton dropped to about 4.5 cents a pound, flour and lumber markets evaporated, and an exodus from the city began. The population, which had peaked at approximately 44,000 in 1892, declined to less than 39,000 by 1894; at the official census of 1900, it had still only recovered to 42,638.

63. LINZ BUILDING, c. 1900
Construction of the Linz Building at the southeast corner of Main and Martin streets (1898) was physical evidence of the end of the depression years following the Panic of 1893. The structure, which awkwardly tried to make the transition from the traditional Romanesque to the newer Chicago commercial style, was demolished in 1963 for a parking lot. *Courtesy of Dallas Public Library*

64. FIRST PRESBYTERIAN CHURCH, c. 1890
The First Presbyterian Church was one of Dallas' earliest attempts at permanent, monumental ecclesiastical architecture. Instead of logs or clapboards, brick and stone were used, accented by the Victorian splendor of stained glass and variegated ornamentation. Built in 1882 on the northeast corner of Main and Harwood streets, the church was demolished about 1917 after construction of the new First Presbyterian Church at Harwood and Wood streets. *Courtesy of First Presbyterian Church*

65. FIRST CUMBERLAND PRESBYTERIAN CHURCH, c. 1901
The stylistically similar yet ideologically opposed First Cumberland Presbyterian Church was constructed in 1898 at the northwest corner of Commerce and S. Harwood streets and razed in 1919 to build a Perfection Oil Company service station. *Dallas Historical Society Archives*

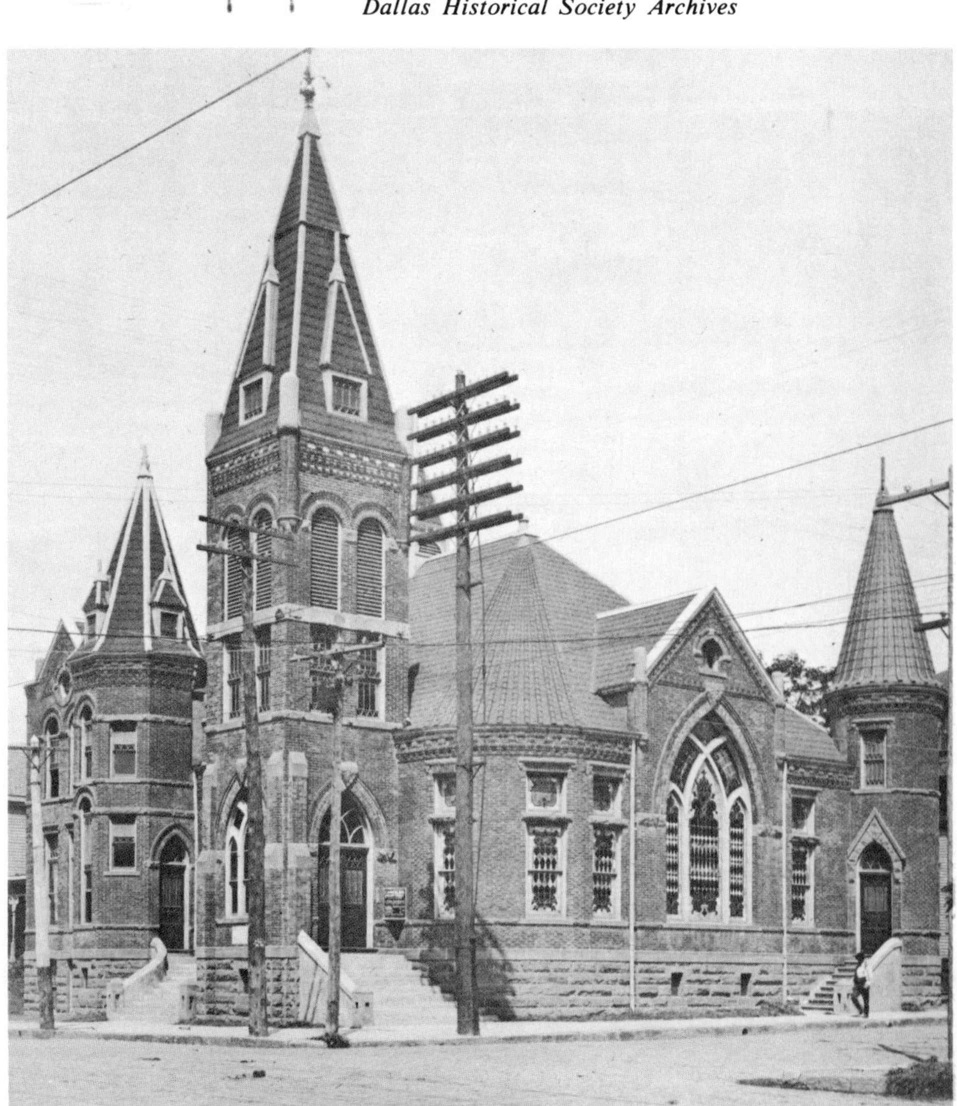

66. HIPPODROME THEATER, c. 1912
The Hippodrome Theater, shown under construction on Elm near Field Street, was the Egyptian Revival creation of Lang & Witchell. It was demolished in 1960. *Dallas Historical Society Archives*

Dallas' most illustrious victim of the depression was Thomas Field's Oriental Hotel (59), a daringly extravagant and visionary undertaking for the city in 1893. Planned as the most elegant hotel west of St. Louis, the depression caught Field with only half the construction completed, and it gained a local reputation as "Field's Folly." Field had made a fortune early as a pioneer real estate developer and promoter, a feat which propelled him into the inner sanctum of Dallas' "good old boy network," of capitalists, bankers, and industrialists like Captain Gaston, Cockrell, the Sangers, Flippen, Dilley, Ferris, Trezevant, and Blankenship. Field, whose enormous Queen Anne mansion (133) in East Dallas was the site of many lavish social functions and masterful business deals, had been one of the principals involved in attracting the railroads, had organized the Opera House, and had sat on the governing board of the State Fair. But his dream of building the South's finest hotel was shattered by the depression.

Field was forced to sell his interests in the hotel to a consortium of St. Louis investors including Adolphus Busch and Otto Herold, who retained Field's imaginative plan and finished construction of the 200-room hotel late in 1893 at a cost of over $500,000. It was a palace of such dazzling interior grandeur, with Italian marble, mahogany woodwork, impeccable food service, and fully electrified rooms and elevators, that many visitors wondered what it was doing in a frontier city like Dallas. Ironically, its exterior Richardsonian Romanesque design, conceived by the St. Louis architect Isaac S. Taylor, made it look more like a mercantile house than a palatial hotel, but Dallas' Oriental remained unchallenged in its internal splendor until 1914, when the Adolphus Hotel was opened.

One of the two notable buildings that did manage to materialize in the depression year of 1894 was the Shell Building (60). This cavernous structure with twenty-foot ceilings and a wonderfully-articulated cast-iron facade, complete with full-scale sculptures of

67. DETAIL OF ENTRANCE, QUEEN THEATER, c. 1915
Dallas Historical Society Archives

68. QUEEN THEATER, c. 1915
By 1920, dozens of ornate vaudeville palaces, smaller "live" theaters, and movie houses had firmly established Elm Street as Dallas' Theater Row, drawing hundreds of people every night with the brilliant glare of the stagelights or the flickering pulse of the motion picture projector. One of the most popular was the Queen Theater, designed in the Northern Italian mode of the Renaissance Revival by Donald Orlopp and built in 1913 on the corner of Elm and Akard streets. The Queen was demolished in 1956.
Dallas Historical Society Archives

"Liberty" and "Independence," was the largest iron-front building ever erected in the city. It was exclusively occupied by John F. Zang's Texas Installment Company, purveyors of furniture, carpets, stoves, and queensware, and utilizers of that revolutionary marketing concept — the installment credit plan.

The other major Dallas landmark to rise during the depression was the National Exchange Bank Building (61) on Main between Poydras and Martin Streets. Erected in 1894, probably by the J. B. Legg Company of St. Louis which built the equally formidable looking North Texas Bank Building, the National Exchange Bank Building was sold in 1904 to Colonel C. C. Slaughter, who renamed it after himself and hired C. W. Bulger and Son to expand it. Bulger's son Clarence, a graduate of the University of Chicago and chief designer for the firm, was a well-trained and knowledgeable architect who would soon become famous for his Praetorian Building design.

Considering his background, Clarence developed a very curious concept for the enlarged Slaughter Building. He added, in 1905, a Chicago commercial-style west wing to a distinctly Romanesque building. Then in 1909, he returned to the original rough stone style for a three-story addition above the main structure, but further added (at the expense of the 1885 Murphy-Bolanz Building, seen to the right in the photograph) an east wing that duplicated the Chicago mode of the 1905 west wing. The result, one of the most incredible and unique hybrids in the history of American architecture (62) & was a remarkable symbol of the adaptability required for architecture and architects to survive on the frontier.

C. W. Bulger, Sr., was born the son of a farmer in Delphi, Indiana, in 1851, and without formal training got his start in architecture as a contractor and designer of flour mills in Kansas. He opened an office in Trinidad, Colorado, in 1887, doing architectural work exclusively, including all the city's schools and the First National Bank Building there. In 1891, he left for the rowdy metropolis of Galveston where he received commissions for the YMCA Building, the Levi and Security buildings along the Strand, and the city's water works.

Bulger's son Clarence authored several notable articles for architectural journals before graduating from the University of Chicago in 1903, and father and son set up a joint practice in Dallas in 1904. Bulger and Son specialized in Baptist churches and built over 100 including the McKinney Avenue Baptist Church (214), the Gaston Avenue Baptist Church (168), the remodeling of the First Baptist in Dallas (36), and the $1 million Baptist Memorial Sanitarium (154). The firm was also responsible for the extant Crockett and Colonial schools and numerous private residences, but Clarence Bulger's greatest contribution to the city was the construction of Dallas' first steel-framed skyscraper, the Praetorian Building (85), only twenty-five years after the form was created in Chicago.

The effects of the depression were devastating and long lasting in rural areas, but by 1898 the city had made its recovery. Daily bank clearances were averaging $300,000 and daily balances $7 million. From the tentative installation of the first phone line in 1879, Dallas had built the largest telephone system in the state, and had also become the world's largest inland cotton market and producer of cotton gin machinery, the world's second largest distributor of agricultural implements, and the second largest publishing center south of St. Louis.[35] The only thing it really lacked was a good, reliable water supply.

Until 1872, the city had obtained its water from small springs or wells which every business, hotel, and residence drilled on its own property. In that year, Browder Springs in the City Park was tapped as an abundant source and the old wells were fazed out; wooden mains were laid, and a stand pipe was erected at Main and Harwood streets (where the Municipal Building was built in 1912). By 1888, the city had outgrown Browder Springs with its meager 300,000-gallon daily flow and so built a pumping station in Oak Lawn which drew nearly 10 million gallons a day from the Trinity. But pollution from Fort Worth had contaminated the river so badly by 1896 that a new pumping station had to be built on the Elm Fork at Record Crossing. With the construction of Bachman's Dam in 1903 and White Rock Dam in 1911, it was believed that the resulting lakes would permanently provide Dallas' water supply.

The year 1898 marked construction of the first substantial downtown building in four years — the closest thing to a skyscraper in Dallas until 1907, when the cornerstone of the Praetorian Building was set into place. The Linz Brothers Building (63), headquarters of the Linz Brothers Jewelry Company, was a fireproof high rise that relied on the antiquated use of a structural cast-iron and wood-beam skeleton rather than steel for its support. The building's architect, H. A. Overbeck, utilized the more conservative elements of the Second Empire and Richardsonian Romanesque styles in its design rather than the advanced Chicago school techniques seen in Sullivan's Bayard Building in New York or the Chicago Stock Exchange Building, both of which were contemporaneous to the Linz.

This discrepancy in style was not an indication of Overbeck's lack of ability. On the contrary, he was responsible for some of the finest, most beautiful structures in the city including the MK&T Building at the corner of Commerce and Market streets, the University of Dallas Building (224), the magnificent St. Paul's Sanitarium (164), several elegant Prairie style homes (including the residence of I. G. Bromberg at 2617 South Boulevard), and the $600,000 Dallas County Criminal Court and Jail Building (1913), one of the few such facilities in the nation to be planned with the humanistic treatment of prisoners in mind, including shower facilities, ice water supply, ventilated air flow, and adequate sanitation quarters.

The Chicago skyscraper did not receive much serious attention in Dallas simply because the conditions that warranted its use in the Midwest were not strongly felt until much later in the Southwest. The cost of prime downtown property was not really an expensive factor in Dallas construction in the late nineteenth century, as it was in Chicago. Open space was still abundant, and Dallas, like many young cities of the period, contented itself with the various historical revival movements in architecture for a sense of identity and a continuity with a past it had never known.

This attitude was readily apparent in two

69. ELM STREET THEATER ROW, c. 1920
At the heart of Dallas' Theater Row were two of the city's finest "Big Time" vaudeville houses. The Hope Theater, built in 1921 as a motion picture palace, was named after Hope Hampton, the famous Broadway musical star of the 1920s. Within a year it was sold to the Loew's chain, renamed the Melba, and converted to vaudeville. The Majestic, Dallas' premier theater, was built 1920-21 by John Eberson, the Interstate chain's principal architect, assisted by Lang and Witchell. *Courtesy of Texas State Historical Association*

70. WASHINGTON THEATER, c. 1915
The Washington Theater, one of the city's most dazzling movie houses, featured stars like Charlie Chap-
lin and Tom Mix, accompanied by the huge house
organ (right). Dallas' early theaters often had live
shows — bands, chorus lines, and comics — but the
introduction of musical "talkies" in the mid-1920s
forced them out of business or into film; the Great
Depression reduced some of these to dime-reelers and
closed many more. With the advent of suburban
theaters and television after World War II, Dallas'
downtown theater district shrank to a few struggling
holdouts like the Majestic (which closed in 1969),
the Tower (1971), the Palace (1971), and the Mel-
ba/Capri (1976). Though the Washington held the
Dallas premier of Al Jolson's "The Jazz Singer" in
1925, it was caught in the Great Depression and leveled for a parking lot by 1932. *Dallas Historical
Society Archives*

71. NIGHT VIEW, WASHINGTON THEATER, c. 1915
Dallas Historical Society Archives

72. INTERIOR, WASHINGTON THEATER, c. 1915
Dallas Historical Society Archives

73. QUEEN CITY RAILWAY CAR HOUSE, c. 1895
The Queen City Car Barn at the southwest corner of Elm and Peak streets was begun in 1891 as the Dallas Cable Railway's power station, the proposed duplicate of the Portland (Oregon) Cable Railway plant. Construction of the streetcar barn was completed in 1894 after the all-electric Queen City Railway took over the bankrupt cable car line. (Dallas had adopted the title "Queen City of the Plains" after the arrival of the railroads in 1872-73 in a civic response to Cincinnati's claim to be the "Queen City of the West.") The barn was occupied by the Dallas Transit Company's bus repair facilities after World War II and razed for a parking lot in 1971.
Courtesy of Dallas Public Library

of the city's major church buildings, the Romanesque First Presbyterian (64) and the Gothic First Cumberland Presbyterian (65). Though one was constructed sixteen years later than the other, both persisted stylistically in the same obsolete Ruskinian display of colors and textures in the brickwork of the facades and the roofing tiles.

These two churches represented over 100 years of bitter controversy within the Presbyterian Church which culminated at the beginning of the nineteenth century in the Great Awakening and the Schism of 1813, dividing the church into two halves, the Presbyterians and the Cumberlands. The Schism occurred over the Cumberlands' evangelic zeal and the Presbyterians' foot-dragging advocacy of educational standards, the authority of the central Synod, and a strict adherence to the Confession of Faith.[36]

Since the Cumberlands wanted to expand quickly onto the frontier, using any means to convert the hordes of infidels and unbelievers in the West, they were the first to arrive in Dallas in 1868, and proceeded to build one of the town's first houses of worship, a small wood-framed church near the corner of Jefferson and Pacific. About 1880, the church found itself deep in the heart of Frogtown and the T&P warehousing district. The church history records that the Reverend W. G. Templeton decided to move the building to the "suburbs on N. Harwood, between Bryan and Live Oak streets. So drawn by mules, the rickety, old church was moved, lock, stock and barrel, up the center of the street to its new site. Halfway there the procession halted, the people entered the church, and Mr. Templeton held Sunday Services, 'squarely in the middle of Pacific Avenue.' "[37] That church remained in use until the newer one was built in 1898.

The Presbyterians finally arrived in Dallas with the railroad in 1872. In that year they built a small wooden church on Elm at Ervay (now the site of the Wilson Building) and then built the larger building in 1882. Around 1907, a reconciliation occurred between the two factions, and the congregations agreed to merge, celebrating the event in 1913 with the construction of the present elaborately Neo-Classical First Presbyterian

80

74. DALLAS CONSOLIDATED STREET RAILWAY, c. 1889
During the golden age of the streetcar, Dallas' street railway companies utilized or experimented with various kinds of power equipment. Mules and horses provided the original power source; use of steam locomotives began in 1887 but were obsolete by 1895. Cable cars were attempted on Elm Street without success in 1890 because they could not efficiently compete with the more adaptable and profitable electric lines. The Pearl Street line was one of the first to convert to electric power, inaugurating its new service in the fall of 1889. *Dallas Historical Society Archives*

75. DALLAS CONSOLIDATED STREET RAILWAY, c. 1889
Dallas Historical Society Archives

76. CARNEGIE LIBRARY, c. 1901
The Dallas Public Library Association, for years confined to a rented room above a Main Street music store or a basement corner of City Hall, found its first permanent home in the $50,000 Carnegie Library Building at the southwest corner of Commerce and Harwood. Constructed of "Roman" pressed brick with terra cotta detailing and Ionic columns of gray Bedford stone, this classical monument to the advancement of learning contained over 10,000 volumes when it opened to the public in 1901. The library was demolished in 1954 to build a more modern facility. *Dallas Historical Society Archives*

77. MAIN ENTRY, CARNEGIE LIBRARY, c. 1901
Courtesy of Dallas Public Library

78. READING ROOM, CARNEGIE LIBRARY, c. 1901
Courtesy of Dallas Public Library

79. WILSON BUILDING, c. 1915
The incomparably beautiful Wilson Building, a masterpiece of design by the Fort Worth architectural firm of Sanguinet and Staats, was a Second Empire elaboration of the Paris Grand Opera House designed by Charles Garnier in 1874. It also displayed striking similarities to two of the finest examples of American architectural artistry — Adler and Sullivan's Auditorium (Chicago, 1879) and H. H. Richardson's Marshall Field Store (Chicago, 1887). Built in 1902-03 at the northwest corner of Main and Ervay streets, the Wilson Building remains, without question, one of the most noble buildings ever constructed in Dallas. *Courtesy of Dallas Public Library*

84

Church which stands at the corner of Harwood and Wood streets.

The turn of the century found Dallas eagerly anticipating all the wondrous marvels of the new advancing technologies of the Industrial Revolution. In a time when the whole world was betting on the golden age of the machine (before all its horrifying coexistent properties were known or felt), Dallas recognized its role as the provincial capital of a 250,000-square-mile empire — the railroad, business, agricultural, and entertainment hub of North and West Texas, Oklahoma, and Arkansas — and took full advantage of it. The city had developed a garment district and a banking district; Market Street had become a regional center for fruit and vegetable dealers of all manner and reputation; the State Fair had become the largest in the nation, drawing thousands of people every year; and the central business district, the length of Elm, Main, and Commerce streets, was astounding visitors and citizens alike with its cosmopolitan flavor. Rapid technological developments in engineering were beginning to allow for the construction of dozens of new buildings, some up to seven stories in height, with larger sheet-glass windows and elaborately carved stone heads, eagles, gargoyles, and scrolls. Even the humblest shops boasted cast-iron fronts, turned out in any architectural style the builder wanted, and with enough arches, columns, brackets, and acanthus leaves to turn the head of even the most sober farmer or rancher when he brought his family to town for the month's shopping.

Henry Ford's noisy contraption, probably the single most important factor in changing the shape and destiny of American life in the early twentieth century, began to appear on the city streets, scaring women, children, and horses with its clattering unpredictability. Colonel E. H. R. Green, president of Texas Midland Railroad and son of Hetty Green, "the witch of Wall Street," drove the first one into town from Terrell in October of 1899, and by 1901, cars had multiplied so rapidly that the first traffic ordinances had to be enacted. By 1905 with the opening of the Dixie Theater on Elm Street, soon to be known as "Theater Row," the first whirrings of the city's "Great White Way" were beginning to be heard. The Dixie was followed by scores of movie houses, amusement arcades, "Kodak" galleries, and famous vaudeville palaces of the twenties and thirties like the Majestic and the Hope. Theaters such as the Hippodrome (66), the Queen Theater (67), and the Washington (70) lined both sides of Elm, beckoning with a crooked finger into the noise and bright lights. Every Halloween the street was closed off to traffic and the theater owners hosted a Mardi Gras-inspired carnival complete with costumed revelers, pickpockets and drunks.

The dry goods emporiums of the Sanger Brothers, A. B. Mittenthal, and A. Harris and Company displayed the imported finery of exotic places in their crowded windows, while electric streetcars clanged up and down the streets, whisking people wherever they wanted to go in the city, or to the far-off suburbs around Forest Avenue, St. Paul's Sanitarium, and Cole Park.

These suburban residential areas were growing at a prodigious rate, and had been since 1886 when the first streetcar lines were extended to the outlying areas and outside capital interests began investing in land. Among these real estate speculators and investors were the Texas Land and Mortgage Company of London; the Jarvis-Conklin Mortgage Trust Company of Kansas City, with capital stock of $6 million; the National Loan and Trust Company of Kansas City, $1 million capital stock; the George W. Baylor Real Estate Company, representing interests from Liverpool, London, and New Orleans, with $25 million in capital stock; the Philadelphia Land Association, a syndicate which included Anthony Drexel and J. Pierpont Morgan and which owned most of the land north of town that eventually became Highland Park; and Pierre S. du Pont of Wilmington, Delaware.

Pierre du Pont, the grandson of Eleuthère Irénée du Pont, founder of E. I. du Pont de Nemours Powder Company, was a young man of thirty seeking new investment fields for the family fortune when he spotted the

80. DOWNTOWN, c. 1910

This view, looking east on Main from the corner of Murphy Street, shows at the far left the Greek-temple facade of the City National Bank as it originally appeared when completed in 1903. To the far right is the Hotel Southland (1906-07), another Dallas landmark, leveled in 1963 for a parking lot.

Dallas Historical Society Archives

opportunity that Dallas streetcar properties afforded. After a trip to Dallas in 1901, Pierre wrote:

> The whole street railway outfit here is strictly "bum" ... the road is operated very badly, cars are dirty and run with very little system. The track is so rough that riding is very uncomfortable, in fact, everybody keeps a horse and buggy and the streets are crowded with vehicles in the evening. Three railway companies, owning 43.45 miles of track with 56 good cars, can be purchased for $1,300,000. And considering the earnings of the Electric Railway during the past year, which amounted to $114,000, and the condition of the property, it [Dallas] seems to be an excellent field for investment.[38]

In June, 1901, Pierre purchased the Dallas Consolidated Electric Street Railway Company and the North Dallas Circuit Railway Company from J. B. Wilson and Royal Ferris for $1.075 million plus $50 thousand in stock in the new company. He immediately made plans to expand the operation but quickly ran into opposition from the two major electric companies in town, which provided power for the railways. The utilities, Dallas Electric Company and the Standard Light and Power Company, both owned by the General Electric Company, were in financial disorder and wanted to raise rates to du Pont. In retaliation, Pierre promised his streetcar line contract to C. H. Alexander's small Dallas Ice Factory, Light and Power Company. In 1902, General Electric countered this move by assisting A. K. Bonta, manager of the Dallas Electric Company, to charter the Metropolitan Street Railway Company, a rival line which would parallel and even duplicate some of the du Pont line routes. Armed warfare nearly broke out between the competing firms and their gun-

81. DOWNTOWN, c. 1925

The same view, fifteen years later reveals Lang and Witchell's famous Roman-inspired Beaux-Arts expansion of the City National Bank. This magnificent facade was removed during renovation in 1952 and the entire building was demolished in 1964 to build One Main Place. The large skyscraper in the mid- background, also the work of Lang and Witchell, is the extant American Exchange National Bank Building, completed in 1918. In the right background is the Southwestern Life Building.

Courtesy of Mr. Charles Coldwell

toting workmen, but was averted by the death of Eugene du Pont in Wilmington, who left control of the du Pont Company to Pierre, necessitating his return to Delaware. Pierre then sold his streetcar lines to General Electric and Stone and Webster of Boston for a $300,000 profit.

The full history of Dallas' streetcar and transit system is a complex and convoluted one, including dozens of mule-drawn, electric, steam- and cable-powered operations involved in an intricate system of expansion, bankruptcies, and take-overs; but the streetcar was unquestionably the most influential factor in the growth of the suburbs, and the traffic patterns it established help to explain why certain areas developed while neighboring ones did not.

Dallas' pioneer street railway entrepreneur was Captain George M. Swink who came to Dallas from Alabama in 1868 and established, along with Captain Gaston and a group of local investors, the original 1872 mule-drawn line along Main Street from the Courthouse to the Union depot. In 1875, W. J. Keller took over the operation of this line and added a second, the Dallas Street Railroad Company which ran on San Jacinto Street; the following year, his brother, Dr. C. E. Keller, and W. C. Connor opened the Commerce and Ervay Street Railway line as far as Pocahontas Street to promote their real estate venture, which in the next few years would grow into the very elegant and affluent area known as The Cedars. In 1887, these three lines and a fourth, the Dallas Belt Street Railway Company (chartered in 1884), were purchased by a local syndicate of bankers and merchants, including Royal Ferris, Jules Schneider, and T. J. Oliver. The resulting Dallas Consolidated Street Railway Company held a monopoly in the downtown area for about three years, but by 1890 poor management, bad service, and inadequate,

82. DALLAS FEMALE COLLEGE, c. 1885
The Dallas Female College, founded in 1865 as a privately operated, Methodist boarding school for girls, was the first major educational institution established in the city. Its main building, on Bryan Street between Pearl and Crockett, was the work of Albert Ullrich in 1876. After the College went bankrupt in 1886, the building was sold to the city and became Dallas' first public high school. Central High School, as it was called, was demolished in 1906. *Dallas Historical Society Archives*

83. DALLAS HIGH SCHOOL, c. 1910
Lang and Witchell completed the extant Dallas High School in 1908 on the site of the old Dallas Female College (Central High School). *Dallas Historical Society Archives*

84. YMCA BUILDING, c. 1910

The YMCA Building (1907) on Commerce near
South Harwood, served as the Dixie University
School of Law between 1933 and 1937; it was later
converted into the less-than-reputable Savoy Hotel
before its demolition in 1950 to build the Dallas Hilton. The house to the left, built c. 1885 by Charles
Kribs, manager of the Middlesex Banking Company,
survived until 1917; it illustrates the not uncommon
residential use of downtown property well into the
20th century. *Dallas Historical Society Archives*

85. PRAETORIAN BUILDING, c. 1930

The home office of the Praetorian National Fraternal
Insurance Order on Main Street at Stone Place became Dallas' first true skyscraper upon completion in
1909. The building's architects, C. W. Bulger &
Son, described it as "a model of up-to-date, fireproof
construction, being equiped with many modern and
unusual devices such as ice water circulation and
individual vaults throughout." The original structure
still remains behind its 1961 exterior renovations.
Courtesy of Cushman and Wakefield, Inc.

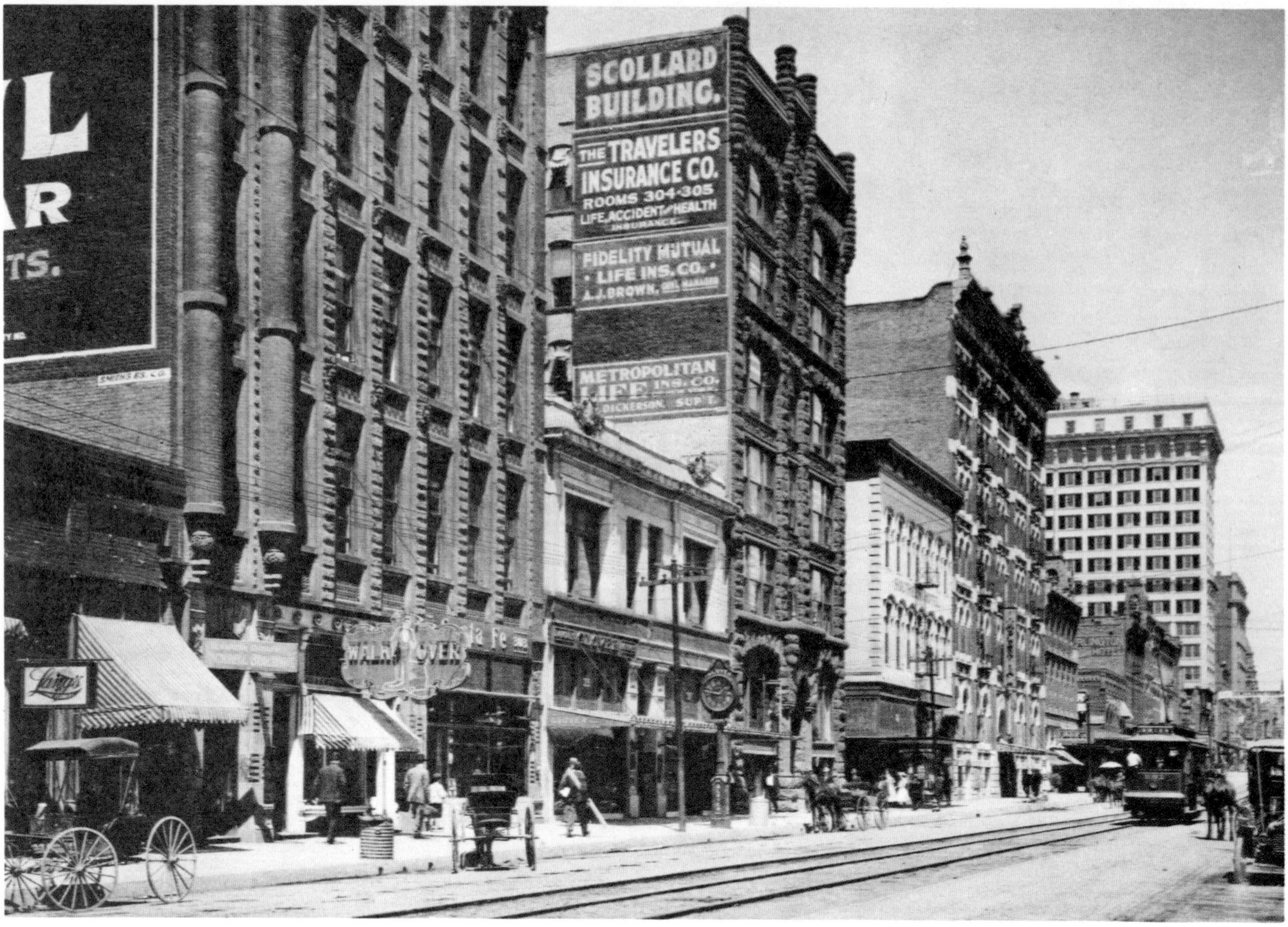
SCOLLARD BUILDING.
THE TRAVELERS INSURANCE CO.
ROOMS 304-305
LIFE, ACCIDENT and HEALTH INSURANCE
FIDELITY MUTUAL LIFE INS. CO.
A. J. BROWN
METROPOLITAN LIFE INS. CO.
DICKERSON, SUPT.
WALK-OVER

LUZIANNE
COFFEE
REGAL CHOCOLATES
BROWN'S
IMPERIAL HOTEL
Putnam
WELCOME VISITORS
OWL
CIGAR

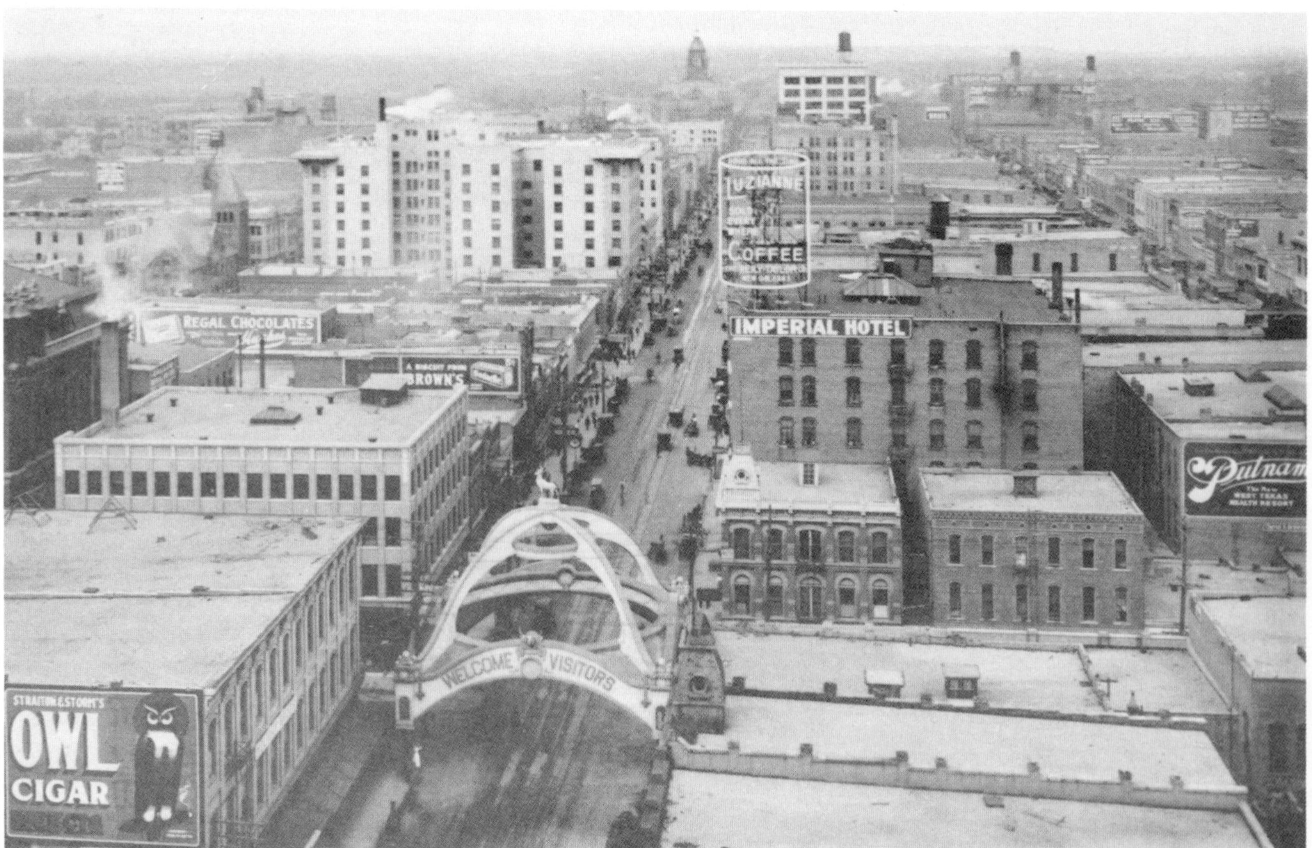

uncomfortable equipment had forced it into bankrupt foreclosure by the Farmers Loan and Trust Company. Only months later it was resurrected as the Dallas Consolidated Traction Company.

In 1887, the expansion of the city's rail system escalated outrageously. Several new lines were built by real estate promoters into essentially wild, overgrown farmland miles from the city. A distinct operating formula emerged which became widely used by nearly every Dallas promoter. Either the land around an existing lake or park would be subdivided for resale, or a lake and/or park would be built on salable property; a streetcar line would then be built to connect the property to the city, enticing Dallasites with the nickel fares to ride out on Sundays to "take in the pure country air," have a picnic, swim, or canoe about the lake and (just incidentally) to look over the beautiful, rustic lots offered for sale. There were several important examples of this phenomenon: the Dallas Rapid Transit Company's steam rail line was completed in 1888 by J. D. Trammel as a southern loop down Lamar Street to Forest Avenue and across to the fairgrounds, promoting the Colonial Hill development; W. J. Keller created Shady View Park at the corner of San Jacinto and Washington streets

86. MAIN STREET, c. 1909
From left to right are the Cockrell Building, the Scollard Building, and the Italianate facades of the Southern Hotel, the Imperial Hotel, the Rowan Building, and the Arlington Hotel. The Imperial was built in 1889 as Dallas' most luxurious accommodation but burned beyond repair in 1914. In the background is the fourteen-story Praetorian Building.
Dallas Historical Society Archives

87. LOOKING WEST FROM THE PRAETORIAN BUILDING, c. 1910
In the foreground is the infamous Elks' Arch, spanning the intersection of Main and Akard streets. Built for the Elks' Convention of 1908, the arch was the site of Dallas' last lynching when Allen Brooks, a black man accused of raping a white woman, was thrown from the second-floor window of the city jail by a mob in 1910. Though the fall killed him, the crowd hung him anyway from a telephone pole next to the arch. The arch was torn down soon after.
Dallas Historical Society Archives

as an inducement to visit his addition; Colonel Henry Exall dammed Turtle Creek and created Exall's Lake to boost sales of the projected Philadelphia Place Addition (now Highland Park); and the North Dallas Circuit Railway was completed in 1888 by Royal Ferris, Frank Cockrell, Major Alexander Lemmon, and Oliver Bowser to serve two separate North Dallas developments.

In 1890, another fantastic street railway enterprise was born when Albert W. Childress, backed by the Philadelphia bond firm of William T. Tiers, organized the Dallas Cable Railroad Company and began to install the South's first cable car line along Elm Street (the last major downtown thoroughfare to get a mass transit system) from the river to Haskell Avenue and across to the fairgrounds. The $600,000 steam-powered cable line was to have been built by the Pacific Cable Construction Company of San Francisco and by contract was to be made "the equal in construction and operation of the Market Street Railway in San Francisco."[39] The cable system was opposed by the financial interests that controlled the existing electric street railways and suffered from their zealous competition. The older, established lines had converted to electricity by 1889 (after Frank Sprague invented the necessary power-relay system for the streetcars of Richmond, Virginia in December, 1888) which gave them more flexibility and less expense in their development and operation. Because of financial problems and construction delays, only about one-third of the cable line was built before the company went bankrupt. In 1893, the Queen City Railway Company purchased the Elm Street rights from Childress and completed the construction of the tracks and powerhouse (73) as an electric powered operation. In 1898, most of the lines in the city were merged into the Dallas Consolidated Electric Street Railway Company under C. H. Alexander and J. B. Wilson, which is where du Pont stepped in in 1901.

Outside influence figured heavily in the city at this time, not only in business and real estate investment, but also architecturally. In this period, the Fort Worth architectural firm of Sanguinet and Staats was to Dallas what the firm of Adler and Sullivan was to Chicago — designers and builders of the most modern, monumental, and classically "correct" structures in the city. Formed in 1897 by M. R. Sanguinet of Fort Worth and Carl Staats of New York City, the firm soon became the most prestigious in the state, opening branch offices in Dallas, Houston, and Wichita Falls, employing nearly fifty associate draftsmen, and constructing the most sophisticated and refined buildings in the Southwest.

The firm's first Dallas commission came in 1901 when Andrew Carnegie, founder of United States Steel Corporation, donated $50,000 to the city for a library — one of over 2,800 libraries the millionaire-philanthropist endowed. The Carnegie Library (76) was built in the style of the Neo-Classical Revival, a movement which began in 1883 with the construction of the Villard Houses in New York by the firm of McKim, Mead and White. This revival was a reaction against what some considered the licentiousness and capriciousness of the High Victorian styles, representing a return to symmetry, discipline, simplicity, and order in the general, classical tradition of Rome and Greece.

The next year Dallas got its second Sanguinet and Staats structure, the eight-story Wilson Building (79). This magnificent Second Empire edifice was begun in 1902, the same year Dallas hosted the Confederate Reunion, a convention which brought over 7,000 Southern veterans of the Civil War and nearly 25,000 visitors into the city (252). The building was commissioned by J. B. Wilson, a wealthy cattleman, banker, and investor who demanded only the finest in craftsmanship and materials in its construction. The interior was richly appointed with Honduras mahogany woodwork and doors, imported Georgia marble on the floors, wainscotting, and pilasters, and elaborate wrought-iron cage elevators and ornamentation; the exterior utilized fireproof reinforced concrete, covered by pressed brick and intricately carved and enameled terra cotta moldings.

The city's third Sanguinet and Staats structure came in 1903 with the erection of Edward Tenison's City National Bank (80).

The City National was a principal link in the direct evolution from Dallas' first bank, the private firm of Gaston and Camp (1868) to the First National, organized in 1930 as a merger between the American Exchange National Bank and the City National. Over the years its officers included such notable Dallas capitalists as J. T. Trezevant, Thomas Marsalis, Bartholomew Blankenship, C. A. Keating and Alex Sanger, and its rich, Greek-inspired facade reflected this almost royal inheritance. The bank was one of the most important early customers of the newly founded architectural firm of Lang and Witchell, soon to become the most renowned and respected in the city. Between 1910 and 1942, the firm dominated Dallas construction and made such a profound and indelible visual impact that its influence still constitutes a major portion of the Dallas skyline.

About 1920 Lang and Witchell were commissioned to expand and redesign the City National Bank Building. The result was an impressive Neo-Classical Revival structure (81) that placed Lang and Witchell squarely in the mainstream of that national phenomenon known as the American Renaissance (less politely termed the Academic Reaction by some architectural historians). This was a movement back to the simplicity and order of the classical tradition, in reaction to the very different qualities admired in the High Victorian period. American architects believed they were at last elevating the country from a second-place status to place it, architecturally, on a level equal to the older, richer cultures of Europe. Ironically, they created a characteristically overpowering American style, best exemplified by the numerous, massive government buildings designed by John Russell Pope in Washington, D.C. (such as the Justice Department Building and the National Gallery of Art). Nowhere in Europe had such an extravagant quantity of fine materials been used so lavishly; in fact, more architectural marble was used in the United States between 1900 and 1917 than in the Roman Empire during its entire history.[40]

This well-intentioned but slightly misplaced classicism was reflected in two early Lang and Witchell buildings, the Dallas High

88. SOUTHWESTERN LIFE BUILDING, c. 1920

Begun in 1911 and finished in 1913, the Southwestern Life Building was a Sullivanesque masterpiece of the art of skyscraper construction. Located at the southeast corner of Main and Akard streets, the crisp lines and classic beauty of the magnificent structure were destroyed in 1972 when it was leveled for a parking lot. *Courtesy of Southwestern Life Insurance Company*

School (83) and the YMCA Building (84). Both incorporated elements of the Second Renaissance Revival and the Beaux-Arts styles in a distinctly non-European, yet highly nimble and appealing, manner. Their unique "Americanness" is pointedly revealed in the photograph of the YMCA Building; with its elaborate facade pinned to an otherwise plain structure in anticipation of other high-rise buildings adjoining it on either side, it was a good example of what Mark Twain referred to as a "Queen Anne front with a Mary Anne behind."

Although the firm was founded during an uninspired, transitional period in American architecture, Lang and Witchell did not languish long in the backwaters of the Academic Reaction. In 1911, they laid the cornerstone of the finest Sullivanesque skyscraper ever to grace the city of Dallas. The Southwestern Life Building (88), finished in 1913, came as close to fulfilling Louis Sullivan's concept of a tall building in the form of a classical Corinthian column — the first two stories corresponding to the base of the column, the next twelve to its shaft (with the equivalent of fluting found in the recesses of windows and spandrels) and the top two floors, with their rich Gothic-inspired terra cotta moldings and terminal cornice, corresponding to the capital — as any major American skyscraper since Sullivan's 1890 Wainwright Building in St. Louis.

Lang and Witchell built several major structures in the Sullivanesque style including the American Exchange National Bank Building (now called the Metropolitan Savings and Loan Building), the Dallas Athletic Club, the incredible Sears and Roebuck complex with a total of over eighteen acres of

89. LOOKING NORTHEAST FROM THE SOUTHWESTERN LIFE BUILDING, c. 1920
Notice how close to downtown the residential section was as late as 1920. The large white homes fronting the open square to the left were, until they were closed about 1917, expensive bordellos along the storied Federal Street red-light district. *Courtesy of Southwestern Life Insurance Company*

floor space under one roof, the Adolphus Hotel Annex, the White Plaza Hotel, the huge Higginbotham-Bailey-Logan block, the Fair Park Auditorium, and the Lamar Street Sanger Brothers Department Store (now El Centro College), as well as serving as associate architects on the twenty-eight-story Mobil Building and the Majestic Theater.

Otto Lang, the leading force in the firm, was born in Freiburg, Germany, in 1864 and educated in engineering at the Karlsruhe Polytechnic Institute. He decided to immigrate to the United States in 1888, and was lured to Dallas by colorful tales of adventure and economic promise. For two years he worked for local architectural firms, gaining experience until he was hired as chief designer by the T&P Railroad in 1890, a position which made him responsible for the construction of the second Gould Building in Dallas as well as Fort Worth's magnificent T&P Depot. In 1904, Lang met Frank Witchell, who had come to Dallas from San Antonio in 1898 to work as a designer for Sanguinet and Staats, and the two men formed their partnership the next year.

By the late 1920s, the firm was moving out of the Chicago School and into the burgeoning modern style popularized by the 1925 Paris Exposition des Arts Décoratifs. Lang and Witchell soon proved to be masters at the stark, rectilinear ornamentation of the Art Deco style, as seen in the Lone Star Gas Company Building (90), the Southwestern Bell Telephone Company Building, the Dallas Power and Light Company Building, and the original twelve-story Mercantile Bank Building. In later years they began to dabble in the Spanish Colonial style, popularized by Bertram Grosvenor Goodhue at the Panama-California Exposition at San Diego in 1915, with the construction of the Highland Park Town Hall and the J. S. Bradfield School, also in Highland Park.

90. LOBBY, LONESTAR GAS BUILDING, c. 1925
Lang and Witchell's Art Deco motif. *Dallas Historical Society Archives*

STATE
HOTEL
WICHITA TRUNKS
SPECIAL SALE
LUNCH

91. ADOLPHUS HOTEL, c. 1915
The world famous Adolphus Hotel, the house that
Budweiser and Adolphus Busch built on the northwest corner of Commerce and Akard streets, replaced
the old Gothic City Hall in 1913. The detail of the
elaborately decorated Beaux-Arts roof — complete
with copper-capped, beer-bottle turret — emphasizes
the monumental grace of this grand hotel. *Dallas
Historical Society Archives*

92. DETAIL, ADOLPHUS HOTEL, c. 1915
Dallas Historical Society Archives

The crowning glory to Dallas' early skyline came in 1913 with the construction of Adolphus Busch's Adolphus Hotel (92). The beer baron's fortune enabled him to spare absolutely no expense in the construction of this masterpiece of the Beaux-Arts style. Tom Barnett of the St. Louis firm of Barnett, Hayes and Barnett, did the design work, taking as his models the famous Plaza Hotel of New York and Chicago's Blackstone Hotel. The Adolphus quickly established a reputation as the finest, gaudiest and most raucous hotel west of the Mississippi River, offering such delights as the Palm Garden, the Grand Ballroom, the Century Room nightclub, and the Victor Proetz-designed "Roof," a stark-white and polished-black ebony pavilion that hosted many a revelrous night of Big Band dancing, with Hal Kemp or Phil Harris, during the bleak years of World War II. In 1914 the "French Room" dining salon was renowned for its "mirrored fountain surrounded by a wrought bronze balustrade, draperies hung in rose silk damask, candle-lit fixtures of Ormolu gold, walls of Breccia Violette marble in the Louis XIV style and bas reliefs in Hautville marble of sculptured Naiads and Nymphs."[41] The Adolphus' interior was remodeled in the 1950s, exorcising its earlier grandeur, but the exterior remains as one of Dallas' few untouched landmarks in a progressive downtown.

93. ADOLPHUS HOTEL, c. 1915
The Edwardianly decadent "French Room" dining
salon as it appeared before remodeling in the 1950s.
Dallas Historical Society Archives

94. CITY TEMPLE, c. 1920
The City Temple of the Central Presbyterian
Church, the product of C. D. Hill's blending of Art
Deco and Norman Gothic styles, was built in 1915
at the southeast corner of Patterson and N. Akard
streets. It stood, arrogantly transfiguring the traditions of religious architecture, until 1964, when the
congregation dispersed to the suburbs, and the cathedral was demolished for commercial construction.
Courtesy of Northpark Presbyterian Church

OWL
Uneeda Biscuit
BLUE VALLEY
BUTTER
CAFE

95. LOOKING SOUTH FROM THE COURTHOUSE, c. 1915
In the center foreground is the livery yard of
Joseph G. Britain, flanked by the former Farmers
Alliance Building on the left and the Union Terminal
(under construction on the right). The building with
the tower at right is the County Jail (1879) and in
the background are the industrialized Trinity River
bottoms, bridged by the recently finished Houston
Street Viaduct. *Dallas Historical Society Archives*

96. COTTAGE RESIDENCE, c. 1895
This simple Victorian cottage was typical of the
profusion of "Carpenter Gothic" homes built from
Maine to California in the last half of the 19th century. Hailed in its day for its "picturesque effect,"
this type of construction began to appear in Dallas
in the early 1870s and examples of it can still be
seen in the older sections of the city. *Dallas
Historical Society Archives*

4 SOUTH DALLAS

In the thirty years between Dallas' founding and the arrival of the Houston & Texas Central Railroad in 1872, the town gradually began to move out of the Trinity River bottoms and into the tangle of undergrowth that lay to the east. With John Neely Bryan's township survey acting as the guiding pattern of settlement, a concentric ring of small stores and mercantile houses began to cluster around the courthouse square, followed by a second ring of log cabins and clapboard houses.

South Dallas, that part of Bryan's township that stretched southward from the courthouse between the river and Poydras Street, had developed only a scattering of small homes, boarding houses, and grist mills by 1852 when Bryan's claim was purchased by Alexander Cockrell, who began to repromote the unsold sections of the town. But the southward flow of settlement was slow and irregular, primarily because of Mill Creek, a formidable barrier of water and mud which remained unbridged until after the Civil War. (It is now approximately the site of the I-30/I-35 Mixmaster.)

The pattern began to change in the late 1860s, however, when news of the coming railroads stimulated several fledging efforts to build residential areas in South Dallas in anticipation of the phenomenal growth the railroads were expected to bring. The first real estate subdivision, a small section bounded by Akard, Wood, Browder, and Young streets, was opened in 1869 by William Tuberville; when it was first laid out, it seemed so distant that Dallasites thought of it as an entirely separate village, named Tuberville. In 1871, Henry Ervay (Dallas' Reconstruction mayor, who had become a local hero when he was jailed for opposing the Union Army's martial edicts) began to cut streets and subdivide lots in an area between Akard, Canton, South Harwood, and Pocahontas streets; his Ervay's Addition stood ready and waiting when the H&TC Railroad steamed into town.

A third development, located to the north and east of Ervay's Addition, was begun by the Reverend W. C. Young. Having come to Dallas in 1865 as a circuit preacher and staying on to build the Lamar Street Methodist Church (the forerunner of today's First Methodist), Young received title to forty acres, bounded by what are now Wood, Canton, Ervay, and Harwood streets, in lieu of outright payment from his struggling congregation. In 1872, hoping that the H&TC might build its depot on his property, the pastor opened Young Street through what had previously been a deserted cedar brake. But the next year the T&P Railroad intersected the H&TC line six blocks to the north, and Young divided his land into lots which sold, like Ervay's, for about $150 to $200 apiece.

The arrival of the T&P Railway in 1873 proved to be a decisive event for South Dallas. By making Dallas the first rail crossroads in the Southwest, it assured at least a degree of future prosperity and brought an immediate influx of over 5,000 people to the city, while its route effectively blocked the town's expansion north of Pacific Avenue and created a profusion of new subdivisions to the south. The general southern area of town became widely known as "The Cedars" because it was "covered by a magnificent forest of Oak and Red Cedar trees, rapidly giving way to houses, gardens and orchards."[42]

By 1876, the residential attractiveness of The Cedars was assured by John J. Eakins, who offered to sell Dallas ten acres near

Browder Springs for its first public park. A deal was negotiated whereby the city exempted Eakins from all property taxes until such time as he had received $400 in credit; the remainder of his $600 asking price was paid by Dr. C. E. Keller, owner and operator of the Commerce and Ervay Street Railway Company. This transaction not only created City Park, but also struck a milestone in Dallas' urban development with the first partnership between a streetcar owner and a land speculator. Land values in The Cedars escalated in direct response to the streetcar line and park, and the tremendous boom in real estate prices was a lesson to later speculators, investors, and developers all over the city. (The very same year, Henry Ervay offered Keller several acres along Pocahontas Street as an inducement to build the line into his development.)

As South Dallas began to grow, prosper, and expand, caught up in the national fever of the Railroad Age, several other housing subdivisions were opened in The Cedars such as the Browder Addition in 1873, just north of Browder Springs (City Park), and Sarah Cockrell's Addition, in 1884, south of the Masonic Cemetery (now the Convention Center) and west of Akard Street.

The first homes built in The Cedars were mostly small, wood framed Victorian cottages (96). These modest structures were built by unschooled, mostly anonymous carpenter-builders, using plans from one of several house-pattern books for inspiration in design. Among the most popular of these pattern books were Andrew Jackson Downing's Gothic-oriented *Cottage Residences* (published in 1857) and Gilbert Bostwich Croff's, *Progressive American Architecture* (1875).

In 1875 Alfred Benners, a lawyer from Alabama, recorded in his journal that he purchased such a plan from "John M. Archer, architect, at a cost of ten dollars"[43] for use in building his house at the corner of St. Louis and Ervay streets. The fact that Archer stayed in business peddling his designs for only three years before moving on, while Benners sold the house (which had cost him $2,300 in 1875) just a few years later for $7,300, is an indication of the changing financial condition of the time. Charles Bermeister wrote to his brother in Wisconsin in 1877, "Property here is very high and only a few men with money can make something here, other men keep away."[44]

As the 1880s drew near, larger, more elaborate Victorian mansions began to appear in The Cedars. One of the first of the now completely extinct Victorian manors was built by Dr. Jesse M. Pace (97), a physician whose family migrated to Dallas from New Orleans and Mississippi in the 1870s.

Another of the large, early homes was built by the Eakins family (98) on the original forty-acre Eakins homestead which had been under cultivation since the arrival of John J. Eakins from Kentucky in 1849. John Eakins built a small frame house on the property when he married Ophelia Crutchfield, whose father, Tom, began operation of the Crutchfield House soon after his family arrived in 1847. In the 1880s, the encroaching city had made the land much too valuable to farm, so Eakins' son, Edward, built a large Queen Anne residence about 1884, a "model home" designed to spur public interest as he developed not only the family farm, but also several other large South Dallas tracts which the family had acquired over the years.[45]

The year 1884 also saw the opening of a new housing subdivision by two Jewish real estate speculators, Gerson Meyer and Max Rosenfield. Their development, bounded by Akard, Corsicana, Browder, and St. Louis

97. RESIDENCE OF DR. JESSE M. PACE, c. 1895
Dr. Pace's French-influenced town house was a direct descendent of those built by the New Orleans architect, James Gallier, in the Crescent City's French Quarter. The home, built c. 1880 at the corner of Young and Browder streets, was destroyed for commercial use by 1915. The property now forms part of the grounds of the new, I. M. Pei-designed City Hall. *Courtesy of Dallas Public Library*

98. EAKINS HOUSE, c. 1890
Edward Eakins' enormous Queen Anne tribute to the wood lathe and the carpenter's skill cost $5,000—a large sum for its time. The house, near the corner of S. Harwood and Gano streets, was built in 1884 to enhance the promotion of the family's South Dallas real estate. It burned near the turn of the century. *Dallas Historical Society Archives.*

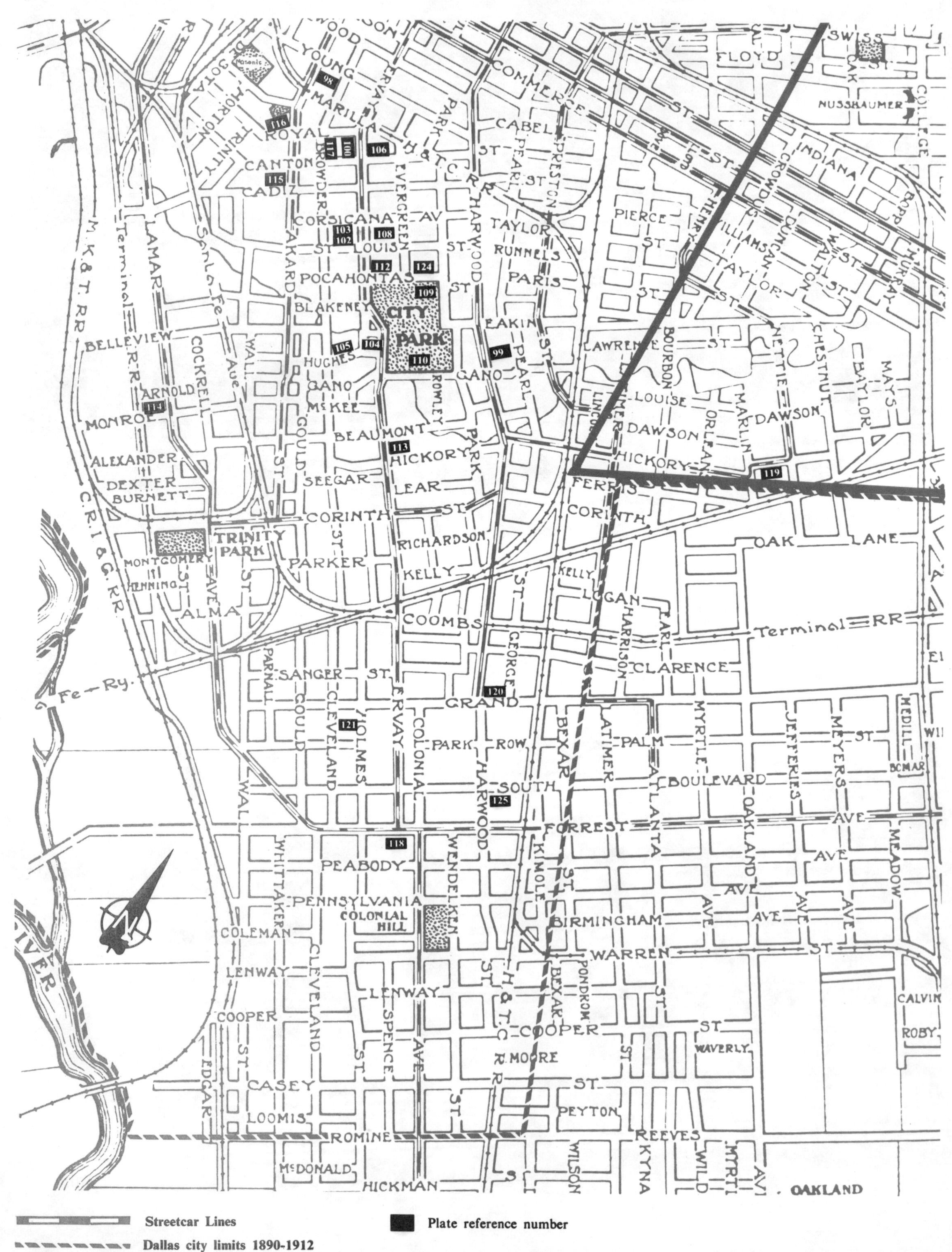

CITY PARK
TRINITY PARK
COLONIAL HILL
MONTGOMERY
Masonic
RIVER
Streetcar Lines
Dallas city limits 1890-1912
East Dallas corporate limits 1883-1890
Plate reference number

99. RESIDENCE OF ALEX SANGER, 1895
The crowning achievement of the 19th-century architect's art was the treatment of even the bulkiest enclosed space with so delicate a touch that it appeared ready to float away, were it not moored to the earth. The Eastlake splendor of Alexander Sanger's home, built c. 1882 at the northwest corner of S. Ervay and Canton, was just such an achievement. *Courtesy of Dallas Public Library.*

100. RESIDENCE OF ALEX SANGER, 1910
The original design contrasted sharply with the heavier, more solid appearance of the house after it was remodeled c. 1905 by Lang and Witchell in a variation of the Prairie style. The house was destroyed in 1925 to build a flophouse for transients. *Dallas Historical Society Archives.*

streets, was sold primarily to Jewish families who had begun to arrive as early as 1872 as part of the "Corsicana crowd" — the terminal merchants who followed the construction of the H&TC. (By 1905, South Dallas held over ninety per cent of the 1,200 Jews in the city.)

The bulk of the Dallas' Jewish population settled in The Cedars after fleeing the pogroms or forced military service of Germany and Russia in the last half of the nineteenth century. Yet the community was by no means a Jewish ghetto; they constituted less than half of the population of The Cedars in 1890 and an even smaller percentage of South Dallas as a whole. Dallas' Jewish population has always been small in comparison to their impact on the city, but the education, resourcefulness, and ability they brought with them contributed greatly to the early city when it needed it most. The Cedars gained the reputation of being the Jewish section of town primarily because its counterpart, Ross Avenue, was so thoroughly Gentile.

The Cedars predated Ross Avenue by about five years, making it the first affluent, "silk-stocking" residential area in Dallas. The northern section of South Ervay Street, little more than a cow path called Miller's Ferry Road in the 1850s, became one of the most exclusive addresses in Texas by the 1890s.

One of the earliest mansions of the area was that of Alex Sanger, built at the corner of South Ervay and Canton streets about 1882 (99). Sanger was one of Dallas' famous terminal merchants who became president and directing spirit of the Sanger Brothers Dry Goods and Department Store. He was also one of those compulsive, driven men who was constantly engaged in a variety of enterprises, always of great scope. Almost immediately upon his arrival in Dallas in 1872, he helped launch the Hebrew Benevolent Association, the cultural and religious progenitor of the Temple Emanu-el. He also served as vice-president of the Dallas Cotton and Woolen Mills (established in 1888 at the corner of South Lamar and Corinth streets), as a director of the Texas State Fair and Dallas Exposition, as a regent of the University of Texas, as a director of the City National and the Dallas Trust and Savings Banks; in short, he was an extremely potent and influential figure in the fate and prosperity of the early city.

Alex Sanger's residence was one of those aerie, Eastlake variants of the Victorian style, a design which has variously been termed Gingerbread, Parvenu, or the Reign of Terror, depending on one's point of view and perspective in time. The style took its name from the English architect Charles Locke Eastlake whose book, *Hints on Household Taste,* became an obsession with builders and craftsmen upon its publication in America in 1872. It passed through six editions in eleven years and sparked an explosion, especially in the western United States, of this extravagantly ornamental and exuberant style. Characterized in this country by the frenzied overuse of chiseled, gouged, and lathed knobs, brackets, spindle rows, openwork friezes and circular perforation motifs, its excesses horrified and embarrassed Eastlake who wrote in 1882: "I now find, to my amazement, that there exists on the other side of the Atlantic an 'Eastlake style' of architecture, which, judging from the specimens I have seen illustrated, may be said to burlesque such doctrines of art as I have ventured to maintain ... I regret that my name should be associated there with a phase of taste in architecture and industrial art with which I can have no real sympathy, and which, by all accounts seems to be extravagant and *bizarre*."[46]

Sanger's house, designed by the local firm of Stewart and Fuller and later remodeled in an attempt to convert it to the fashionable Prairie style (100), was richly decorated inside with rose silk damask walls, velvet draperies, elaborately carved oak and mahogany mantels and paneling, and both crystal and Tiffany chandeliers.

Further down Ervay, Alex's brother, Philip Sanger, built his home (101) next door to that of Judge George N. Aldredge (102), a wealthy attorney and ex-Confederate soldier who served as United States District Judge from 1878 to 1888.

Across from the City Park, Dr. F. E. Hughes and Sons built, about 1885, their Hughes Brothers Manufacturing Company (103). One of the best loved industries in the city, its capability as a manufacturer of baking powders, bluing, mineral and soda waters, champagne cider, vinegar, flavoring extracts,

101. RESIDENCE OF PHILIP SANGER, c. 1890
Philip Sanger, vice-president of Sanger Brothers Dry
Goods and Department Store, built an enormous
mansion on the northwest corner of S. Ervay and
St. Louis streets in 1885. Constructed at a staggering
cost of $15,000, it resembled a Long Branch, New
Jersey, resort house where the Sanger family spent
many summers. Philip's home remained standing
until 1953—the last of Dallas' large Victorian manors to survive into the 20th century. The house,
which Philip constructed at the expense of a mule
barn belonging to an early streetcar company, was
ironically demolished to build the R.L. Thornton
Expressway. *Dallas Historical Society Archives.*

HUGHES BROS. MFG. CO.

102. ALDREDGE HOUSE, 1895 *(Above left)*
The residence of Judge George N. Aldredge was built c. 1888 on the southwest corner of S. Ervay and Corsicana streets. It was converted into a rooming house in the early 1920s and leveled in 1928. *Courtesy of Dallas Public Library.*

103. HUGHES BROTHERS FACTORY, 1892 *(Left)*
When it began production of sweet ciders and candies from this factory about 1885, the Hughes Brothers Manufacturing Company was among the most respected industries in Dallas. Yet within twenty years, this plant and others like it had become contributors to the decline of The Cedars as people became increasingly less enamored with industries in their back yards. Though the original building on S. Ervay at the corner of Sullivan was de-stroyed, one of its additions, built in 1903, today houses the ice cream cone production facilities of the Gulf Cone Company. *Courtesy of Dallas Public Library.*

104. BELLEVIEW PLACE, c. 1890 *(Above)*
Dr. Frederick E. Hughes, shown here with his wife, children, servants, and the family cow, built Dallas' first "apartment house" on Sullivan near the corner of Browder Street about 1890. The concept was just a little advanced for its time and in 1902 the immense structure was sold to the Keeley Institute, a branch of the world-famed Dwight Institute, for the cure of "Inebriety, Morphine, Cocaine, and Tobacco Diseases and Neurathenia." The clinic was demolished in 1927. *Dallas Historical Society Archives.*

105. ST. MATTHEW'S EPISCOPAL CATHEDRAL, 1910
The third St. Matthew's Episcopal Cathedral, see of
the Episcopal Diocese of North Texas, was built on
the northeast corner of S. Ervay and Canton streets
in 1894-95 by the firm of Sanguinet and Messer.
Accommodating over 900 worshipers, it was constructed in a cruciform pattern of blue-gray
Comanche sandstone, at a cost of over $100,000. The
church was demolished in 1937 for a used car lot.
Dallas Historical Society Archives.

106. INTERIOR, ST. MATTHEW'S EPISCOPAL CATHEDRAL,
   1910
Dallas Historical Society Archives.

107. TEMPLE EMANU-EL, c. 1898
The second Temple Emanu-el, a stately, Moorish-influenced Reform synagogue, was built at the northeast corner of S. Ervay and St. Louis streets, only after it became clear that the Jewish community was settling in The Cedars and after the Commerce Street temple had to be abandoned about 1898. The pattern was that of the synagogue following the congregation rather that the opposite. The second temple was converted into a Unitarian Church in 1913 and finally demolished in 1961 for R.L. Thornton Freeway. *Courtesy of Dallas Public Library.*

preserves, jellies, fruit butter, and candies was pointed to with pride as an example of Dallas' growing cosmopolitanism.

The Hughes family came to Dallas in 1872 after having made a considerable fortune in cotton with plantations in Virginia and South Texas along the Guadalupe River basin. Dr. Hughes, who had attended the Medical College of St. Louis in 1848-49, set up practice in Dallas in 1872 and bought about twelve acres of land west of Browder Springs. The doctor and his son, John V. Hughes, built large homes on the property in the 1880s, fronting on their own private street which they called Hughes Circle (now Sullivan). About 1890, Dr. Hughes imported the radical New York concept of "apartment" residences and built the first apartment house in town which he named "Belleview Place" (104), a remarkably innovative and farsighted investment for this part of the country.

Across Ervay from Alex Sanger was built, in 1894-95, the Norman Gothic third St. Matthew's Episcopal Cathedral (105) which would have been built, had the Panic of 1893 not intervened, by one of America's most brilliant and original architects, Bertram Grosvenor Goodhue. Jobless, but young and full of fire, Goodhue wandered into Dallas the year St. Matthew's held a design competition for the Ervay Street commission. He won the contest with his plan for a perpendicular Gothic style cathedral, (modeled after the chapel of the University of Chicago), but as the depression advanced, financing became impossible, the plans were scrapped, and Goodhue went back to Boston to become a

partner with Ralph Adams Cram and design such masterpieces as St. Thomas' Cathedral in New York City, the campus of the United States Military Academy at West Point, and the Nebraska State Capitol Building at Lincoln.

Across Ervay from Philip Sanger, one of Dallas' most notable landmarks was constructed in 1899. Architects J. Reilly Gordon, H. A. Overbeck, and Roy Overbeck were paid the princely sum of $528.30 for the design and construction of the second Temple Emanu-el (107), a classically beautiful Richardsonian Romanesque structure with a minaretlike Moorish tower which dominated the heavily Jewish community.

The jewel of Ervay Street was of course the City Park (109) with its languid lagoon, its forest of willow, oak, and cedar, and its fragile pavilions and gazebos from which open air concerts were given on summer nights. When John Eakins sold the property to the city in 1876, it was considered as a location for a public park primarily because two public facilities already occupied the site — the city water supply, Browder Springs, and the Pest House, a city-run cottage for the quarantining of contagious diseases. However, the most important aspect of the immense popularity of the City Park was that it strongly influenced the expansion of the city southward by attracting the thrust of Dallas' growth for more than a decade.

Land values in the Cedars escalated in direct response to the streetcar line and park, as illustrated by the city's subsequent purchases to expand City Park. In 1882 Dallas bought an additional eight acres adjacent to Eakins' original ten for about $2,200 — or nearly four times its cost six years earlier.[47] In the 1880s the city continually added to and improved the acreage with such delights as several greenhouses, where orchids and other exotic plants flourished, and a zoo.

Although some prominent families continued to live in the area as late as the 1920s, the height of The Cedars as a very elegant and fashionable residential area was short-lived, lasting only from about 1880 through about 1890. During this period The Cedars functioned as a relatively isolated enclave,

108. CONFEDERATE MONUMENT—CITY PARK, 1910
In the spring of 1897, the Daughters of the Confederacy raised a memorial to the Confederate war dead in the northeast corner of the City Park. The monument, bearing statues of President Davis and Generals Lee, Jackson, and Johnston, was created by the sculptor Frank Teich and dedicated by Jefferson Davis' daughter and the widow of Stonewall Jackson. In 1961 it was moved to the Masonic Cemetery near the Convention Center to make room for the R.L. Thornton Freeway. *Dallas Historical Society Archives.*

109. VIEW IN CITY PARK, 1910
Dallas Historical Society Archives.

110. **LOOKING NORTH ON SOUTH ERVAY STREET, c. 1895**
These large frame homes were typical of those built in The Cedars between 1880 and 1900, only to be destroyed within the next thirty years. The structures to the far left, beyond Pocahontas Street, were leveled c. 1902 to build the Columbian Club, and several just out of the photograph to the right were removed in 1904 for construction of Dallas' oldest remaining luxury hotel, the Park (now called the Ambassador). *Courtesy of Dallas Public Library.*

111. **COLUMBIAN CLUB, 1910** *(Above right)*
The Columbian Club originated in the early 1890s as the Pheonix Club, a social organization for Dallas' prominent Jewish families. Many Jewish girls made their debuts in the handsome Second Renaissance Revival style clubhouse, the first collaborative design of Otto Lang and Frank Witchell. Built in 1904-05 at the northeast corner of S. Ervay and Pocahontas streets, the structure burned in 1931. *Dallas Historical Society Archives.*

112. **RESIDENCE OF T.A. MANNING, 1895** *(Right)*
Thomas A. Manning, special agent for the North British and Mercantile Insurance Company, built his home c. 1890 at the northeast corner of S. Ervay and Ophelia (now Hickory) streets. It was demolished in 1922 for commercial construction. *Courtesy of Dallas Public Library.*

116

protected from downtown, from the black and white "lower classes," and from too much industrial development. But between 1880, when Dallas' population stood at 10,358, and 1890, when it had swelled to 38,067, the city experienced an industrial and real estate boom which eventually left little room for such sheltered sanctuaries.

The number of Dallas real estate transfers filed in 1880 did not quite reach 300, yet by 1886, 3,739 were on record and by 1887, 5,784 were filed with an aggregate value of $9,378,184. Promoters and developers were wildly subdividing any parcel of land they could lay their hands on. Between 1887 and 1890, Chestnut Hill, South Park, E. M. Kahn's Addition, Cotton Mills Addition, Edgewood, and Exposition Park were opened for new housing starts in far South Dallas between the City Park and Pennsylvania Avenue. Most of these developments contained middle- to lower-class, one- or one-and-a-half-story frame homes with little style and a tendency toward rapid deterioration. For example, the Cotton Mills Addition, built in a marshy area known as Wahoo Lake, was a working-class development rented primarily by black people who worked in the mills along the Santa Fe and the Rock Island railroad lines. The homes were substandard from the beginning, with no running water or indoor toilets, and five years after its construction, the Cotton Mills Addition was the most economically depressed area in Dallas, plagued by consumption, pneumonia, poor city services, inadequate sanitation, crime and housing segregation.

As in so many sectors of Dallas' growth, the influence of the railroads was strongly apparent in the generation of the very poor housing districts. The H&TC had begun developing its right-of-way, which lay just to the northeast of the Eakins family property (along what is now Central Expressway east of Harwood and west of Good-Latimer), for industrial use. By the late 1880s such heavy industries as the Gulf Refining Company, the Howard Oil Works, and the Dallas Waste Mills had located in the H&TC Addition,

causing a great demand for housing for the mill workers.

An important corollary to the growth of industry in South Dallas was the large number of black squatters and tenants who settled there, creating the residential sector of Deep Ellum; the H&TC encouraged black people to locate on its right-of-way because no one else would settle this property along the tracks and their presence acted as a lure to industry with the offer of cheap, readily accessible labor. The railroad could build inexpensive shotgun houses (so named because a shotgun could be fired through the house — in the front door and out the back door — without hitting the walls) for rentals or allow squatters to erect makeshift shanties for homes.

This pattern, which forced low income blacks to cluster in squalid hovels near the railroad tracks, was repeated all over the city, creating a spidery network of black communities permeating nearly every white area. Negro residences, interspersed with low-income whites and Latins, could be found along the H&TC from Haskell Avenue on the north through Freedmantown and Stringtown to Deep Ellum; extending along the Santa Fe almost to Grand Avenue on the south in what was known as Boggy Bayou; and along the MK&T in Frogtown, as far north as the Booker T. Washington Addition which bordered Highland Park, near the intersection of the MK&T and Monticello Street.

The Boggy Bayou area west of Lamar

113. COCKRELL HOUSE, c. 1884
In 1884, Sarah Cockrell and her son Alexander began to subdivide and promote their land between Lamar Street and the river. Though most of the property attracted only heavy industry or workers' shantytowns after the Missouri, Kansas & Texas Railroad built through it in 1889, Alexander, shown here with his family, insisted on building his beautiful Eastlake mansion in the same area on a full city block along S. Lamar between Arnold and McKee streets. Surrounded by commercial properties, it was finally demolished in 1913. *Courtesy of Old City Park, A Museum of Cultural History, Dallas, Texas.*

114. RESIDENCE OF L. PHILIPSON, 1895
The home of Ludwig Philipson, a wholesale tobacco
dealer, was built c. 1890 at the northwest corner of
S. Akard and Cadiz streets. It survived until 1942.
Courtesy of Dallas Public Library.

115. COLUMBIAN SCHOOL, c. 1900 *(Left)*
One of several stone and brick Romanesque Revival schoolhouses designed for the city by James Flanders, the Columbian School was completed in 1893 at the northwest corner of Akard and Royal streets. After attendance became negligible due to the commercialization of the South Dallas neighborhood it served, the building was converted into the school district's administration offices in 1923. It was razed in 1954 to build Memorial Auditorium. *Dallas Historical Society Archives*.

116. RESIDENCE OF R. LIEBMAN, 1895
Rudolph Liebman, president of the Texas Paper Company, built his residence c. 1894 at the northwest corner of Canton and Browder streets. It was destroyed in 1930 and the property is now part of the City Hall grounds. *Courtesy of Dallas Public Library*.

117. COLONIAL HILL ADDITION, c. 1900

Looking west along Forest Avenue near its intersection with S. Ervay Street, this view shows the affluent Colonial Hill Addition. An area approximately bounded by Grand Avenue, Warren Street, Akard Street, and the H&TC tracks, this fine neighborhood contained many large homes similar to the expansive, Neo-Colonial residence of Thomas Scollard (right foreground), owner of the Scollard and Jennie buildings downtown. Built in 1890, Scollard's home was demolished in 1927 as Forest Avenue began to commercialize; about this time, the Jewish residents of South Boulevard and Park Row began to desert the homes they had built between 1900 and 1915 for Highland Park and North Dallas. *Dallas Historical Society Archives.*

118. ALAMO SCHOOL, c. 1898

James Flanders' Alamo School, built in 1893 at the southwest corner of Nettie (now Jeffries) and Ophelia (now Hickory) streets, served the working class families of the Santa Fe and the H&TC Additions to the city. Its most notable feature was, of course, the Alamo-inspired, trapazoidal pyramid over the front entrance which was taken down due to structural instability in the 1930s. The school survives today only as a shell. *Dallas Historical Society Archives.*

Street (which lay in the marshy floodplain of the Trinity until the levee system was created in 1927-33) began to see industrial development in the 1890s. Alexander Cockrell II (113), whose father had purchased this southern strip of John Neely Bryan's claim in 1852, encouraged industries such as the Trinity Cotton Oil Company, the Dallas Cotton Mills, the Dallas Union Stockyards, and the Armstrong Packing Company to establish plants along the Rock Island's sidings all the way from the Houston Street Viaduct to Corinth Street. The Armstrong Packing Company was incorporated in 1890 as the Dallas Dressed Beef and Packing Company and by the time it was purchased in 1899 by John S. Armstrong (with the backing of Philip Armour of Chicago) it had become, in conjunction with the Union Stockyards, a major rival of Fort Worth, employing over 1,500 people. It was sold to Swift and Company in 1928 which later closed it down in order to concentrate the business in Fort Worth.

This tremendous rise of industrial plants along the railroads flanking both sides of South Dallas had a direct cause-and-effect relationship with the growing prosperity of the core residential area of The Cedars. Many of the capitalists who owned these plants and mills lived in that sheltered province between South Harwood and South Akard streets just north of the City Park. Between 1880 and 1890 a map of the area almost resembled a medieval fiefdom: the financier-prince built his palatial Victorian mansion in the core area and his industrial concerns in the outlying fields, with a buffer zone of low-income workers between himself and the noise and smell of his plants.

In the eighties and early nineties this kind of social pattern remained possible in The Cedars, but by the turn of the century, the enormous growth and spread of the industrial areas and the buffer zones, coupled with the deterioration of the core area and the competitive lure of newer residential developments, led to the increasing undesirability of The Cedars as a place to build one of these Victorian palaces.

In 1888, the Dallas Rapid Transit Company opened a steam-driven excursion line from the courthouse down Lamar Street to Forest Avenue, across to the Fairgrounds and back downtown, as a promotion for the new Colonial Hills Addition (117). To meet the competition, the Dallas Consolidated Street Railway Company extended its lines down Akard, Ervay, and Harwood streets and east along Hickory Street toward the Fairgrounds and the Alamo School (118). This opened up the entire South Dallas area — which had heretofore been wilderness, accessible only by carriage or rickety, mule-drawn cars which only came as far as the City Park — to anyone with a nickel and a few hours of leisure.

This loss of exclusivity quickly killed The Cedars' appeal to wealthy, snobbish home buyers, who after 1905 turned toward the contractually-guaranteed exclusive Munger Place and Highland Park Additions. As the older Cedars homes came up for sale, the owners found a declining market for expensive mansions which were rapidly aging out of style and favor. (In contrast to Frank Lloyd Wright's new Prairie style homes which became enormously popular between 1900 and 1920, the Victorians styles suddenly appeared "gaudy" or distasteful.) But the continuing influx of people allowed The Cedars a second phase of development, approximately between the years 1890 and 1905.

Some nice, moderately priced, Victorian homes were built in this period (121 and 122); and even a few mansions, like Simon Linz's Prairie style home on the corner of Ervay Street and South Boulevard (which survives as the McGowan Funeral Home) and J. Ashford Hughes' home (123), rose across from the City Park, like the specters of J. P. Morgan and Jay Gould roaring at the insolence and impudence of the picketing masses. The times had changed, however, and apartment houses, duplexes, and cottages were being erected in the gaps between the large estates; sometimes even the great houses themselves were ignominiously rented to boarders. With the expansion of downtown, the property also began to appeal to small businesses like laundries, saloons, restaurants, and repair shops — enterprises which traditionally cluster at the periphery of the business district.

119. SECOND CUMBERLAND PRESBYTERIAN CHURCH, 1892
Displaying the wide variety of colors and textures used by Victorian craftsmen, the Second Cumberland Presbyterian Church was a grand example of the potential of wood construction. Built in 1889 at the northeast corner of S. Harwood and Grand Avenue, this was the first church to venture into the newly developing suburbs of far South Dallas. It was demolished in the mid-1960s. *Dallas Historical Society Archives.*

120. RESIDENCE OF G.S. LEACHMAN, c. 1905
As The Cedars began to deteriorate, many of its former residents relocated in the new, more fashionable developments further south. There, the 1901 home of George S. Leachman, president of the Dallas Steam Laundry and Dye Works, displayed the popular pattern book design of a transitional period between older Victorian ornamentation and the emerging Prairie style. The house on Holmes Street near Grand Avenue was destroyed in 1973. *Courtesy of Mrs. Manning B. Shannon, Jr. (Elizabeth Leachman Shannon).*

To some extent, the deterioration of The Cedars came from the large home owners themselves. Their many little barns, outhouses, and servants' buildings created a crowded, unsightly clutter around almost every house. As late as 1911 the Sanger brothers retained a large stable near their homes to house delivery van animals (even after trucks came into general use).

The coup de grace to the rapidly declining situation occurred when the industrial expansion along the railroad lines surrounding The Cedars began to spill over into the residential area. An increasing number of cotton mills, petroleum distillation plants, cottonseed oil presses, lumber yards, and ice factories (with attendant workers' quarters, black shantytowns and subsidiary businesses) began to constrict that protected, isolated pocket of big homes, further decreasing their desirability and value. Even Mill Creek, the meandering stream which had been such a pleasant attraction only a few years before, evolved into an open sewer, filled with foul-smelling human and industrial wastes, and lined with refuse as if it were the city dump.

Since Dallas' earliest days, Mill Creek had been very attractive to the city's industry. Several of the early grist mills, Scott's Flouring Mill, and the City Cotton Compress located along its banks because it was the largest waterway in the city aside from the Trinity River system. Larger than Turtle Creek or Five Mile Creek, its waters ran all year, and it also had a tremendous amount of cedar and oak for lumber. As the city grew, the mills and other industries obliterated the tree cover and began to use the stream primarily to flush away wastes. The foul sight and smell contributed greatly toward making South Dallas an undesirable place to live. George Kessler, in his city plan of 1911, called for the cleanup of Mill Creek and for its development as a greenbelt-parkway, but by then the area had declined past any hope of breaking the destructive momentum. The city decided to lay pipe in the creek bed for drainage and then covered it up in the mid-1930s.

By the early 1920s, this process of deterioration had reached its peak. The business district was perilously close, less than two minutes by automobile, which effectively reduced the area to a commercial extension of downtown. Homes were being demolished in order to build businesses and warehouses, and those in less attractive locations remained only as low-rent boarding houses and tenements. With the construction of the R. L. Thornton Freeway in the early 1960s, the last remnants of those tattered old hulks which had been lurking in unexposed corners were swept away.

Most of The Cedars' residents, anticipating this commercialization, had moved out by 1910 to 1915. About that time, a large segment of the Jewish community moved to South Boulevard, Park Row, and Forest Avenue, creating a serene alternative to Highland Park and Swiss Avenue (some of the homes still exist today and are being restored). Two of the finest homes in this far South Dallas area were built in 1913 and 1914 by the architect J. Edward Overbeck: the Levi Marcus home at 2707 South Boulevard, and the Isaac Bromberg house at 2617 South Boulevard both remain standing today. A library was built by the Sanger brothers at Harwood and South Boulevard and the third Temple Emanu-el (124) was constructed on South Boulevard at Harwood in 1917, the same year that Forest Avenue High School was built. The school (now called James Madison) enjoyed a reputation as the finest, best-equipped and best-staffed school in the city for a number of years. Yet by the 1930s the same problems that had plagued The Cedars caught up to this far South Dallas area. Industry along the H&TC tracks grew steadily; lower income, bungalow-style homes were erected haphazardly over the area; a lack of zoning ordinances helped to commercialize Forest Avenue by the late 1920s; and a growing black community, called "the Prairie" upon its establishment after the Civil War because it was so far out of town, began to engulf the entire South Dallas community. The construction of Central Expressway and I-45 along the old H&TC track in 1952 was the final addition to those destructive forces which created the conditions that exist today.

122. SCENE ON SOUTH AKARD STREET, 1895 *(Left)*
Built in the mid-1890s, most of the homes along
S. Akard where it crossed Mill Creek belonged to
middle-class Jewish salesmen, clerks, and shop owners
until the 1920s and 1930s. This photograph reveals
the deplorable condition of the streetcar tracks
which, combined with the precarious financial
condition of the streetcar companies, allowed Pierre
du Pont to gain control of Dallas' street
transportation system in 1901. *Courtesy of Dallas
Public Library*

123. RESIDENCE OF J. ASHFORD HUGHES, 1910 *(Above)*
The monumental home of J. Ashford Hughes,
financial officer of the Trinity Warehouse Company,
was constructed at the northeast corner of
Pocahontas and Evergreen (St. Paul) streets c. 1902.
By 1945, it was in use as the Dallas Gospel Center
Church and was demolished in 1960 to build R.L.
Thornton Expressway. *Courtesy of Dallas* Times
Herald

124. TEMPLE EMANU-EL, c. 1920 *(Right)*
The third Temple Emanu-el, a Neo-Classical creation
of the firm of Hubbell and Greene, was constructed
in 1917 on South Boulevard at the corner of
Harwood Street. It was leveled in 1972. *Courtesy of
Temple Emanu-el*

125. BOLL HOUSE, c. 1885
The home of Henry Boll, very likely the first brick
residence built in the frontier village of Dallas,
resembled the narrow, one-room-deep provincial
dwellings common to Europe in the 17th and 18th
centuries. Boll and his fellow colonists brought the
style with them when they immigrated from
Switzerland to La Reunion in 1855. Built in 1859 at
the northeast corner of Swiss Avenue and Germania
(changed in 1914 to Liberty), the home was torn
down for its brick in 1905. *Dallas Historical Society
Archives*

5 EAST DALLAS

The earliest incidence of settlement in the wild, tangled undergrowth east of Dallas occurred in 1855 when Captain Jefferson Peak purchased and settled on a large tract of land lying far to the northeast beyond the original limits of the city of Dallas. Peak's farmhouse, built at what is now the corner of Worth and Peak streets, was the first indication to westward-bound travelers of the presence of the town, and was the only human habitation of any kind for miles. This property (which Captain Peak's son, June, subdivided and sold as Peak's Addition beginning about 1897) originally sold for as little as fifty cents an acre, a price very attractive to many of the survivors of the troubled La Reunion colony who moved to East Dallas in the late 1850s. Several of the French, Belgian, and Swiss immigrants settled the area rather than return to Europe after their Utopian dream collapsed in great agony on the west bank of the Trinity. These early East Dallas pioneers included Julien Reverchon (the expert naturalist for whom Reverchon Park is named), Jacob Nussbaumer, and Henry Boll (125). Boll, a native of Aargau, Switzerland, settled in 1859 on a small property adjacent to the old White Rock Road (now called Swiss Avenue in deference to these early families), and carried on his trade as a butcher. His brother-in-law, Jacob Nussbaumer, purchased a sizable tract, also along Swiss Avenue between what are now Cantegral and Hall streets, which he and Boll began to subdivide and sell soon after they returned from service in Colonel Nat Burford's 19th Texas Cavalry in 1865.

Some of the property was sold to a second wave of European immigrants recruited and brought to Dallas in 1870 by Major Ben Long, another Reunion colonist who believed the town to be a haven from the disruptive in fluences of nineteenth-century Europe. Among those who came in this second group were Jacob Boll, Henry's brother and a naturalist colleague of Reverchon, Charles Ott (180), and Louis Wagner (126), whose cast iron-fronted grocery store on Main Street stood until the 1960s as a symbol of the strong bonds of faith and family so characteristic of these people's American Dream. Most of these new European arrivals settled in East Dallas near Moon Lake, a small natural pond created by Mill Creek on Nussbaumer's property (near what is now a parking lot on the southwest corner of Gaston and Hall, across from Baylor Hospital's complex).

These French, Belgian, and Swiss immigrants were later joined by small groups of Germans, Italians, Austro-Hungarians, and Greeks, who at first gathered together instinctively in East Dallas for mutual support and protection, much as their counterparts did in New York's Little Italy. Yet foreign enclaves did not persist long in Dallas because the city greatly needed their skills, craftsmanship, and artistic talents; they were almost completely assimilated into the urban life by the turn of the century. While very little remains of this European community today other than a few street names, a row of nineteenth-century homes and back buildings known as the Wilson Block, located across Swiss Avenue from the site of Henry Boll's old homestead, does miraculously survive.

Frederick P. Wilson and his brother John B. Wilson came to Dallas in 1872 from Toronto, Canada, to enter business as cattle dealers. By the 1880s, they were driving Texas

126. WAGNER HOUSE, c. 1890

Louis Wagner and his two brothers immigrated to Dallas from Frankfurt, Germany, about 1870 to avoid induction into the Prussian Army. After establishing a green grocery on the courthouse square, Louis built his family a spacious, comfortable home on the corner of Bryan and Germania streets c. 1885. The house was moved to Live Oak Street and restored in 1976.

Courtesy of Musti and Robert M. Roller

longhorns to summer pasture in Wyoming and then shipping them by rail to St. Louis and by ship to Europe through the Gulf port of Galveston. In 1894, Frederick Wilson married Henrietta Frichot, Jacob Nussbaumer's niece, and by 1898 he had acquired all of the Nussbaumer property. On that land he built a magnificent Queen Anne style home (127), said to be a miniature replica of the Czarina's summer palace in Belorussia. Wilson built three smaller rental houses on the block behind the main house, all of which still survive. One, at 2902 Swiss (128), was built for Dr. T. E. Arnold, a famous eye surgeon whom Boll had persuaded to immigrate from Geneva, Switzerland, in 1891. Arnold's son, Charles Erwin Arnold, was sent to medical school in Zurich but never practiced, preferring instead to follow a brilliant career as a professional photographer. He became a contract researcher of chemicals and papers for Eastman Kodak in the 1920s, the chief of micro-photography for Baylor Dental School, organized Dallas' first police ballistics and crime lab, and took hundreds of wonderfully crafted "portraits" of the city.

Other remnants of this early European community include St. Joseph's German Catholic Church, built about 1910 at the corner of Swiss and Texas streets, and the gambrel-roofed Beilharz home at 2723 Swiss, built about 1885 by Laura Beilharz (Mrs. F. P. Wilson's sister) and her husband Theodore, a Swiss-born stonemason who did the

130

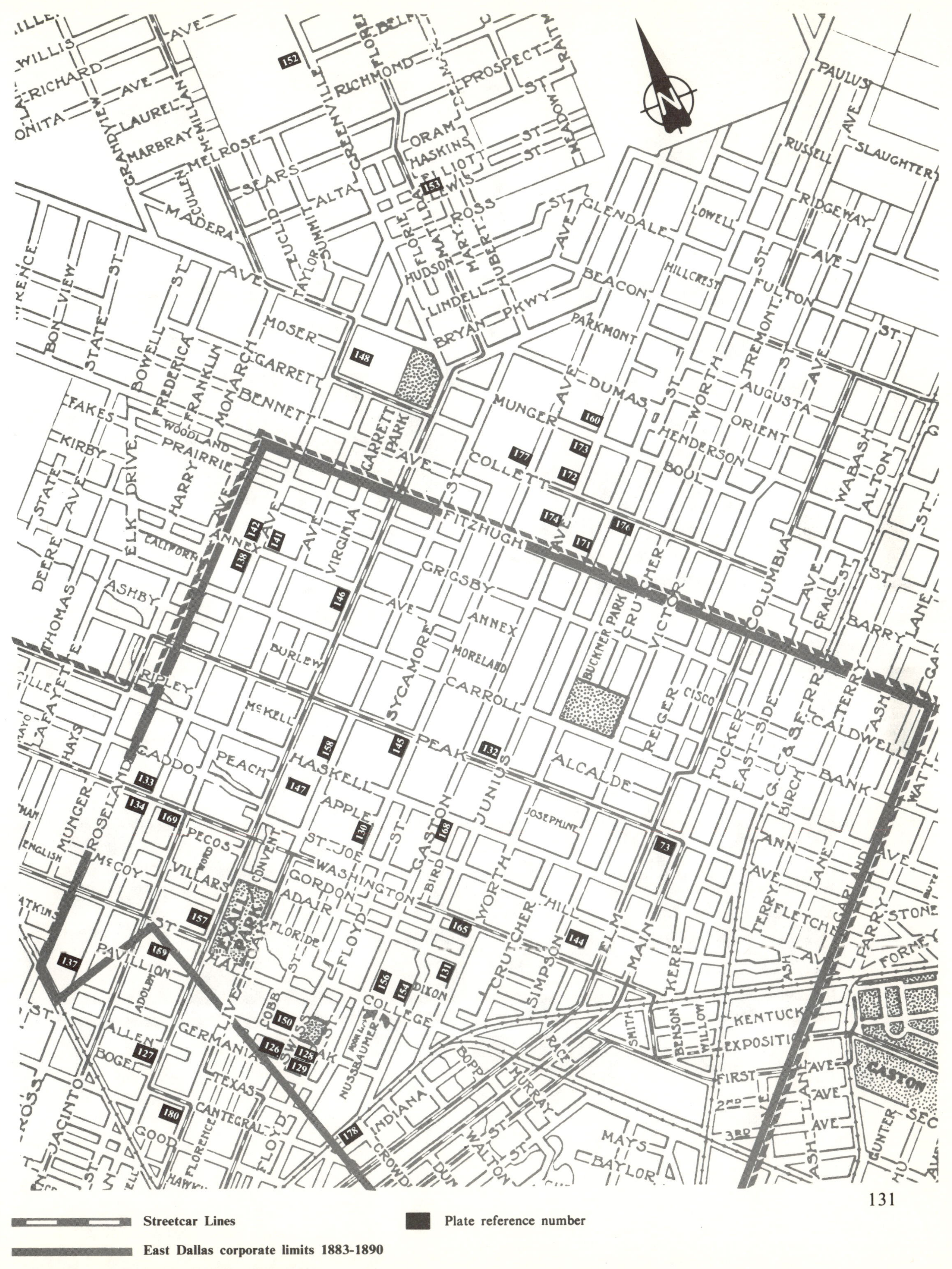

131

Streetcar Lines

East Dallas corporate limits 1883-1890

Dallas city limits 1890-1912

Plate reference number

127. WILSON HOUSE, c. 1900 *(Above left)*
The residence of Frederick P. Wilson, a rare and beautiful example of the gracious qualities of the Queen Anne style, was built c. 1898 on the corner of Swiss Avenue and Oak Street. The home is the last survivor of the hundreds of grand, 19th-century Victorian mansions that once flourished throughout the city. *Dallas Historical Society Archives*

128. WILSON BLOCK, c. 1901 *(Left)*
This backhouse on the Wilson property was for many years the home of photographer Charles Erwin Arnold and his family. Built in 1901 on the southeast corner of Swiss and Germania, the house was equipped with both electrical and gas lighting to spare the occupants the loss of either unreliable utility. *Courtesy of Mrs. Claude L. McGlamery*

129. GASTON MANSION, c. 1885 *(Above)*
Captain William H. Gaston, Confederate soldier, banker, financier, and empire builder, designed and constructed his own Greek Revival home in 1873 on the northeast corner of Swiss Avenue and St. Joseph Street. This elegant mansion, headquarters of the 400-acre plantation that became the town of East Dallas, was demolished in 1927 to construct the Dallas Theological Seminary. *Courtesy of Mrs. John N. (Sallie Bell Flippen Gaston) Jackson*

exterior stonework on many early Dallas buildings.

Without question, the most important spur to the growth of East Dallas was the arrival of the railroads. Their intersection a mile east of the courthouse not only drew the entire city eastward, away from the river, but also established the primary focus for an alternate city, which began to grow in the otherwise vacant area. A small business district, composed of drummers' hotels, restaurants, and dry goods stores which catered to the rail traveler, grew up around the Union Depot, forming, in effect, East Dallas' downtown. In the 1870s, the cattle trade helped to make this depot area into a tenderloin district full of outlaws, prostitutes, and gamblers who plied their trades from shoddy little hotels and tent saloons. It was also a haven for displaced black people from all over the South who began erecting squatters' shacks on railroad property; by the 1880s, the Houston & Texas Central Railroad had built a large switching yard there, the Texas & Pacific Railroad was constructing a huge roundhouse across Gaston from the Wilson Block, and the area began to take on the well worn look of Deep Ellum as many industrial concerns also located there to take advantage of both the rail junction and the cheap, readily available labor.

Until 1871, the land on which the Union Depot was built had been Dallas' first fairgrounds, the site of the Dallas County Agricultural and Mechanical Association Fair. In 1871 Captain William H. Gaston purchased the site in anticipation of the railroad's arrival and relocated the fairgrounds further east on land where Baylor Hospital is now situated.

130. HUGHES/SLAUGHTER HOUSE, c. 1890
The beautiful "Steamboat Victorian" home of Colonel Christopher Columbus Slaughter was built c. 1880 by Colonel W.E. Hughes, owner of the Grand-Windsor Hotel. Situated on a large expanse of East Dallas real estate, the structure was destroyed in 1939 to build the Washington Place Apartment Project. *Courtesy of Old City Park, A Museum of Cultural History, Dallas, Texas*

131.132. INTERIOR, HUGHES/SLAUGHTER HOUSE, c. 1900
Courtesy of Old City Park, A Museum of Cultural History, Dallas, Texas

Captain Gaston was exemplary of the kind of men who created and shaped Dallas' entire 140-year history. In January of 1868, he and Aaron Camp opened the firm of Gaston and Camp, Dallas' first bank, which Gaston later parlayed into the City National Bank (predecessor of the present First National). He began investing his bank profits in East Dallas real estate and in 1871, acquired a 400-acre tract along old White Rock Road on which he built an enormous Greek Revival home two years later (129).[48] To insure that the railroad would not bypass Dallas, Gaston donated the old fairgrounds to the T&P for a depot in 1873 and the land became a sort of public grazing lot for all the ranchers shipping cattle out through this terminus.[49]

One famous rancher who sometimes used the pasture facilities was Colonel Christopher Columbus Slaughter, the president of the Texas and Southwestern Cattle Raisers Association, owner of the C. C. Slaughter Cattle Company, and at one time, during the 1880s, the largest single taxpayer in the state of Texas. Colonel Slaughter began herding cattle with his father about 1870, driving them north along the Chisholm Trail to Abilene, Kansas, and investing the profits in land. By 1890, he owned or controlled over one million acres of land under the "Long S" brand, stretching all across the West Texas caprock between Big Spring and Lubbock, with additional ranches located in Mexico, New Mexico, and the Dakotas. Slaughter was a contemporary and friend of the legendary cattle barons who once ruled Texas — men like Colonel Charles Goodnight, who in 1876 founded the first ranch in the Texas Panhandle, the 700,000-acre J. A. Ranch in Palo Duro Canyon; like Major George W. Littlefield, owner of the 275,000-acre LIT Ranch; and like John Chisum, unquestionably the largest individual cattle owner in the United States, who by 1877 was running nearly 80,000 head on the unlimited range of the lower Pecos.

Like these men, Slaughter epitomized the rugged Texas individualist who achieved wealth and power through sheer strength of will. Yet Slaughter was more than just a cold-blooded cattle king; he was an innovator,

133. FIELD/WILSON HOUSE, 1895

Thomas Field, a pioneer Dallas real estate broker and developer, built his fashionable Eastlake style mansion on Peak Avenue between Gaston and Junius in 1884 when East Dallas was little more than open prairie. In 1894 the prominent cattleman and banker J.B. Wilson bought the home, which stood on an entire city block, and it remained an area landmark until 1922 when the house was demolished in order to subdivide and redevelop the land. *Courtesy of Dallas Public Library*

134. CLARK HOME, c. 1897

The modest residence at the northest corner of Ross Avenue and Washington Street was home to a succession of powerful and wealthy Dallas men. Built in 1886 by W.J. Keller, it was sold in 1889 as a town house to William Brown Miller, the county's largest cotton grower and owner of the antebellum mansion Millermore. In 1897 the house was acquired by Judge William Clark, whose son Tom became Associate Justice of the Supreme Court in 1949 and whose grandson, Ramsey, was appointed U.S. Attorney General in 1967. The home was destroyed in 1928 and was replaced by a gas station. *Courtesy of Mrs. Elizabeth Clark Capers (Mrs. Julian Capers, Jr.)*

a devout Christian, an astute practitioner of the modern corporate philosophy of diversification of capital, and a lavish philanthropist, donating millions of dollars to Baptist-affiliated churches, schools, and hospitals. He was the first rancher in Texas to breed improved hybrid stock by importing, in 1873, several thousand head of Durham shorthorn cattle from Kentucky, and he was also one of the few ranchers to recognize the limitations of cattle raising and to branch out into banking (as vice-president of the American Exchange National Bank) and industry (as president of the First Texas Chemical Company). For many years, he was chairman of the Baptist General Convention of Texas and the story goes that he opened the 1886 Cattle Raisers Association meeting with a prayer (and God knows that praying cattlemen have always been scarce in Texas).

In 1885, Slaughter moved his headquarters from West Texas to Dallas, purchased a home on Worth Street between Hall and Adair (130), and began to purchase large parcels of East Dallas property, much of which is now the grounds of Baylor Hospital.

Another of the large East Dallas estate owners was Thomas Field, one of Captain Gaston's associates in bringing the T&P and the H&TC to town. A pioneer real estate developer, Field flamboyantly promoted his extensive East Dallas holdings in 1884 with the construction of a palatial residence in the middle of his property (133). Field's real estate activities in East Dallas in the late 1880s and the early 1890s were very important to its growth and development, for at one time he owned, controlled, or influenced the sale of large sections of the area. But his firm, Field and Field, Real Estate and Financial Agents, sold or developed the land in such an unstructured manner — with no zoning and little planning — that he actually hastened its eventual deterioration in some ways.

Publicly, Field was primarily known for opening Dallas' first opera house in 1873 and for his great doomed vision, the Oriental Hotel. The depression in 1893 put such a burden on his finances that he sold not only the unfinished Oriental to St. Louis interests but also his East Dallas residence to John B. Wilson in 1894.

Wilson had accumulated a sizable fortune by investing his profits from the family cattle business (which he shared with his brother Frederick, owner of the Wilson Block) in several stable, prosperous, and essential Dallas enterprises. By 1894 he was president of the Trinity Cotton Oil Company, president of the Dallas Electric Street Railway Company, vice-president of the American Exchange National Bank, chairman of the board of the City National Bank, treasurer of the Titche-Goettinger Company, and well into the planning of the Wilson Building downtown. As a result, his newly acquired home sparkled throughout the season with the many varied social functions his position demanded.

The decade between the arrival of the railroads and the incorporation of East Dallas as a separate city in 1883 witnessed little activity beyond the establishment of these large estates and the buying of cheap property by men of wealth and foresight. The area was heavily wooded, especially along the course of Mill Creek as it meandered through what is now Exall Park and along Hall Street toward The Cedars. It boasted a scattered population of 2,000 to 3,000 and very little development or street construction past Washington Avenue. There was only one streetcar line, the mule-drawn Dallas Street Railroad Company, built out Ross and San Jacinto in 1875 by Colonel William J. Keller. But within ten years, East Dallas began to experience the same wild, uncontrolled growth that was afflicting South Dallas, and the town's quiet tranquility slowly became a memory.

One of the area's first organized real estate developments began about 1886 when Colonel Keller extended his streetcar line down Washington Avenue to Gaston's new fairgrounds and created the small picnic grounds called Shady View Park to attract prospective buyers on Sunday outings. The first home built in Keller's Addition was one he constructed for himself that year at the northeast corner of Ross and Washington streets (134). The house was sold in 1897 to Judge William H. Clark, whose family would span five generations of

135. CRAWFORD HOUSE, c. 1894 *(Above left)*
Between 1885 and 1920, a Ross Avenue address held great cachet in Dallas social circles—a prominence easily maintained by Colonel William L. Crawford in his magnificent Eastlake mansion. The house was built in 1894 as part of the Keller Addition, and boasted not only one of the finest and most expensively furnished interiors in town, but also an adjoining private art gallery, maintained and supported by the Colonel's wife, Katherine. The home was dismantled by the family in 1946 because of the neighborhood's steady deterioration, but the staircase and much of the carved paneling, fixtures, and murals were reinstated in a Greenway Parks home which still stands. The gallery's artworks were eventually sold or given to various museums throughout the country. *Courtesy of Mr. William Crawford*

136. ART GALLERY, CRAWFORD HOUSE, c. 1905 *(Left)*
Dallas Historical Society Archives

137. INTERIOR, CRAWFORD HOUSE, c. 1894 *(Above)*
Courtesy of Mr. William Crawford

138. RESIDENCE OF T.J. WORD, c. 1885
In order to oversee development of his several-hundred-acre property on upper Ross Avenue, Thomas Jefferson Word commissioned an unpretentious but spacious home from the architect A.B. Bristol. Built c. 1885 at the corner of Germania Street, the house survived until 1948 when it was torn down for a used car lot. *Courtesy of Old City Park, A Museum of Cultural History, Dallas, Texas*

139. MUNGER HOUSE, c. 1904 *(Left)*
Among the most spectacular of the mansions along
"Dallas' Fifth Avenue" was the imposing Colonial
Revival home of Stephen I. Munger, president of the
Continental Gin Company and brother of the
inventor and real estate genius Robert Munger. The
house was built in 1904 at the northwest corner of
Ross Avenue and Annex Street with an intimidating
front portico of classical Corinthian columns. The
Munger family, apprehensive about the progressive
degeneration of Ross Avenue, demolished the home
in 1954 to prevent its conversion to commercial
usage. *Courtesy of Mrs. Samuel A. Shelburne*

140. MUNGER HOUSE, c. 1904 *(Above)*
The last vestiges of the frontier were exorcised by
such genteel rites as the Terpsichorean Club Ball,
held in the third floor ballroom of the Munger home.
Courtesy of Mrs. Samuel A. Shelburne

141. RESIDENCE OF HENRY COKE, 1910 *(above left)*
The dignified self-confidence of Dallas' city leaders expressed itself in Ross Avenue, a nearly two-mile-long boulevard of splendid homes. Among these were the turreted residence of Henry Coke, founder of the prominent legal firm of Coke & Coke and vice-president of the Commercial Bank and Trust Company. Built c. 1890 at the southeast corner of Ross and Annex, it was razed in 1958. *Dallas Historical Society Archives*

142. ALEXANDER HOUSE, 1910 *(left)*
The residence of Charles H. Alexander, an enormously wealthy banker, manufacturer, and entrepreneur, was built in 1906 on the northeast corner of Ross and Annex at a phenomenal cost of $125,000. It was purchased in 1930 by the Dallas Women's Forum and restored. *Dallas Historical Society Archives*

143. THORNE HOUSE, 1910 *(above)*
The last of the great houses built on Ross, the home of Texas & Pacific Railroad Executive Vice-president Lansing S. Thorne, was erected in 1908 on the northeast corner at Grigsby. It was demolished in 1969 for a parking lot. *Dallas Historical Society Archives*

prominent public service in this country's legal profession.[50]

With the profits from his real estate venture and the sale in 1887 of his streetcar lines to Royal Ferris' Dallas Consolidated Street Railway Company, Keller founded the Banker's and Merchant's National Bank. In 1893, he began to construct a second house in Keller's Addition, on the northwest corner of Ross and Washington (135), but died before it was completed. The family sold it to Colonel William L. Crawford, a veteran of the 19th Texas Cavalary who had read law under Judge (soon to become Governor) David Culberson in Jefferson, Texas, after the Civil War.

Crawford left Jefferson for the bustling city of Dallas in 1871 to establish the firm of Crawford, Muse and Crawford, and a personal reputation as the foremost criminal advocate in the South. His wife, Katherine, the daughter of a wealthy plantation family in Oxford, Mississippi, was educated in Europe and studied art in New York, Berlin, Paris, and Rome as a young woman. In 1903, she instigated the most avant-garde happening in Dallas' history with the opening of the first private art gallery in the entire Southwest. Displayed in the north wing of the Ross Avenue home (136). Mrs. Crawford's unique collection included paintings and sculpture by such artists as Van Dyke, Kunz-Meyer and Bougereau, along with her own work; hers was also one of the first galleries to showcase regional artists like John Knott and Frank Reaugh.

The house was decorated with murals, tapestries, and intricately carved and handpainted Louis XVI furnishings in museumlike abundance (137). The Crawfords were well known in the highest social circles of the state — the Colonel for his gracious Southern gentility and lavish parties, and Mrs. Crawford as the artistic grande dame of a frontier town with a growing social and artistic consciousness. Even in a time when the city and nation were mobilizing for the first World War, their activities were avidly followed by the press, as revealed in a *Morning News* report: "Following the close of the Fair, during which the Crawford Art Gallery was a distinguished attraction, the second season of

144. RESIDENCE OF MR. AND MRS. BARRY MILLER, c. 1895 *(above)*
The newlywed cousins Minerva Hortense and Philip Barry Miller lived in a modest wood-frame home on Simpson Street, a wedding gift from the bride's father William Brown Miller. Constructed about 1894, the home was dismantled in 1970. *Courtesy of Dallas Public Library*

145. RESIDENCE OF M. B. TERRILL, c. 1910 *(above right)*
Walter Sharp, an oilman active in the development of Spindletop and later one of the first directors of what is today Texaco, Inc., built his home, a variation of the Georgian Revival style, c. 1900 on Swiss Avenue at the northwest corner of Peak. In 1906, the home was purchased by M. B. Terrill, who converted it for use as the Terrill Preparatory School for Boys, predecessor of the St. Mark's School. The house was essentially destroyed in 1938 when it was stuccoed and remodeled for a clinic, but actual demolition occurred in 1973. *Dallas Historical Society Archives*

146. RESIDENCE OF W. H. DANA, c. 1890
The finest example of the Eastlake cottage-type residence in Dallas was built c. 1885 by William H. Dana at the corner of Annex and Bryan streets. It was torn down in 1913. *Courtesy of Dallas Public Library*

147. URSULINE ACADEMY, c. 1895
The magnificent Ursuline Academy, built in a French-inspired High Victorian Gothic style at a cost of $250,000, occupied the entire block bounded by Live Oak, Bryan, St. Joseph, and Haskell streets. When the main section was finished in 1884, it rose like a misplaced Alsacian chateau in a remote sea of cotton fields worked by black sharecroppers from Freedmantown. The main tower building, begun in 1882 and completed in 1884, was designed and constructed by Nicholas J. Clayton, the brilliant architect responsible for most of Galveston's grand structures, including the Bishop's Palace (or Gresham Home) on Broadway. Using Clayton's drawings and plans, the Dallas architect W. H. Harrell constructed two wings in 1889 and 1902 respectively, which served as classrooms and living accommodations for the sisters. After the school moved to North Dallas, this beautiful complex of buildings was casually demolished in 1949. *Courtesy of Dallas Public Library*

1914-1915 was brilliantly introduced by . . . a program of music and literature given in the gracious Ross Ave. home of Col. and Mrs. W.L. Crawford, distinguished for its hospitality, brilliant entertainments and artistic fittings."[51]

This upper extension of Ross Avenue, northeast of the H&TC depot, had in the mid-1880s taken on a very important role as the boundary zone between the rest of East Dallas and the North Dallas black areas known as Freedmantown and Stringtown. By 1890, the Dallas Consolidated Street Railway Company and the Queen City Railway Company had opened access to all of these communities and were quickly filling them with the thousands of newcomers who arrived each year. Ross Avenue became the most elegant address in town, and its spacious, fashionable homes were staffed by servants drawn from the large numbers of black people living in Freedmantown (immediately behind Ross) on Flora, Roseland, Juliette, Cochran and Trinidad streets.

Thomas Jefferson Word, a prominent Dallas attorney, was one of the largest landowners along this upper end of Ross, the so-called Fifth Avenue of Dallas. He assured the street its exclusive reputation by selling property along its course only to his friends, knowing they would build large homes much like the one he constructed at the northeast corner of Ross and Germania streets (138). Stretching almost the entire length of the city from Akard Street near downtown to St. Mary's Institute (where Ross turns into Greenville Avenue near Captain Walter Caruth's former homestead), this elegant row of impressive Gothic, Italianate, Neo-Classical and Queen Anne style mansions — broken only by a short stretch of black servants' quarters along the H&TC tracks — was daz-

zling to behold at its height, about 1908.

As Dallas' real estate boom of the late 1880s and early 1890s progressed, all of East Dallas prospered. The most important factor in this success was the proliferation of streetcar lines during the period. The areas that received transit service were, of course, almost invariably the areas with the largest subsequent growth, and the decision as to where the lines would run very often was made by a land developer who either owned the streetcar company himself, or influenced its policy through a deft donation of land to the right people. Streetcars quite dominated the city's pattern of evolution and growth, simply because they were the easiest and the cheapest (though not always the quickest) means of getting out of the rapidly commercializing downtown.

In 1890, the idea of living in the suburbs and commuting to downtown was an alien and revolutionary concept. People customarily lived and worked in a small central area, with business and entertainment no more than a short walk or buggy ride away. This small-town approach to life persisted in Dallas (with people actually living downtown as late as World War I), but the growing specialization and segmentation of commercial and residential life near the turn of the century caused many people to leave the increasingly commercial and industrial downtown for the pure "country" atmosphere of the suburbs. Until the advent of the personal automobile in the twentieth century, this process was almost entirely governed by streetcars.

One of the earliest and most important lines in East Dallas, inaugurated about 1888 by the Dallas Consolidated Street Railway Company, ran out Bryan Street to Garrett Park. Its primary goal was to provide public

148. ST. MARY'S COLLEGE, c. 1890
The monumental Victorian Gothic St. Mary's College
was built in 1884-86 on the block bounded by Ross,
Henderson, Garrett, and San Jacinto streets. The
college remained insulated on its tranquil campus
for years until worsening conditions in The Cedars
forced the Episcopal Diocese to abandon its Ervay
Street Cathedral in 1927 and move to St. Mary's
attractive twenty-acre suburban site. The college
chapel, built in 1908 (partially visible to the left in
the photograph), was converted into the St. Matthew's Cathedral which it remains. The towering
stone college building, the work of the Dallas architect A. B. Bristol, was demolished in 1948. *Dallas
Historical Society Archives*

149. ST. MARY'S COLLEGE, c. 1890 *(above right)*
Aside from its statuary and Minotaur's mask, the
Greek studies classroom of St. Mary's College
reflects the sober austerity of the period and of
Bishop A. C. Garrett's (seen in the portrait over the
fireplace) educational philosophy. *Dallas Historical
Society Archives*

150. GARRETT HOUSE, c. 1890
The Right Reverend Alexander C. Garrett, Bishop of
the Episcopal Diocese for North Texas and founder
of St. Mary's College, built a distinctive, Italianate
rectory at the corner of Greenwood and Oak streets
in 1880. Bishop Garrett, whose family had spawned
four generations of Irish clergymen, graduated from
the University of Dublin in 1855, was ordained in
1857 as a priest of the Church of England, and
spent the next seventeen years in various missionary
posts in British Columbia, San Francisco, and
Omaha, Nebraska. In 1874 he was named Missionary Bishop to North Texas, at the time an area of
over 100,000 square miles with a total of three
small, wooden churches. After he died in 1924, the
rectory was used as an orphanage until its destruction in 1963. *Dallas Historical Society Archives*

151. EAST DALLAS, c. 1895 *(above)*
The sporadic redevelopment of East Dallas after World War II often bypassed large pockets of small, wood-framed, lower- to middle-class housing. These homes, built between 1880 and 1920, had by the mid-1940s naturally reached a state of neglect and disrepair, and the failure to remove them and redevelop the property was one factor contributing to the disinterest in maintaining or restoring the area's larger homes. Only recently has the general trend been reversed. *Dallas Historical Society Archives*

152. RESIDENCE OF SAMUEL DARNELL, c. 1895 *(below)*
The residence of Samuel P. Darnell, president of the Burton Lumber Company, was one of the few homes built in the old Ross Avenue Heights subdivision (later known as the Belmont Addition). Constructed c. 1891 at the northeast corner of Lewis and Hope streets, it stood, a solitary sentinel surrounded by cornfields, for nearly two decades awaiting East Dallas' expansion. *Courtesy of Dallas Public Library*

153. BOSQUE BONITA, c. 1920
"Bosque Bonita" was the name of Captain Walter Caruth's elegant, three-story farmhouse, situated at the end of Ross Avenue on 900 acres he called "the most fertile black soil in Dallas County." Built c. 1885, the home was sold in 1919 to Ela Hockaday who transformed it into the first Hockaday School for Girls. It was torn down in 1962 for apartment development. *Courtesy of Hockaday School*

154. TEXAS BAPTIST MEMORIAL SANITARIUM, c. 1910
The Texas Baptist Memorial Sanitarium, constructed in 1905-09 at the northeast corner of Junius and Hall streets, was the predecessor of the huge East Dallas Baylor Medical Complex. This superbly crafted Neo-Classical structure, designed by C. W. Bulger & Son, remained in service as a hospital until 1969 when it was renovated for administrative use. *Courtesy of Dallas Public Library*

152

access to the Ursuline Academy, convent, and chapel (147), which had been founded in 1874 by a group of Ursuline Sisters sent to Dallas by the Diocese at Galveston. The secondary goal of the Bryan Street line was to reach another of Dallas' foremost educational institutions, St. Mary's College (148), a private, women's preparatory school run by the Episcopal Church.

Aside from providing access to these institutions, the Bryan Street rail line opened the entire length of East Dallas to development. Between 1888 and 1892, the Middleton Brothers' Addition, Hunstable's College Hill Addition, Livingston Place, Peak's Addition, Caruth Heights, Nussbaumer and McCoy's Addition and the Belmont Addition were opened, often with lots sold even before streets and utilities could be laid out. This reckless and exploitive method of growth was rarely criticized because the voracious demand for land so overshadowed its supply.

155. LOOKING NORTH ON BOPP STREET AT THE T&P TRACKS, c. 1910
In the background is the Texas Memorial Sanitarium of Baylor Hospital. In the foreground are the shotgun row houses of the predominantly black Deep Ellum district, an industrial-poor residential area which began in the 1860s as a freedmantown. *Courtesy of Dallas Public Library*

156. EAST DALLAS CITY HALL AND SCHOOL, c. 1900
When East Dallas incorporated as an independent municipality in 1883, it needed a city hall to mark its legitimacy. Although Captain Gaston, the city's largest landholder, politely declined the town's mayoral offer, he did commission the architect Albert Ullrich to build a striking, Neo-Colonial, red brick and white-quoined municipal office and public school on the southeast corner of College (now Hall) and Gaston Avenue for $15,000. Built in 1886, the structure was demolished in 1948 to build the present Baylor Dental Clinic. *Courtesy of Dallas Public Library*

157. 1420 HALL STREET, c 1910 *(near left)*
The awkwardly foreshortened Neo-Classical Revival building at 1420 Hall Street changed ownership too often in its brief life to acquire a permanent name. Built in 1905 as the Texas College of Physicians and Surgeons, it became the Southwestern University Medical College in 1906, the SMU School of Medicine in 1911, the State Dental College in 1915, and finally Baylor Dental College in 1918. It was demolished in 1950 and remains a vacant lot. *Dallas Historical Society Archives*

Much of East Dallas at this time was also under cultivation by small farmers who did not want to relinquish their means of livelihood, leaving such a limited quantity of land available to developers that an outstanding seller's market was created. This boom was illustrated by the rise in the value of real estate transfers, which went from just under $6 million in 1886 to over 14 million by 1890.[52] The only guiding principle in the development of most of East Dallas (and for much of the rest of the city, whether done by large estate owners like Field or Gaston, or by individual farmers seeking to cash in on the land rush) seems to have been a belief in the absolute free will of the individual to control and promote his own property in whatever manner he wished.

One specific example of this type of ill-planned development was the Caruth Heights Addition, a middle-class subdivision begun in 1889 on a portion of the old Caruth homestead. William Caruth and his brother, Captain Walter Caruth, had come to Dallas from Scottsville, Kentucky, in 1848 and 1849 respectively, with the sole intention of founding an empire. They opened a general store, "W. Caruth and Bro.," on the banks of the Trinity when Dallas was a settlement of only twelve white Indian traders. The mercantile business was simply a means to an end and very shortly they began to purchase vast amounts of the rich cotton land north of town. Buying the land at $5 to $10 an acre, they had by 1885 amassed a plantation of nearly 30,000 acres between what are now Inwood and Abrams roads, extending north from the city limits past the rambling mansion house built by William in 1875 (near the current intersection of Central Expressway and Northwest Highway).

About 1885, Captain Walter Caruth built his own Victorian estate home at what is now the northwest corner of Greenville Avenue and Belmont (152), and four years later sold a 170-acre section of his property to a St. Louis syndicate for $117,800 — a price of nearly $700 dollars an acre and a profit of almost 7,000 percent. John Webster and Charles Wood were hired as local agents and managers of the property but the promotion,

158. RESIDENCE OF DR. JOHN McREYNOLDS
Dr. John O. McReynolds, Dean of Southwestern Medical College and Professor of Physiological Optics at SMU School of Medicine, commissioned C. D. Hill and Company to design a massive, Prairie-influenced home at the northeast corner of Live Oak and Haskell. Built in 1904, it was leveled in 1971 to construct the Dallas Medical and Surgical Clinic, which McReynolds had also founded.

Dallas Historical Society Archives

called Ross Avenue Heights, was almost a complete failure because the streetcar line had advanced only as far as St. Mary's College by 1889. One major exception was the home of Samuel P. Darnell (153), built on land surrounded by empty fields.

About 1892, the St. Louis investors sold the property to the prominent New York financier, August Belmont, who had the streetcar line extended, graded the streets, marked lots, built sidewalks, and changed the name to the Belmont Addition.[53] The economic crash of 1893 intervened just as Belmont put the property back on the market and, of course, it did not sell. For many years not a house was erected in the addition and the whole tract grew up in sunflowers and other weeds. The area's big boom came in the early 1900s, reaching its peak in 1919 when Captain Caruth's residence was sold to Miss Ela Hockaday to become the Hockaday School for Girls. But the pressures of the en-

croaching commercial development along Ross, south of Belmont (which finally forced Hockaday to move to its present location in far North Dallas in 1961), coupled with the deterioration of the neighborhood's numerous frame homes, placed the area at the end of a long line of declining neighborhoods throughout East Dallas. As some of these East Dallas subdivisions got older and reached that critical period in the 1950s and 1960s when the destructive momentum might have been halted and even reversed, many residents instead chose to move to Lakewood or the Park Cities, or even satellite towns like Richardson or Garland because of the sheer bulk of substandard homes and dwellings which had been erected between the 1890s and the 1920s.

The Baylor Medical Center has always been a source of deep civic pride for East Dallas, and for the Slaughter family who were instrumental in founding it. It was

154

located on property bounded by Hall, Gaston, Worth, and Washington streets, which was originally pastureland for Colonel Slaughter's cattle awaiting shipment north to market. In 1872, the land became the site of the North Texas Fair after Captain Gaston moved the festivities from the Union Depot grounds. The hospital itself was begun in 1903 when the Texas Baptist Convention purchased the fourteen-room brick residence of Judge M. L. Crawford and converted it into the Good Samaritan Hospital. By 1905, this hospital had proved inadequate to the city's needs and was torn down in order to build the Texas Baptist Memorial Sanitarium (154), a monumental Neo-Classical building finished in 1909 through the herculean efforts of Colonel Slaughter, who donated over $500,000 toward its construction; Dr. C. M. Rosser, its chief surgeon; Reverend R. C. Buckner, (166) its first president; and C. W. Bulger, the architect. In 1921, the sanitarium, Baylor Medical College, and Baylor Dental College were merged under one board of directors to form the present Hospital of Baylor University of Dallas.

Baylor Medical College was founded in 1900 by Drs. C. M. Rosser and E. H. Cary as the University of Dallas Medical Department, a private institution located on Commerce Street in the old abandoned Temple Emanu-el building (46). In 1903 it was incorporated into the Texas Baptist Memorial Sanitarium until 1922, when it moved into Cary Hall.

Cary Hall (156) was originally built as East Dallas' city hall three years after the wild, sparsely populated lands east of the H&TC tracks incorporated as a separate municipality in 1883. The first floor served as the municipal office and the top two floors as the East Dallas School until the city voted to merge with Dallas in 1890. (This merger was strategically timed to take place in a census year so that Dallas could boast being the largest city in the state — the first and only time this occurred in the city's history. That year East Dallas' acreage was larger than that of Dallas, but its approximate population of 8,000 was only one third of the 23,000 in Dallas.) After East Dallas' assimilation by

Dallas, Cary Hall became the Stephen F. Austin School until it was sold to Baylor Hospital in 1922 for use as classrooms and labs for the college of medicine. The sale of Austin School to Baylor Hospital was delayed for a short time by an organized neighborhood protest which charged that the medical college was causing servants to flee the area in droves, complaining that they would not work close to a place "where young boys cut up dead men."[54]

Baylor Dental College was formed in 1918 when the State Dental College, a private institution located at 1420 Hall Street, was sold to Baylor University. The Hall Street building (157), a pubescent Neo-Classical curiosity by an unknown architect, had been erected about 1905 to house the Texas College of Physicians and Surgeons. Founded by Dr. John McReynolds (158), the Texas College had numerous problems. It affiliated with Southwestern University at Georgetown, Texas, in 1906, but changed its affiliation in 1911 to become the Southern Methodist University Medical College — a venture which failed miserably. The institution did not stabilize until it became a part of the large East Dallas medical complex which included not only Baylor's hospital and colleges, but also the majestic St. Paul's Sanitarium (164), founded by the Daughters of Charity of St. Vincent de Paul, who came to Dallas in 1896 from the Catholic Diocese in Emmitsburg, Maryland.

In 1905, a real estate development began which was conceptualized and promoted as a direct alternative to the problem of the declining exclusiveness of the other East Dallas areas. Called Munger Place, it was contractually guaranteed by certain deed restrictions to remain "strictly a high class residential district."[55] The Munger Place Addition embraced over 300 acres (about fifty city blocks) between Fitzhugh, Live Oak, Henderson, and Columbia streets, which "served to emphasize the important fact that its occupants need never fear the encroachment of factories, shops, or any other undesirable class of neighbors within its boundaries."[56] Its promoters pledged that there would be "no unattractive environments to mar the beauty of its

159. ST. PAUL'S HOSPITAL, c. 1940 *(right)*
Dominated by a bell tower and arched entrance
porch of medieval inspiration, H. A. Overbeck's
distinguished design for St. Paul's Hospital was
completed in 1898 at a cost of over $350,000. The
architect's Victorian Romanesque concept was
enhanced by two later additions — the first constructed in 1916 by C. D. Hill, the second in 1952
by M. C. Kleusner — making the structure one of
the most imposing in the city. Unfortunately, it was
also the least advanced in terms of technology; the
350-bed institution was closed in 1963 when the new
St. Paul's facility opened, and the building was
demolished in 1968. *Courtesy of St. Paul's Hospital*

160. ENTRANCE PORCH, ST. PAUL'S HOSPITAL, c. 1900
(below) Dallas Historical Society Archives

161. ST. PAUL'S HOSPITAL, c. 1910 *(facing page, above)*
This typical operating room in St. Paul's Hospital
remained essentially unchanged throughout the hospital's seventy-year life. *Courtesy of St. Paul's
Hospital*

162. ST. PAUL'S HOSPITAL, c. 1910 *(facing page, center)*
A figure of St. Mary kept watch over the maternity
ward. *Courtesy of St. Paul's Hospital*

163. ST. PAUL'S HOSPITAL, c. 1910 *(facing page, below)*
St. Paul's Hospital chapel. *Courtesy of St. Paul's
Hospital*

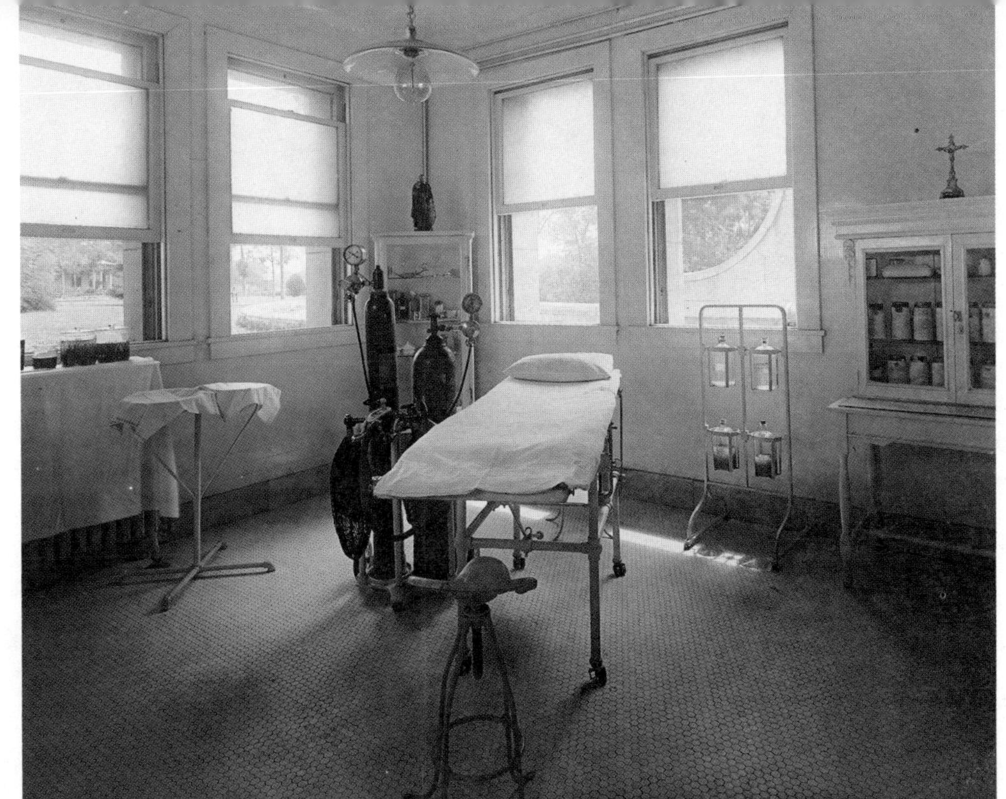

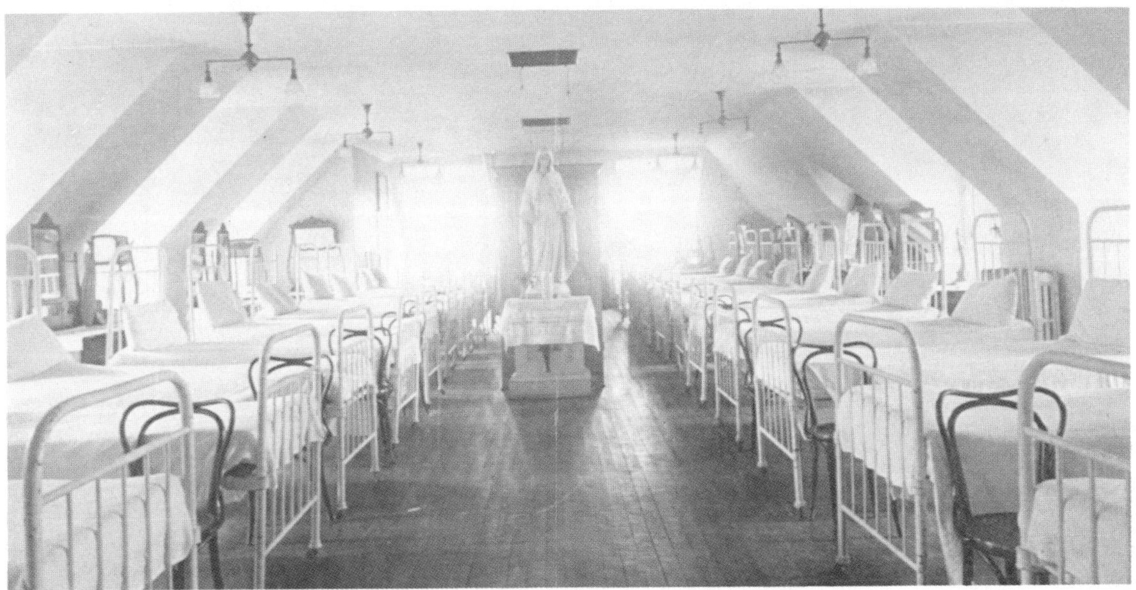

164. ST. PAUL'S HOSPITAL, c. 1940
This aerial view of St. Paul's Hospital illustrates the extent of the economic and social intermix in the patchwork fabric of East Dallas. *Courtesy of St. Paul's Hospital*

165. ALEXANDER COCKRELL HOME, c. 1938
When the industrial pressures from small factories became too great, Alexander Cockrell II moved from his S. Lamar Street home to the corner of Worth and N. Washington streets. Built in 1907, his Colonial Revival residence became a boarding house in the 1950s and was demolished in 1960 for a parking garage. *Dallas Historical Society Archives*

166. BUCKNER'S ORPHAN HOME, c. 1895
Reverend R. C. Buckner's Orphan Home was founded about 1885, six miles east of the city limits along the T&P Railroad (now Loop 12 at I-20). The Girl's Dormitory (above) built in 1890, was razed in 1936, the same year John Neely Bryan's cabin was moved from the basement of the chapel where Reverend Buckner had been safeguarding it, to the Courthouse grounds and restored. The chapel, built in 1895, still stands along with the orphanage's Dallas Annex, built in 1897 on Junius Street. *Courtesy of Dallas Public Library*

167. BUCKNER'S ORPHAN HOME CHAPEL, c. 1900
Dallas Historical Society Archives

perfect surroundings or to disturb the peace of its occupants."

Munger Place was very carefully planned and laid out with all the best city conveniences: gas for fuel and lights, water and sewage connections, street railway service, fire stations, schools, churches, concrete sidewalks, and streets paved by the new bitulithic process on a solid concrete foundation. Telephone lines and electric wires were discreetly placed in the alleys "to insure more sightly streets and avenues." Homes on Swiss and Gaston were required to show a *minimum* investment of $10,000 in an era when the average cost of a home was $2,000 to $3,000. Prices on side streets like Worth and Junius were scaled down to $4,000 or $5,000 with "lots sold to white persons only." Interestingly enough, the Munger Place planners consciously designed a definite social hierarchy by these investment restrictions, which placed the presidents and board chairmen of Dallas' corporations on Swiss and Gaston, their mid-level and junior executives on flanking streets, and delegated the clerks and workers to the bungalow subdivisions south of Fitzhugh and east of Columbia streets.

The man behind Munger Place was a cotton gin genius named Robert S. Munger who had come to Dallas from Birmingham, Alabama, about 1883. Through his Munger Improved Cotton Machine Manufacturing Company (later called the Continental Gin Company) at the corner of Elm Street and the Texas Trunk Railroad (now Hall Street), Munger made a fortune and a sizable reputation for himself by improving Eli Whitney's cotton gin. He held numerous patents for such things as gin saw cleaners, gin saw sharpeners, spiked belt elevators, and revolving double box presses — devices which made Dallas the world's leading manufacturer of cotton gin machinery and the largest inland cotton market in the United States in the 1890s.

Robert Munger eventually turned the daily operation of the company over to his brother Stephen (139), and began to devote himself to researching the real estate market. He gained an intimate understanding of what could best be marketed in East Dallas by living in the area (at the northwest corner of Swiss and Gordon streets) and by studying several restricted-residence parks in St. Louis, Kansas City, Birmingham, and Atlanta. With this knowledge he began buying raw farmland near St. Mary's College, and as a result of his efforts, Munger Place was an instant success from the day it was opened in 1905. Dallas welcomed its first opportunity to be modern and progressive, and consequently some of the city's largest and finest homes were built there, especially along Gaston (175) and Swiss (177), between 1905 and 1925.

Several Dallas architects established lucrative practices by building homes on Swiss and Gaston and later in Lakewood and Highland Park, including Hal Thomson, Fooshee and Cheek, Roscoe Dewitt, and C.D. Hill. Hill, who constructed a stark and brutally modern home for himself in 1909 at the southwest corner of Junius and Collett (176), came to Texas in 1903 after studying architecture at the Chicago Art Institute. He worked as a draftsman in the firm of Sanguinet and Staats until 1907 when he founded C.D. Hill and Company, a firm which quickly rose to a position of prominence in Dallas. The firm contributed such structures as the French Renaissance-inspired Municipal Building, the First Presbyterian Church with its classical Roman dome and Corinthian portico, the City Temple (95), the second Dallas Country

168. GASTON AVENUE BAPTIST CHURCH, c. 1910
The Gaston Avenue Baptist Church, designed by C. W. Bulger and Son and built in 1902-04 at the southwest corner of Gaston and Haskell, is one of the last survivors of Dallas' era of classical grandeur. *Dallas Historical Society Archives*

169. SAN JACINTO SCHOOL, c. 1900
The San Jacinto School and its anomalous Oriental cupola, the creations of James Flanders, were completed in 1891 at the northeast corner of San Jacinto and Pecos streets. With the population shift away from the Ross Avenue area in the late 1930s, the structure was demolished in 1948 to build the present School Administration Offices. *Dallas Historical Society Archives*

170. MUNGER PLACE ADVERTISEMENT, c. 1909
Dallas Historical Society Archives

171. JUNIUS STREET GATES, c. 1915
The stone entrance gates built in 1905 along Junius, Gaston, and Swiss marked the beginning of construction in the East Dallas pastureland later known as **Munger** Place. They were removed in the mid-1950s **because** they had become traffic hazards. *Dallas Historical Society Archives*

**172. RESIDENCE OF JEFFERSON DAVIS ALDREDGE —
MUNGER PLACE, c. 1910**

Very few of the homes built in Munger Place conformed to the pure, architectural ideals and aesthetics of the Prairie style as envisioned by Frank Lloyd Wright, the preeminent master of the form. Many of the Munger Place homes incorporated various elements of the Mission Revival, the Spanish Colonial Revival, the Colonial Revival, or the Victorian cottage styles in an independent, free-form interpretation of Wright's Prairie style canons. Two fine examples of this architectural audacity were the Day House, built in 1906 at the corner of Gaston and Collett, and the Aldredge House, built next to it in 1908. Both structures were demolished in 1959 to construct the Paree Apartments. *Dallas Historical Society Archives*

173. RESIDENCE OF J. DABNEY DAY — MUNGER PLACE, 1910

Dallas Historical Society Archives

174. RESIDENCE OF R. L. CAMERON — MUNGER PLACE, 1910

The Cameron Auto Company, distributors of Hupmobile, Mason, Regal, and Oakland motorcars, had the distinction of being the first automobile dealership in Texas. From the fortune he made in this far-sighted venture, Russell Cameron built his home, a blend of the Mission Revival and Prairie styles, in 1908, on Gaston near the corner of Fitzhugh. It was demolished in 1958 and replaced by an apartment house.
Dallas Historical Society Archives

Club building (225), the Oak Lawn Methodist Church, and several beautiful homes including those of Edward Tenison (222), Dr. John McReynolds (158), and Edgar Flippen's Mount Vernon (226).

However, in spite of such efforts as Munger Place, Dallas' real estate development was a little too nearsightedly laissez-faire, particularly in East Dallas, for its own good. Many East Dallas home owners constructed smaller wood-frame back buildings and rental houses which deteriorated much more rapidly than the adjoining houses, they built for themselves. Also, the total lack of coordinated planning or conceptualization of future problems, and the absence of municipal zoning policy until 1927, led to the same problems that eventually strangled The Cedars. East Dallas became laden with pockets of servants' shotgun houses, sheds, and outbuildings among the expensive mansions along Swiss, Ross, and Gaston, and randomly placed and often poorly constructed subdivi-

sion bungalows appeared. The major streets were increasingly commercialized, with stables, saloons, and later pawn shops and topless bars, while heavy industry like C.H. Alexander's Dallas Ice Factory, Light and Power Company plant (at the northeast corner of Swiss and Hall) and the W.J. Lemp Brewery (178) invaded the area. This amalgamation contributed to the decline of East Dallas and helped establish its reputation, by the 1960s, as a questionable area for investment in new home construction.

In part this decline dated from about 1941 when the Ford Motor Company plant on East Grand dramatically increased its production capacities for the war effort. With the large influx of new workers into the area, it was considered patriotic for local residents to open up their homes to boarders. After the war, the city zoned East Dallas for multi-family dwellings, hoping to attract apartment developers who would provide permanent housing for these people and in the process,

175. RESIDENCE OF D. E. WAGGONER — MUNGER PLACE, 1910

Before the urban renewal of the late 1950s, Gaston Avenue was considered as prestigious an address as Swiss Avenue. One example was the large Mission/Prairie style home built by Lang and Witchell in 1909 for David Waggoner, president of the Guaranty State Bank and Trust. It was demolished in 1959 for apartments.
Dallas Historical Society Archives

clear out the old, dilapidated buildings in the area. But the developers needed large lots on which to build apartment houses and began to buy and demolish the bigger homes on sizable tracts of land along Gaston, Live Oak, and Ross. They ignored the smaller, less desirable homes and lots, off the major thoroughfares, which continued to decay. These pockets of older residences were unattractive to single family buyers and were eventually converted to rooming houses or cut up into efficiency apartments.

An example of this problem can be seen in the case of Charles Ott, a Swiss immigrant of the 1880s who opened a locksmith shop downtown where he also sold guns, pistols, ammunition, fishing tackle, sporting goods and bicycles. (Ott's Locks, built about 1890 at 909 Elm, is one of the few cast iron-front Victorian buildings left downtown.) About 1888, Ott bought approximately one acre of land at the corner of Live Oak and Cantegral — down the street from where

Jesse James' brother Frank lived while working for nearly two years in Mittenthal's Dry Goods Store on Elm across from the Sanger Brothers.

On this property, Charles Ott built a small, cottage-type home in 1889. Ten years later he built a large two-story residence (180) on the site and moved the smaller structure to the Cantegral side of his acreage for use as rental property. Between 1900 and 1910, Ott built several more small, poorly constructed houses on his land, all without indoor plumbing, which he rented to his servants and other low income families.

This same process was repeated all over East Dallas by both large and small property owners; combined with the city's irresponsibility in zoning the area for multi-family units, it began a severe erosion of the community's exclusiveness — traditionally a very desirable and salable commodity in Dallas' housing market. Gradually East Dallas property became attractive only to apartment

176. RESIDENCE OF C. WEICHSEL — MUNGER PLACE, 1910
Christian Weichsel, president of the Zeese Engraving
and Printing Company, commissioned Lang and
Witchell to build his massive home in 1908 at the
corner of Swiss and Collett. The house was
demolished in 1957. *Dallas Historical Society Archives*

177. RESIDENCE OF C. D. HILL — MUNGER PLACE, 1910
Charles Hill, one of Dallas' most prominent, early
20th-century architects, built his home, a strong,
starkly modernistic structure, in 1909 at the corner
of Junius and Collett. The house, which stands
within the Munger Place Historic District, has been
restored. *Dallas Historical Society Archives*

178. LEMP BREWERY, c. 1895
The brewery built 1890-91 at the southeast corner of
Crowdus and the T&P tracks (Pacific Avenue) was
the Dallas headquarters of William J. Lemp's
St. Louis Beer and the local licensee for what later
became the Falstaff Brewing Company. The company
went out of business in 1919 due to Prohibition, but
parts of the old brewery are still standing and in use
by the American Cold Storage and Ice Company.
Courtesy of Dallas Public Library

179. DELIVERY WAGONS, LEMP BREWERY, c. 1895
Dallas Historical Society Archives

180. RESIDENCE OF CHARLES OTT, 1910
James Flanders is credited with having built the large rambling home of Charles Ott in 1899 at the corner of Live Oak and Cantegral. The house was demolished in 1951 when irregular sections of East Dallas were redeveloped as commercial properties and is now a used car lot. *Dallas Historical Society Archives*

builders, boardinghouse owners, and in Ott's case commercial developers who demolished his house in 1951 to build the College Stop Drive Inn. These conditions were only reinforced by the city and by the Federal government when they funded Washington Place Apartments, a low-income Dallas Housing Authority project built between 1941 and 1945 directly behind the Baylor Medical Center. Not only did it demolish a number of large homes in the Slaughter family compound, but it also perpetrated the wide discrepancy between rich and poor in the area.

6 NORTH DALLAS

Although Dallas later expanded primarily south and east, the city's first residential subdivision was situated to the north of the courthouse. William Caruth opened Caruth's Addition in 1854 in an area bounded by Ross, Orange, McKinney, and Lamar streets; it was a dirt-street tract with no amenities, on which a few very crude, single-room frame homes were built. Just after the Civil War, Judge J. M. Patterson opened a second addition along Patterson and Camp streets (near what is now the first Baptist Church) and the town began to give every indication that it would grow northward first.

The primacy of the northern expansion seemed assured in 1868 when Andrew J. and William Ross began to survey and subdivide Ross Avenue from Orange Street toward East Dallas where rumor and speculation held that the Houston & Texas Central Railroad would soon arrive. The Ross brothers had been well-known fruit growers, horticulturists, and wine merchants in Smith County, Texas, before the Civil War; in 1866 they decided to try their hands at the mercantile business in Dallas, but soon recognized the profit potential in real estate. About the same time, Colonel John M. Stemmons purchased and began to advertise for sale "several beautiful and desirable residential lots, situated on Pearl St." between Ross Avenue and Bryan Street. A Tennessee lawyer and Confederate war hero, Colonel Stemmons utilized the Ross brothers' survey to help promote his own land, and between them they built the nucleus that would ten years later blossom into Dallas' finest residential thoroughfare. However, their visions of North Dallas development were temporarily disrupted in 1873 when the Texas & Pacific Railroad

steamed down Pacific Avenue and blocked off the north side of town with a series of dangerous crossings. The noise and unsightliness of the railroad's operation, along with the attendant commercialization that soon followed, caused a sharp decline in real estate values in these neighborhoods, and the "respectable" families that had originally settled there moved across the tracks to resettle along with the thousands of new arrivals in either the Elm-Main-Commerce corridor, or southward toward J. J. Eakins' new park.

The vacuum they left behind swiftly filled with floaters, gamblers, and a class of women of doubtful reputation and dubious social standing (including Belle Starr, who reputedly dealt stolen horses from her livery stable on Camp Street). This was the genesis of Frogtown, one of Dallas' most notorious turn-of-the-century red-light districts. Frogtown was a general designation given to the area composed of the northern section of Bryan's town plot and the Caruth and Patterson Additions to the city, all of which now constitute the West End Historical District. The brothels in this area centered around the lower end of McKinney Avenue and along Emma Street (now Federal) near St. Paul. Beginning about 1900, Frogtown attained a quasi-legal status, similar to the red-light districts in Galveston and New Orleans: state law still officially prohibited prostitution, but city officials recognized the area by requiring the girls to have regular health department examinations and to carry doctor's certificates. This practice continued until 1914 when civic moral indignation finally focused in closing down the brothels.

Starting around 1880 Frogtown began to lose its so-called "residential" status as large

181. FLOYD FARM HOUSE, BRECKINRIDGE, c. 1901
From the time of its founding well into the 20th century, Dallas County was primarily composed of small agrarian communities such as Breckenridge (now known as Richardson). The farmhouse John and Julia Floyd built in 1856 on their 640-acre homestead also served as the Breckinridge Stage Coach Inn through the late 1860s. *Courtesy of Mr. Raymond Floyd*

industrial concerns, attracted by the rail outlets of the St. Louis & Southwestern and the Missouri, Kansas & Texas railroads, moved into the area. Among these were the Dallas Iron Works, built in 1880 at Ross and Orange; the Trinity Iron Works, established about the same time at Ross and Magnolia; Jules Schneider's Dallas City Gas Light Company which built a coal-to-methane gas production plant at the corner of Ross and North Houston about 1881; the Dallas Electric Light and Power plant, built about 1890 where the Dallas Power and Light plant now stands; and the Dallas Brewery, the locally owned producer of "Dallas Splits" and "Tipperary" beers, which located about 1885 at the corner of Houston and Cochran streets. The brewery was converted into the Grain Juice Company in 1918 as the era of national Prohibition approached, but grain juice proved much less profitable than beer and the company went bankrupt in 1926; the plant was demolished in the 1930s.

By about 1910, Frogtown had virtually completed its transition from residential area to warehouse and commercial district, and only a few isolated pockets of homes remained close to downtown. One of these pockets was located across McKinney from Caruth's Addition and became known in the early twentieth century as El Barrio, literally "the neighborhood." This area, bounded originally by McKinney, Alamo, Akard, and Yeargan streets, began development in 1875 as part of a right-of-way grant to the Dallas & Wichita Railroad, an enterprise chartered by the people of Dallas in 1871 to run from Dallas through Denton to Wichita Falls for the purpose of penetrating the reputed rich mineral regions along the northern Red River. The Dallas County Deed Records show that the railroad's president, J. W. Calden, granted to Pointer, Shields and Company of Dallas "40 acres of land around the depot [designated to be built at the corner of Alamo and Ashland streets] to be disposed of or held for the equal benefit of each member of the firm."[57] The railroad was delayed by the Panic of 1873, and the venture also suffered from being north of the T&P tracks along Pacific Avenue. Pointer, Shields and

Company and George Laws began to subdivide the property for homes but it remained only sparsely populated until the early 1890s when a large group of Jewish refugees from Eastern Europe settled in the old Dallas & Wichita Addition because of the bargain prices on property and rents. These poor, Orthodox Jews, many of whom worked as street peddlers or sidewalk vendors, did not easily fit into the affluent, Western European, Reform society of The Cedars and so settled in the north, establishing their own Temple Tefereth Israel Synagogue in 1893 near the corner of Ashland and Akard street. In May of 1911, this Orthodox community began to be displaced by thousands of Latin Americans fleeing Diaz and the Mexican Revolution, and El Barrio was born.

In 1884, however, North Dallas' inaccessibility and its stigma of being "across the tracks" were largely erased by the construction of the Dallas Bell Street Railway Company streetcar line under the direction of J. E. Henderson, Jules Schneider, and Colonel J. T. Trezevant. The streetcar ran up McKinney Avenue to Thomas Street, providing access to the rest of the city and making possible new middle- to upper middle-class development in the Thomas-Colby District, North Dallas' first socially elite neighborhood, remnants of which still exist today. The homes there were smaller than the Victorian mansions that would line South Ervay and Ross Avenue a few years later but they comfortably reflected the city's growing prosperity (184).

About 1885, the commercial success of Dallas' leading capitalists began to express itself in a wave of mansion construction, beginning with the terminal merchants in The Cedars and continuing fervently along Ross Avenue. The Dallas Belt Street Railway line, running the length of Harwood Street from McKinney Avenue to The Cedars, had regenerated interest in the development potential of Ross Avenue, but the threat of the eastward expansion of Frogtown posed a problem. This difficulty was overcome by settling a well-understood boundary along Ervay and Akard streets where they joined at Ross, and enforcing it by controlling the land between

TEXAS MACHINERY & SUPPLY CO.
CRANE CO
NSTON CO.

BORICH. SIGNS
SALOON

182. LOOKING NORTH FROM THE COURTHOUSE
TOWER, c. 1910 *(facing page, above)*
Dallas' early warehouse district. *Dallas Historical
Society Archives*

183. LOOKING NORTH FROM THE PRAETORIAN
BUILDING, c. 1910
In the foreground is the Emma Street red-light dis-
trict, followed by the First Baptist and Central
Christian churches, followed by the flamboyant man-
sions along Ross Avenue. *Dallas Historical Society
Archives*

184. MORONEY HOUSE, c. 1890
James Moroney, president of Moroney and Company
Hardware, built his home c. 1880 at the northeast
corner of McKinney and Harwood streets. At that
time, S. McKinney was a fine residential neighborhood, but by World War I, it had become a commercialized, working-class area. *Courtesy of Mrs.
Max Clampitt*

the boundary and Frogtown. Jules Schneider accomplished this about 1880 when he established an auxiliary facility of his Dallas City Gas Light Company where the Fairmont Hotel now stands, across the street from his home on the northeast corner of Ross and Ervay streets (186). This imposing High Victorian structure, built in 1879 by James Flanders, marked the southern extremity of Ross Avenue, an almost uninterrupted, two-mile Gilded Age promenade lined with French chateaus, Gothic mansions, Italiante palazzi, large spreading shade trees, and manicured gardens, all animated by the hushed clatter of liveried coachmen.

Some of the most prominent men in Dallas' history lived on Ross Avenue. Next door to Schneider was the home of William H. Flippen (185), also built by J. E. Flanders about 1885. Flippen's son, Edgar, married one of the daughters of John S. Armstrong, who lived just down the street (187). Edgar later completed the development of his father-in-law's Highland Park venture, begun in 1907. Armstrong's collaborator in Highland Park, Colonel Henry Exall, owned a home at Ross and Harwood Streets and the North Dallas land baron, William Caruth, maintained a townhouse at the corner of Ross and St. Paul.

Captain W. H. Gaston built his first Dallas home at the northwest corner of Ross and Pearl streets in 1868. Twenty years later, Colonel A. H. Belo purchased the property, removed Gaston's small, frame home and in its place constructed the beautiful Georgian Colonial home (190) which still stands across Pearl from the Cathedral of the Sacred Heart

174

185. FLIPPEN HOUSE, c. 1895
Another of the intimidating expressions of wealth along Ross was the residence of William H. Flippen, founder of the private banking firm of Flippen, Adoue, and Lobit. James Flanders again drew upon his not inconsiderable skills in fashioning this Gothic-inspired palace in 1885. The house was demolished in 1922 and the property is now the home office of the Southwestern Life Insurance Company. *Courtesy of Mrs. John N. (Sallie Bell Flippen Gaston) Jackson*

(195). Designed by Herbert Green, the mansion was constructed about 1900, complete with its classically columned Greek portico in an effort to create a replica of the Belo family home in Asheville, North Carolina.

Just off Ross Avenue, at the corner of Akard and Cochran streets (now Woodall Rodgers Expressway), the Cumberland Hill School (191), was built to serve this affluent neighborhood. Founded by the Cumberland Presbyterians before the Civil War, the school originally offered private classes held in a one-room, wooden schoolhouse. After the establishment of public education in Dallas in 1884, the Cumberland school was sold to the city, which moved the structure four years later to Welborn and Alamo streets in Frogtown for use as a "colored school." In 1888 the city hired A. B. Bristol to build this splen-

did brick structure and its exact duplicate, Oak Grove School (50), at Jackson and Harwood streets.

Just as in East Dallas, Ross Avenue gradually evolved into the southern boundary of North Dallas' Freedmantown, the city's largest black ghetto, which extended northeast of Pearl Street to the H&TC tracks and north of Ross Avenue to Greenwood Cemetery.

Freedmantown's roots began in 1861 when a rural Negro cemetery was established at what is now the intersection of Central Expressway and Lemmon Avenue. After the Emancipation Proclamation and the end of the Civil War, Dallas' estimated 300 former slaves gradually began to settle near the cemetery — the only kind of landmark or symbol of black identity to be found in the city at that time. They gathered together in far

186. SCHNEIDER HOUSE, c. 1895
In 1879, Jules E. Schneider, president of the
Schneider-Davis Wholesale Grocery Company and
the Consolidated Street Railway Company, commissioned James Flanders to build his magnificent, High
Victorian Italianate mansion on the northeast corner
of Ross and Akard. Schneider's home, which initiated
the opulent growth along Ross Avenue, was
demolished in 1919 for an auto sales lot. *Courtesy of
Dallas Public Library*

187. ARMSTRONG HOUSE, 1898 *(facing page, above left)*
John S. Armstrong, president of Armstrong Packing
Company and the founder of Highland Park, built
his charming Queen Anne home at the southwest
corner of Ross and Pearl. The work of the architect
C. A. Gill, it was completed in 1891 and demolished
in 1927. *Dallas Historical Society Archives*

188. MORRILL HOUSE, 1898 *(facing page, above right)*
Mrs. Miranda Morrill's dark, brooding residence,
completed in 1886 by A. B. Bristol at the southwest
corner of Harwood, was leveled in 1920 for construction of the First United Methodist Church. *Dallas
Historical Society Archives*

189. CONWAY HOUSE, c. 1902 *(facing page, below)*
The massive, columned home of John C. Conway,
built in 1902 at the northwest corner of Ross and
Harwood, became the Dallas Academy of Music and
School of Opera before it was demolished in 1930
for a tire store. *Courtesy of Dallas Public Library*

North Dallas for mutual support and protection against attitudes of racial oppression which persisted throughout the postwar South, and culminated in sporadic incidents of violence such as the lynching of Allen Brooks near the Elk's Arch in 1909 (87).

During the turbulent days of Reconstruction, racial tension mounted in Texas because of difficulties over land possession and labor contracts. There was much talk of independence from Negro labor, and bands of whites, determined to establish political and economic supremacy, roamed the rural sections of North Texas, threatening black people with loss of crops and bodily harm, and burning the schools and churches of those who refused to yield in slavelike obedience. As a result, hundreds of rural blacks flocked to Dallas — to Frogtown, Boggy Bayou, and especially the North Dallas Freedmantown around Hall, State, Thomas, and Washington streets. Another sizeable black area was Stringtown, which was "strung out" along the raised grade of the H&TC between the east side of Hall Street, through the San Jacinto, Bryan, and Federal street area to Deep Ellum. By the time the Texas & Pacific Railroad arrived in Dallas in 1873, the Negro

190. BELO MANSION, c. 1940
Colonel Alfred Horatio Belo, a Civil War hero who surrendered his forces alongside General Lee at Appomattox, acquired the Galveston *News* and later founded the Dallas *Morning News*, built his home, a graceful reminder of the prewar South, c.1900. After the Colonel's death, the family leased the premises to the Loudermilk-Sparkman Funeral Home. There, in the late spring of 1934, thousands of people lined up in Dallas' dizzying heat to view the bodies of Bonnie Parker and Clyde Barrow, lying in state after they were killed in an ambush set by Texas Rangers. *Courtesy of Mr. Bill Sparkman*

191. CUMBERLAND HILL SCHOOL, 1895
Once the most fashionable school in the city, with as many coaches lined up at its front door in the afternoons as could be found at the Idlewild Ball, the Cumberland Hill School was forced to close in the 1940s as the families of Ross Avenue fled the encroaching commercialization of the area. Built in 1888, the school was restored in 1970 as the offices of SEDCO, Inc., and has since become one of Dallas' outstanding landmarks and architectural treasures. *Courtesy of Dallas Public Library*

population had climbed to 1,222, and remained at about 15 to 20 percent of the city's population until World War II.[58]

Although North Dallas' Freedmantown did not receive legal recognition from either the federal Freedmen's Bureau or the city of Dallas until the 1890s, it became a focal point for the black people of the city. Its population was composed of laborers and porters who worked in the downtown business district; sharecroppers who worked the cotton fields of East and North Dallas; and servants for the large homes on Thomas Street (which ran through the heart of the black area but remained, curiously enough, almost exclusively white), Ross (which witnessed the same phenomenon), East Dallas, and later Maple Avenue and Highland Park.

Unlike black people in many areas of the South, those in Dallas began to buy and own property in the North Dallas Freedmantown as early as the 1870s. Dallas County records show that in 1872 J. H. Cole sold 13½ acres to William Adam, a freedman, for $337, and a two-acre lot the same year to Lewis Moore, also a freedman, for $35. Several other large Dallas landholders, including Maxime Guillot and H. H. Hall, show record of selling small parcels of property to black men — lots where they would build the shotgun houses common to the area and plant subsistence crops.

There are several possible reasons for this deviation from the general real estate practice. First, the property was not prime real estate. Its sandy soil and scrub oak and mesquite undergrowth were generally used only as woodlots or as cemetery plots — a fact illustrated by the creation of the segregated Colored, Jewish, Catholic, and Protestant (Greenwood) cemeteries on Hall Street in the early 1870s. Chartered in 1896, Greenwood was originally the thirty-three acre Trinity Cemetery, established in 1875 by W. H. Gaston on property he had purchased in 1868.[59] These adjacent cemeteries served as an effective barrier to the further northern expansion of Freedmantown, and almost automatically limited the marketability of the property lying to the south of it to blacks.

Second, like railroad right-of-way property in Deep Ellum, much of the land in the

192. BOOKHOUT HOME, 1895 *(facing page, above)*
John Bookhout, Associate Justice of the U.S. Court
of Civil Appeals, built his home on the corner of
Masten (now St. Paul) and Caruth (now Munger)
streets in 1891. Designed by James Flanders, the
residence was demolished in 1927 for a parking lot
which today remains intact. *Courtesy of Dallas
Public Library*

193. THE NORTHSIDE OF ROSS AVENUE BETWEEN
HARWOOD AND PEARL STREETS, c. 1895
These residences, the homes of Dallas' most
successful leather and lumber dealers, lawyers,
bankers, and manufacturers, were built in 1880-90,
but by the early 1930s almost all had vanished.
Courtesy of Dallas Public Library

194. DESSAINT HOME, c. 1945 *(above)*
The last of Ross Avenue's great houses to be
condemned was the Louis Dessaint home, built in
1885 between Harwood and Pearl. It was demolished
in 1945 for an automobile dealership. *Courtesy of
Mrs. Thomas Burke*

North Dallas Freedmantown was occupied by
squatters. The profit-seeking landlord could
choose between evicting the squatters and
selling the land at $5 to $10 an acre for
woodlots, or selling the property to the squatters, usually sharecroppers, for a lien on their
crops at the inflated rate of $25 to $30 an
acre.

Third, it became fashionable for the wealthier white families to insure a constant source
of domestic help and reliable labor for their
homes and businesses by financing the purchase of their black servants' homes. These
tenants were a good credit risk because they
were likely to work for the family for several
years and were conveniently close by to help
with the young children, the meals and the
gardening.

However, much property remained in the
hands of white absentee landlords like Edward
Belsterling who served for many years as the
city attorney and owned several rental shotgun
houses on Flora, Hall and Roseland streets,
some of which are still in use.

In 1890, a streetcar line was installed on
Hall Street to connect with the Colored High
School at the corner of Cochran Street (199),
and in 1913 Hall was paved, making it the
main street of the black community. In 1921,
the city developed a portion of the old Colored
Cemetery as the Hall Street Negro Park
(which received its present name, Freedman's
Memorial Park, in 1965). This park became
an important center of social life in the black
community with a swimming pool and free
summer movies; later, a black-operated
amusement area with rides, galleries, and food
concessions evolved across the H&TC line
(where the Hall Street Housing Project now
stands).

Before 1886, almost all of the activity in
North Dallas (except for a few isolated, rural
communities like Cedar Springs and Maple
Springs) was confined to areas like Ross Avenue and Thomas Street which were served by
the Belt Street Railway. But in that year, a
dispute arose among the backers and boosters
of the Dallas Fair. The majority of Dallas'
merchants favored Captain Gaston's site in
East Dallas, where the present Fairgrounds

are situated, but some opposed this location. The dissenters, led by Cecil Keating, president of the Keating Implement and Machinery Company and the Texas Disc and Plow Company (200), were primarily farm implement dealers with strong ties or investments in North Dallas, the Knights of Labor, and the Farmer's Alliance. As a result of this feud, two separate fairs were held in 1886 — the Dallas State Fair and Exposition in East Dallas, and the Texas State Fair located in far North Dallas on John H. Cole's homestead (now the grounds of North Dallas High School, built in 1922, and the seven-acre Cole Park, established in 1921). The fairs merged in 1887, agreeing finally on the East Dallas site, but the popularity of the short-lived North Dallas fair, which had attracted thousands of people over its five-day span, triggered one of the strangest real estate developments in the city's history — one which had a profound effect on the subsequent growth of North Dallas.

Frank Cockrell, impressed with the public response to the fair, purchased a small portion of John H. Cole's 5,000-acre farm for a housing development. Cockrell's Fairland Addition stretched from the old fairgrounds between the Missouri, Kansas & Texas and the H&TC tracks as far north as McCommas Avenue. Cockrell apparently was not worried by the fact that the property was nearly three miles from the courthouse with few streets and no streetcar service or utilities. He began by chartering the North Dallas Circuit Railway Company with Walter Caruth, O. P. Bowser, Jules Schneider, Royal Ferris, and $100,000 of capital stock. This steam-driven streetcar line ran through the developed areas of North Dallas to the wild undergrowth of Cole's farm, and out Cole Avenue to a small pond built on Williams Creek at the northeast corner of McKinney and Hester streets. The idea of a lake or park at the end of the streetcar line had been a favorite gimmick of Dallas promoters ever since the concept had originated with J. J. Eakins' City Park, but Cockrell's Addition was simply too remote for success. A few homes were built along Cole Avenue and the streetcar line on lots sold in the early 1890s (some of which still stand today), but most of

the area did not develop until after 1910.

However, Frank Cockrell's North Dallas Circuit Railway did spur development of the North Dallas areas situated a little closer to town — primarily Oak Lawn, Cedar Springs, and Maple Avenue — at a time when the city was growing and expanding at a staggering rate. Between 1880 and 1890, Dallas' population almost tripled, the assessed taxable wealth of the city jumped from $4,374,219 to $31,314,821, a gain of nearly 800 percent,[60] and the number and value of real estate transfers increased by over 2,000 percent. Before 1886, systematic expansion northward had been minimal; farming was essentially the only activity in North Dallas until the fair of 1886 sparked a fervor of new interest in the northern lands. The enormous growth which fed these new subdivisions and real estate developments culminated in 1890 when the city extended its boundaries to include the incorporated city of East Dallas, the unincorporated areas of South Dallas as far as Romine Street, and North Dallas as far as Oak Lawn Avenue.

After the Circuit Railway was completed, the most important factor in the development of North Dallas was probably the chartering, in 1888, of the North Dallas Improvement Company, a loosely associated group of land investors, speculators, and developers dedicated to the general promotion of the northern limits of the city. The Improvement Company, directed by men such as Royal Ferris, Edwin P. Cowan who opened Maple Avenue, Oliver P. Bowser of Bowser and Lemmon's Oak Lawn and North Dallas Additions, Frank Cockrell, and Oliver and J. D. Thomas who subdivided much of the McKinney Avenue-Thomas Street area, did not concentrate its efforts on any single neighborhood, but rather acted as general agent, counsel, and public relations office for many of the twelve subdivisions that sprang up in the north between 1886 and 1894. Easily the most illustrious of these was E. P. Cowan's Maple Avenue development.

The Maple Avenue area had been settled as early as 1843 when John H. Cole arrived from Virginia and began cultivation of an extensive grape vineyard and peach orchard on his

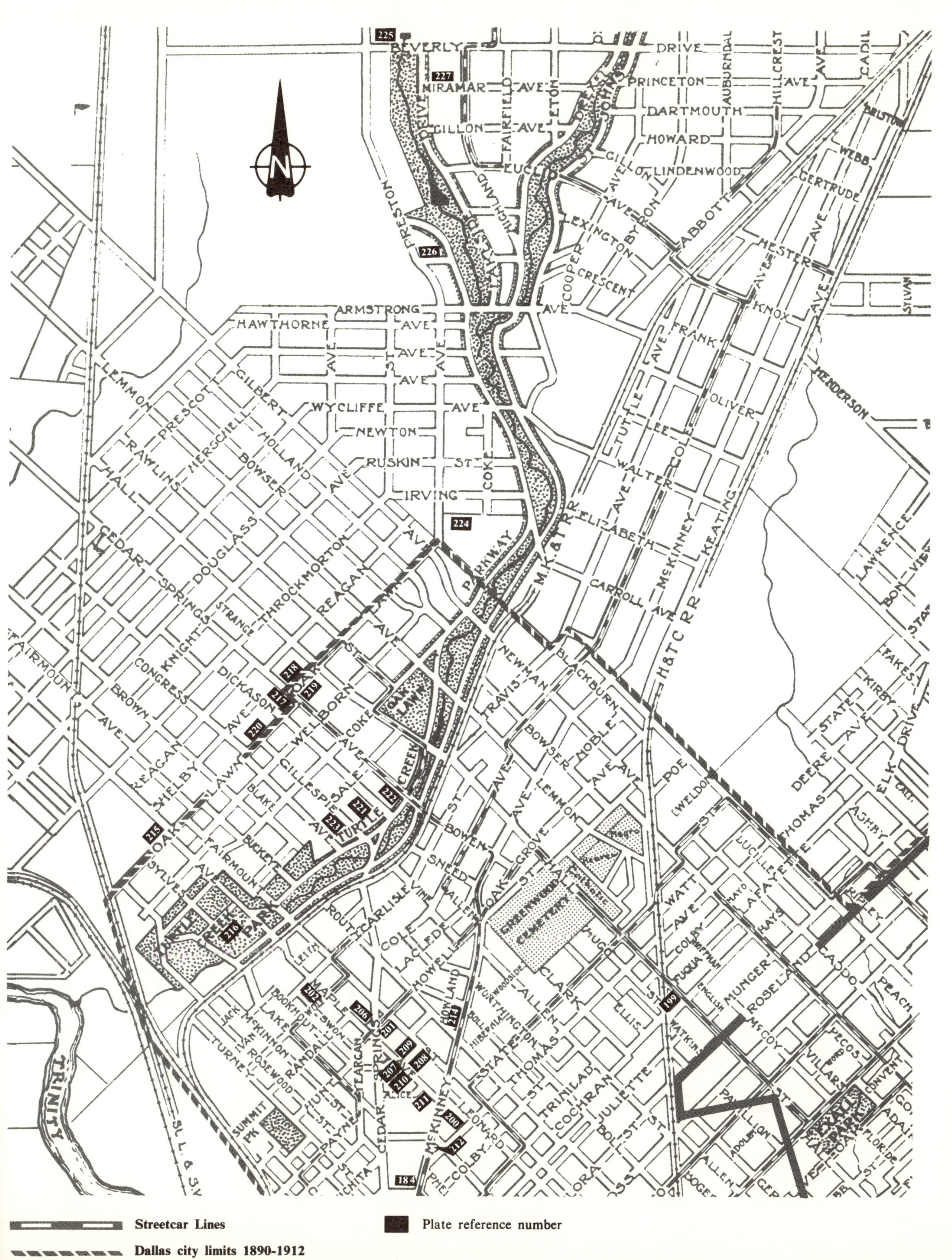
N
TRINITY
BEVERLY
DRIVE
MIRAMAR
PRINCETON
DARTMOUTH
HOWARD
GILLON AVE
LINDENWOOD
FAIRFIELD AVE
EUCLID
LEXINGTON
CRESCENT AVE
GERTRUDE
HESTER
KNOX
WEBB
SYLVAN
COOPER
FRANK
OLIVER
TUTTLE AVE
LEE
WALTER
ELIZABETH
McKINNEY
CARROLL AVE
KEATING
COLE
HENDERSON
HAWTHORNE
ARMSTRONG AVE
WYCLIFFE AVE
NEWTON
RUSKIN ST
IRVING
LEMMON
PRESCOTT
GILBERT
HOLLAND
BOWSER
RAWLINS
HALL
CEDAR SPRINGS
DOUGLASS
THROCKMORTON
REAGAN
KNIGHT
STRANGE
CONGRESS
BROWN
DICKASON
WELBORN
COKE
OAK LAWN
REAGAN
SHELBY
LAWN
GILLESPIE
BLAKE
BUCKNER
FAIRMOUN
SYLVESTER
OAK
TURTLE CREEK
BOWEN
SNEED
OAK GROVE
LEMMON AVE
BOWSER
NOBLE AVE
POE
NEWMAN
TRAVIS
BLACKBURN
WELDON ST
THOMAS
STATE
DEERE AVE
KIRBY
ASHBY
LUCILLE
LAFAYETTE
WATT AVE
MAYO
COLBY
HAYS
HUGO
MUNGER
ROSELAND
CADDO
PEACH
PECOS
VILLARS
ROUTH
CARLISLE
VINE
COLE
LACLEDE
HOWELL
MAPLE
WOODSIDE
HARWOOD
ALLEN
CLARK
ELLIS
WATKINS
McCOY
JULIETTE
MAPLE
BOOKHOUT
SWISS
CEDAR SPRINGS
SEARCY
VANRANDALL
McKINNON
ROSEWOOD
TURNEY
HUNT ST
PAYNE
SUMMIT PK
WICHITA
PHELPS
COLBY
McKINNEY
LEONARD
WORTHINGTON
HIBERNIA
POLK
STATE
THOMAS
TRINIDAD
COCHRAN
BOLL ST
PAUL
ADOLPHUS
GERMANIA
FLORIDA
TRINITY
S.L. & S.W.
M.K. & T. R.R.
H. & T. C. R.R.
PARKWAY
PRESTON
HIGHLAND
Streetcar Lines
Plate reference number
Dallas city limits 1890-1912
East Dallas corporate limits 1883-1890

195. CATHEDRAL OF THE SACRED HEART, 1910
In 1891, the small clapboard Sacred Heart of Jesus Church on Bryan Street was chosen by Bishop Thomas Brennan to be the Dallas Catholic Diocese Cathedral. In 1898, a new edifice, "befitting the majesty and dignity of God," was deemed necessary and J. Edward Overbeck began construction. The result, completed in 1902 on Ross Avenue, was the colorful, High Victorian Gothic marvel known today as the Cathedral Santuario de Guadalupe. *Dallas Historical Society Archives*

196. INTERIOR, CATHEDRAL OF THE SACRED HEART, 1910
Dallas Historical Society Archives

197. CARTER HOUSE, c. 1895
Charles F. Carter made his fortune as a North
Texas cotton broker, and the massive chateau built
in 1891 at the northeast corner of Ross and Crockett
was the outspoken expression of his wealth. It was
destroyed in 1932. *Courtesy of Mrs. Manning B.
Shannon Jr. (Elizabeth Leachman Shannon)*

198. TENISON/HAY HOUSE, c. 1909
Albert Tenison, owner of the Tenison Brothers
Saddlery Company, built a stygian Queen Anne
masterpiece c. 1890 on Ross between Fairmount and
Routh streets. Purchased in 1909 by Stephen J. Hay,
president of the Dallas Trust and Savings Bank and
mayor of Dallas from 1907 to 1911, the house was
ultimately demolished in 1929. *Courtesy of
Mrs. Elizabeth Hay Morse*

199. COLORED HIGH SCHOOL, 1895
Built on the southeast corner of Cochran and Hall streets in the heart of North Dallas' Freedmantown, this austere brick school building was for many years the primary facility for the city's black children. Completed in 1891, it was restricted to the elementary grades in 1922 and renamed B.F. Darrell School. The structure was demolished in 1973. *Courtesy of Dallas Public Library*

200. GARLINGTON/KEATING HOUSE, c. 1895 *(left)*
M.D. Garlington, an early partner of Thomas
Marsalis in the wholesale grocery business, built a
residence in 1889 on McKinney at the head of
Maple that bespoke solid, Victorian respectability.
Purchased in 1903 by Cecil A. Keating, president of
the Keating Implement and Machinery Company and
the Texas Disc and Plow Company, the structure
was demolished in 1948 for a new American Red
Cross headquarters. *Dallas Historical Society
Archives*

201. THE SHINGLES, 1895
Maple Avenue, with its monumental residences
constructed between 1888 and 1905, was the social
and architectural successor of Ross Avenue and the
predecessor of Highland Park in Dallas' inexorable
northern urban march. Edwin P. Cowan, the
developer of Maple Avenue, built the indomitable
"Shingles" in 1888 at a cost of over $20,000. The
home was purchased in 1893 by William H. Abrams,
whose family owned it until its demolition in 1930
when the property became Exline's Evergreen
Farm #1. *Dallas Historical Society Archives*

5,000-acre tract (part of which later became Cockrell's Addition). He later opened Cole's Vineyard Addition to the city of Dallas near the corner of Cole and Vine streets. The Bowen family arrived during the Civil War, purchased a farm near the present Quadrangle, and also began growing grapes, apples, and peaches. John M. Howell, the "father of Dallas horticulture," settled on a sizable acreage between McKinney Avenue and Cedar Springs Road in 1872 and opened a commercial greenhouse at McKinney and Pearl. In 1876, Howell attended the Philadelphia Centennial Exhibition as the official representative of the fledgling Horticultural Society of Texas, and returned with the hope of helping Dallas to produce a city as great as the one he had just visited. Howell decided to develop his own property and began by laying out several streets. The first was named in honor of Philadephia's grounds, Fairmount Park; the second for his father-in-law, Reverend Jacob Routh, a pioneer Baptist preacher; the third for the Howell family; and the fourth he simply called Maple.

Howell's Maple Avenue was really just a primitive trail cut through the tangled growth of wisteria and honeysuckle on his property until 1888. That year, in a promotional move calculated to attract wealthy families to Maple Avenue, Edwin Cowan constructed his spectacular home, called "The Shingles" (201), at the northwest corner of Cedar Springs Avenue. The house, designed by an unknown architect, was undoubtedly the finest example of American Queen Anne architecture ever seen in Dallas and easily compared in boldness and adventurous extravagance with any ever built in California, where the style reached its outrageous peak in the homes of several multimillionaire rail magnates, silver mine barons, and whaling fleet owners.

The Queen Anne style was characterized by its irregular plan and massing, and by the wide variety of colors, textures, and materials used in its construction. Although the style originated in England around 1868, it proved wonderfully adaptable and popular in the United States, primarily because it conjured a vision of romantic fantasy for a country that had just endured a devastating war and lost much of its self-confidence during the financial Panic of 1873. The Queen Anne style reflected the country's need for exuberance and vitality, and was embraced especially on the West Coast with such fervor that in 1883 the architectural historian Montgomery Schuyler called its practitioners "a frantic and vociferous mob, who welcome the 'new departure' as the disestablishment of all standards, whether of authority or of reason, and as an emancipation from all restraints, even those of public decency."[61]

Cowan's promotional gamble worked so well that by 1900 his $20,000 home had attracted a plethora of lavish, expensive Victorian mansions, making Maple Avenue the architectural and social successor of South Ervay Street and Ross Avenue, and in some ways marking the beginning of the population shift away from those areas. Cowan's personal fortunes benefited from only a small part of Maple Avenue's ultimate success because he and the North Dallas Improvement Company became victims of the depression of 1893. Cowan was forced to sell "The Shingles" that year to William H. Abrams, the land and tax commissioner of the T&P Railroad.

Magnificent as the Cowan/Abrams house was, it was overshadowed in 1890 by construction of the arrogantly eclectic, medieval Moorish manor of George Dilley, built on a slight hill at the southwest corner of Maple Avenue and Wolf Street (202). George M. Dilley made his fortune in railroad construction as the principal contractor for Jay Gould's developing railroad empire in Texas and the Southwest. Dilley built sections of the Houston & Great Northern Railroad in 1870, the Sunset & Southern Pacific in Pecos County in 1882, the Houston & Central Arkansas Railroad in 1886, and the Houston Central & Northern Railroad in 1889,[62] using some of his profits to build his $60,000 Dallas extravaganza, called "Ivy Hall."

In 1890, he moved his construction firm to Dallas from Joliet, Illinois, and brought with him the architect F. S. Allen and several stonemasons, engineers, carpenters, and

202. IVY HALL, c. 1895

Eclecticism was a philosophical concept originating in France in the 1830s describing a system of thought which incorporated only the best elements selected from various other diverse systems. In the late 19th century, this concept was enthusiastically applied to architecture in the belief that a free adaptation of motifs would evoke a greater creativity. Nowhere in Dallas was this spirit of eclecticism embraced more fervently than in George M. Dilley's Ivy Hall, undoubtedly the most spectacular private home ever built in the city when it was completed in 1890. Dilley hired hundreds of craftsmen for the construction, imported Texas marble (gray limestone) from Pecos County for the exterior, oak and Honduras mahogany for the interior, and topped the structure off with a Kremlinesque dome and a third-floor ballroom in which the most lavish and talked-about parties in town were given. Even the coach house, which housed Dilley's collection of phaetons, broughams, and victorias, was larger and more stylish than most peoples' homes. The mansion was sold in 1900 to Royal A. Ferris, a prominent Dallas banker, who carried on Ivy Hall's showplace tradition. By 1924, the house had become too expensive to maintain and was demolished to build the present Maple Terrace Apartments. *Dallas Historical Society Archives*

203. PARLOR OF IVY HALL, c. 1895
Courtesy of Mr. Royal A. Ferris III

204. COACH HOUSE, IVY HALL, c. 1895
Courtesy of Mr. Royal A. Ferris III

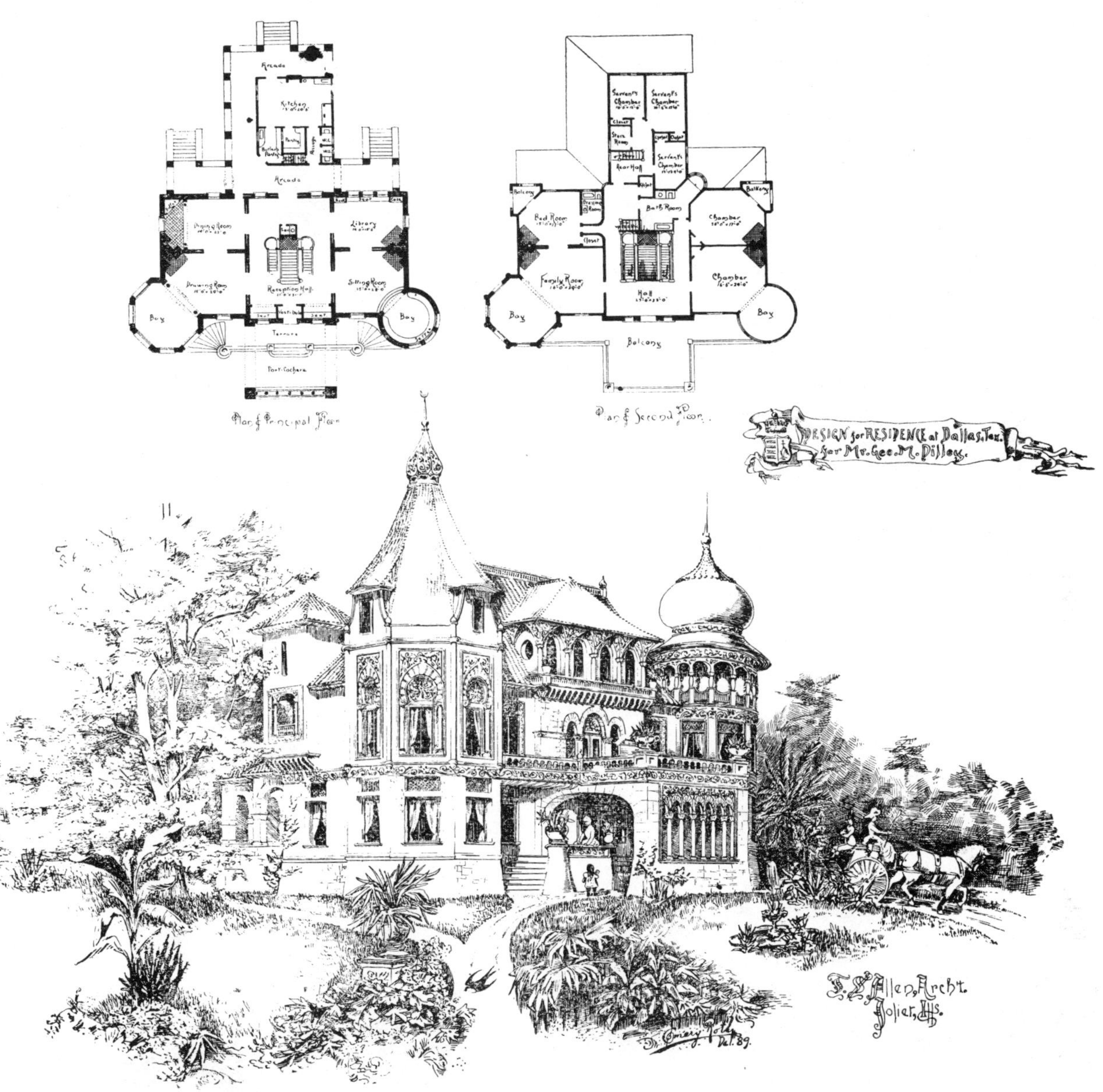

205. ARCHITECT'S PLANS, IVY HALL, c. 1890
Courtesy of the Dilley heirs.

206. WOODWORTH/KNIGHT HOUSE, 1895
The spacious home built in 1889 by C.S.
Woodworth, one of the founders of Dallas' huge
lumber industry, was purchased in 1898 by
Robert E. Lee Knight, the attorney son of Obadiah
Knight, one of the original settlers of Cedar Springs.
It was demolished in 1942. *Dallas Historical Society
Archives*

207. WOLFE HOUSE, 1910 *(below)*
Manson H. Wolfe, a wealthy cotton broker, built his
home in 1905 at the southwest corner of Maple
Avenue and Cedar Springs Road. The Colonial
Revival residence was razed in 1928 and replaced by
the E-A-T Bar and Grill. *Dallas Historical Society
Archives*

208. MURPHY HOUSE, 1910
John P. Murphy, president of Dallas' largest and most active real estate investment and development company, built a large home on Maple at the northeast corner of Mahon in 1901. In 1919, the house was acquired by his father-in-law, Judge Eugene P. Locke, founding partner of the prestigious legal firm of Locke, Locke, Dyer and Purnell. The house is one of the few surviving examples of Maple Avenue's former glory. *Dallas Historical Society Archives*

209. MAYFIELD HOUSE, 1910 *(below)*
Built in 1896 by J.S. Mayfield, president of the Mayfield Lumber Company, the expansive stone home at the northwest corner of Maple and Mahon was leveled in 1959 for a restaurant. *Dallas Historical Society Archives*

210. DEALEY AND ROBINSON HOMES ON MAPLE AVENUE, c. 1901

In 1901 George Bannerman Dealey, publisher of the Dallas *Morning News,* built a home on Maple (left) which was torn down in 1923 for an apartment house. The home of his neighbor William B. Robinson, an Elm Street hardware merchant, was constructed in 1899 and remained standing until 1937.

Dallas Historical Society Archives

craftsmen from the Pullman Railroad Car Company of Chicago to build his home. Dilley was also quite politically motivated and wanted to be remembered not as a railroad builder or mansion owner, but rather for his stand at the Republican Convention of 1880 "as one of the Immortal 306 delegates who held together in one unbroken column for General Ulysses Grant" during the general's unsuccessful bid for his third Presidential nomination.[63]

Dilley sold his mansion in 1900 to the only Dallasite with princely enough credentials to dare to buy it, Royal A. Ferris. Ferris, who at that time was president of the American Exchange National Bank, president of the Commercial Bank and Trust Company, first vice-president of the Hughes Brothers Manufacturing Company, president of the North Dallas Circuit Railway Company, and vice-president of the Dallas Consolidated Traction Railway Company, carried on the Dilley tradition of fanciful, extravagant balls and maintained the house as the showplace of the city.

Both The Shingles and Ivy Hall were beautiful refutations of the twentieth-century notion that Victorian architects produced nothing but architectural "monstrosities." The modern concept of an organic architecture in which outer form follows inner function woefully lacks understanding of the Victorian concept of arrangement of masses for pictorial effect. The Victorians succeeded in bringing the traditional Western idea of architecture as style applied to structure to its logical conclusion with a rich and creatively fabulistic accumulation of past motifs — Classical Greek and Roman orders, Gothic vaulting, and curious Egyptian or Middle Eastern exotica. Later practitioners could add little to this eclectic mode, and so contrived a reaction against it which is often limited and humorless.

Victorian architecture was both a conscious and subconscious parody of the past, and not simply an unimaginative or grotesque duplication of historic styles. How can a structure which incorporates an orgy of gargoyles, leering monsters, pilasters, dangling Cupids,

194

211. WEAVER HOUSE, 1910
The home of John C. Weaver, built in 1898 at the southeast corner of Alice Street, was in 1969 the last old Maple Avenue Victorian to be demolished. During the Depression years, the home was occupied by the Dallas Art Institute which sponsored the famous Alice Street Art Carnivals, and later it served as headquarters of Elmer Scott's Civic Federation of Dallas. *Dallas Historical Society Archives*

belvederes, pseudo-Italian columns, looming minarets, bell towers, flying porches, Byzantine domes, widow walks, cupolas, balustraded ledges, secret passages, recessed alcoves, and hidden perches appear to be anything but symbolic of an exuberant affirmation of life?

The Victorians' stress of truth and character over mere beauty was a reflection of their highly capitalistic appreciation of self-expression, self-determiniation, free will, independence, and individuality, and of a period in time which could allow such passions in its philosophy. Our nineteenth-century architectural heritage, which is mostly lost to us, was the material image of the American dream of Manifest Destiny — of the romantic vision of an open and free western land a continent wide, a land in which the individual could bury the failures of his past, and where anyone could begin life anew, free of the ignominy of war, Reconstruction, and poverty — beliefs and options which now are in great part also lost to us.

At the northwest corner of Maple and Cedar Springs stood another large and well-known Queen Anne home, the Woodworth-Knight house (206), which shared this prominent avenue with several other elegant residences, including those of John P. Murphy, president of Murphy-Bolanz Land and Loan Company (208); George Bannerman Dealey, publisher of the Dallas *Morning News* (210); and John C. Weaver, president of the Briggs-Weaver Machinery Company (later Briggs and Stratton) (211).

One half-block down McKinney from Maple, at the southeast corner of Pearl Street, is the Trinity Methodist Church (212), one of Dallas' last surviving architectural landmarks, which continued its ministerial service to the Maple Avenue and North Dallas district until the early 1970s. Built by James Flanders in 1904, it was unique in utilizing the Chicago School Prairie style, a design rarely adapted to churches but which here achieved a forceful, complex form, expressed in two intersecting gable roofs and three entry towers. Begun in 1846 in a small wood structure in Frogtown, Trinity Church moved to this site in 1895 as a suburban

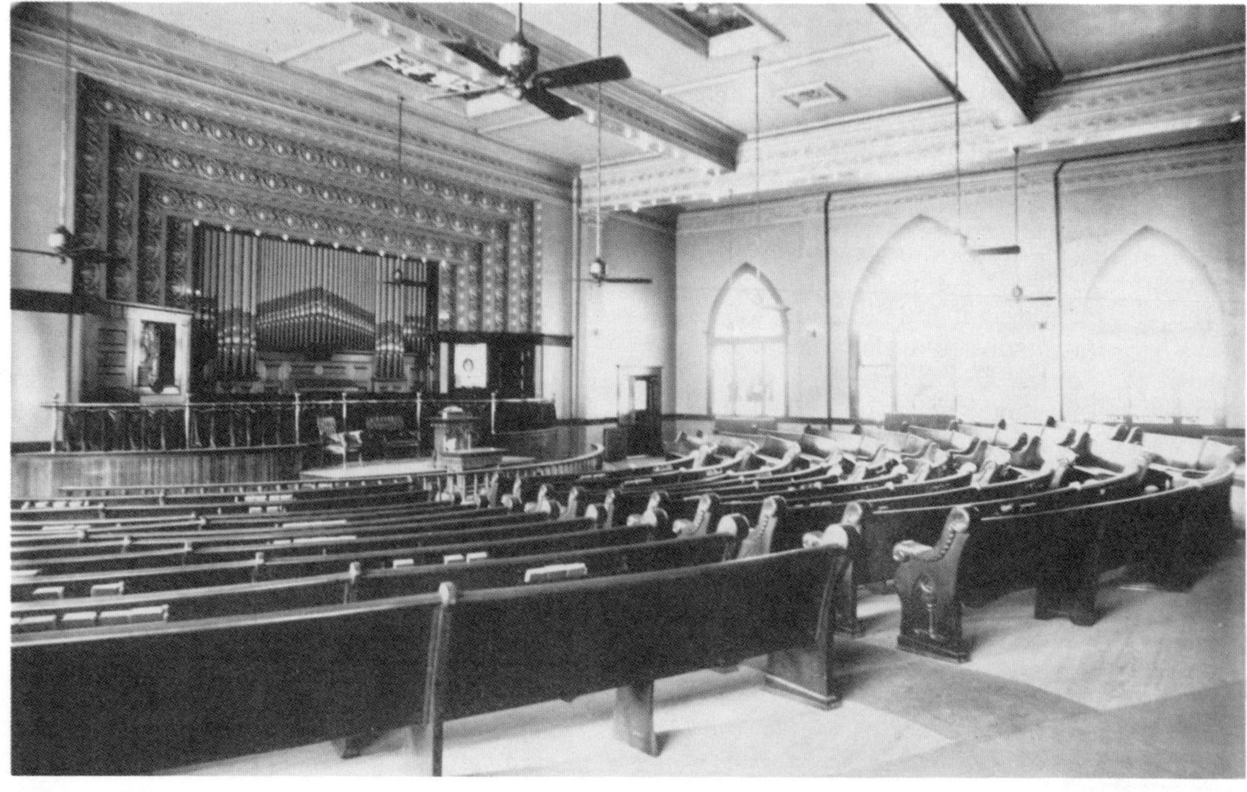

212. TRINITY METHODIST EPISCOPAL CHURCH, SOUTH, 1910 *(facing page, above)*
James Flanders' architectural masterpiece, an impressive combination of elements of the Chicago, Gothic, and Prairie styles, was completed in 1904 as a missionary extention of the downtown First Methodist Church. Through the efforts of local preservationists the Trinity Church was designated as the first Dallas landmark on the National Register of Historic Places. *Dallas Historical Society Archives*

213. INTERIOR, TRINITY METHODIST EPISCOPAL CHURCH, SOUTH, 1910 *(facing page, below)*
Dallas Historical Society Archives

214. MCKINNEY AVENUE BAPTIST CHURCH, 1910 *(above)*
Designed by C.W. Bulger and Son, the stuccoed brick McKinney Avenue Baptist Church was completed in 1906 at the corner of Routh Street, where its shell is today utilized by a shop specializing in structural antiques. *Dallas Historical Society Archives*

extension of the downtown First Methodist Church. In that year, the Methodist fathers decided that several strong suburban churches could serve the expanding community more effectively than one central church, and so a new building was commissioned for Trinity and its congregation was bolstered by First Church members. This is a remarkable illustration of how early Dallas began to let its suburbs take dominance over the central city, a phenomenon which contributed directly to the commercial sprawl of downtown and the ultimate urban corruption of the inner city neighborhoods like The Cedars and Ross Avenue.

This predilection for suburbia was further nurtured when one faction of the North Dallas Improvement Company opened Bowser and Lemmon's Oak Lawn and North Dallas Additions in 1887. Oliver P. Bowser and Captain William H. Lemmon were determined to capitalize on the cheap North Dallas lands opened up by the 1886 fair and the Circuit Railway, and toward that end they subdivided two areas. The North Dallas Addition was located just south of the fairgrounds, approximately between Blackburn, Oak Grove Street, Cedar Springs Road, and the MK&T tracks; the Oak Lawn Addition was bounded by Cedar Springs Road, Gilbert, Hood, and Knight Streets. Lee Park, originally called Oak Lawn Park, was created about 1892 by Bowser and Lemmon in association with the North Dallas Circuit Railway as an attraction to Sunday picnickers, excursionists, and prospective lot-buyers, whom the developers hoped to draw to the area with nickle rides on the steam locomotive.

Oliver Bowser had come to Dallas from Illinois in 1856 and staked out a small farm near Ross Avenue and Boll Street. In 1876, he and Captain Lemmon, who settled in Dallas after the Civil War, formed a farm implement company which they liquidated in 1887 in order to purchase over 1,500 acres of North Dallas property. The development was a tremendous success from the beginning, due to its accessible location and the intense desire of the population to abandon the commercial and industrialized downtown district for the pure, relaxed life in the "country." Lemmon made a considerable fortune and built a large estate home at the corner of Lemmon and Cole avenues called "Elmwood," but the Panic of 1893 caught the developers overextended, and the unsold properties were assumed by Charles B. Gillespie and Jacob Cullum. These unsold sections were primarily across Turtle Creek in the Oak Lawn Addition.

Until about 1891, Jacob Cullum had been a farmer, cultivating several hundred acres west of Cedar Springs and south and east of the St. Louis & Southwestern Railroad (now the North Dallas Tollway). Seeing how rapidly the city approached his property and how much more valuable farmland could be as homesites, he decided, like many other old Cedar Springs families, to subdivide. The depression of 1893 allowed Bowser and Lemmon's properties to be obtained at a bargain price, and the entire area became known as Gillespie and Cullum's Oak Lawn Addition.

Prior to 1885, the Oak Lawn area had been marked only by small, scattered settlements, most often clustered around natural springs. One of these was Maple Springs, a farming community just off Oak Lawn Avenue at Maple between the old Parkland Hospital (215) and the mineral spring in Reverchon Park called the Gill Well (216). Another small settlement was the Cedar Springs community, a village of about 100 people, most of whom were related either to the J. H. Cole family which arrived in 1843, or the family of Obadiah Knight, who settled there on 1,000 acres of land in 1845. A tiny but important watering stop for travelers along the Preston Trail, the village consisted of a steam-powered flouring mill, a small whiskey distillery, and a general store located on what is now Cedar Springs Road at about the corner of Kings Road. (What remains of the springs can be seen now on the grounds of the Kings Road Apartments.)

One of the first large homes to be built in the area was that of Colonel George Mellersh, who came to Dallas in 1873 from Memphis. Mellersh built his home, named "Oak Lawn" after the magnificent trees on his four-acre lot (217), in 1876 on the corner

215. PARKLAND HOSPITAL, 1895
Dallas' first Parkland Hospital was built in 1894 at the corner of Maple and Oak Lawn on the former site of an amusement park and picnic grounds. This all-wood structure served as the city's only public hospital facility until 1913 when it was replaced by the brick building which presently serves as the Woodlawn Detention Center. *Courtesy of Dallas Public Library*

216. GILL WELL BATH HOUSE AND NATATORIUM, c. 1904
In 1903, a test well, authorized by Alderman C.A. Gill, was drilled in front of what is now P.C. Cobb Stadium to determine if artesian water could supply the city's needs. The idea proved unfeasible but in 1904 Dr. J.G. Mills and J.D. Aldredge decided to capitalize on the highly mineralized waters and piped them into Reverchon Park where a series of pools, baths, and fountains had been built for public use. The sale of these mineral waters, whose "restorative qualities as a laxative" were widely renowned, was brisk until the 1930s when the minerals clogged the pipes, the baths were removed, and the well was plugged. The site is now covered by a manhole in the middle of Oak Lawn Avenue. *Courtesy of Dallas Times Herald*

GLEN ROSE (GILL WELL) STRATA.
TRINITY SANDS STRATA DEPTH 2850 FT.

217. MELLERSH/BURGHER, c. 1904 *(above)*
Colonel George Mellersh, a Civil War veteran and agricultural implement salesman, built his home on the corner of Oak Lawn and Cedar Springs Road in 1889 when the area was nothing but open farmland. Colonel Mellersh was forced to abandon the land after the depression of 1893 and for several years the property was used by stockmen as grazing pasture and the house served as a sheep barn. In 1904, the property was purchased and restored by Ballard M. Burgher, a prominent banker, real estate promoter, and street railway entrepreneur whose family owned it until 1924 when the house was demolished to build the Melrose Hotel. *Courtesy of Mrs. B.W.Z. Gordon*

218. GANO/MOSS, 1910 *(above right)*
In 1889, a second large home on Oak Lawn at Cedar Springs was built by William B. Gano. Designed by Stewart and Fuller, the regal residence was sold in 1903 to Colonel S.E. Moss, "the Lightning Rod Man of Texas." Moss, who liked to list his occupation as "capitalist," began his career as a supersalesman of lightning rods and soon built a sizable fortune in livestock, real estate, and manufacturing. The house was demolished in 1929 to build Dallas' first suburban shopping center. *Dallas Historical Society Archives*

219. WOMACK HOUSE, 1910 *(right)*
William O. Womack, vice-president of the Texas Drug Company, built a formidable Colonial Revival residence on the remaining corner of Oak Lawn and Cedar Springs in 1907. It remained standing only until 1920. *Dallas Historical Society Archives*

that would later be the intersection of Oak Lawn and Cedar Springs. He also owned about forty additional acres behind his residence, north to Throckmorton Street and west to Congress Avenue, which he began to develop about 1889, retaining the name Oak Lawn which Reverend Marcus Hiram Cullum adopted for the entire area when he organized the Oak Lawn Methodist Church in 1874. Across the street from the Mellersh house was the residence of a prosperous Dallas attorney, William B. Gano, built about 1889 (218).

The development boom of the late 1880s and early 1890s which invigorated and populated what previously had been the wild, outlying areas of not only North Dallas, but East and South Dallas as well, was slowed considerably by the depression of 1893. Residential growth and expansion in these areas continued much more moderately into the twentieth century, but finally was almost halted by two very fashionable and exclusive housing additions which attracted most of the new growth in Dallas for decades. These were the Munger Place Addition in far East Dallas, begun in 1905, and Highland Park in far North Dallas, which was started in 1907.

The idea for Highland Park was generated in 1889 when J. T. Trezevant and Henry Exall traveled to Philadelphia to sell 1,300 acres of North Dallas property to the Philadelphia Place Land Association, a syndicate of Eastern investors composed primarily of the banking house of Anthony J. Drexel and J. P. Morgan. In what the Dallas *News* called "the biggest single deal in suburban real estate ever made in Texas," the association paid over $500,000 (an average of $377 per acre) for the 288-acre Mart Cole tract, the 311-acre Isaac Carter tract, the 235-acre Joe L. Cole tract, and the 492-acre Walter Caruth tract — all of which had originally been land grants made by the Republic of Texas as homesteads or in recognition of military service at San Jacinto in 1836.

Both men returned to Dallas greatly impressed by Philadelphia's elegant cosmopolitanism. Trezevant was so inspired by Fairmount Park, site of the Centennial Exposition of 1876, that he urged that Turtle Creek be developed as a parkway and greenbelt, announcing that "Dallas has an opportunity to compete with Philadelphia in the matter of parks. Along what is known as Turtle Creek, there is found a greater natural attractiveness . . . which could be made into a sylvan delight and the most beautiful drive in all this broad state."[64] As local agent for the investors, Exall immediately began laying out gravel roads and later built Exall's Lake (along what is now Lakeside Drive). Had the Panic of 1893 not arrested the plan, what is now Highland Park would have been called Philadelphia Place and might be graced with huge Victorian mansions of the Ross and Maple Avenue vintage. Instead, the land was simply utilized by Exall as the Lomo Alto Stock Farm, where he specialized in the breeding and raising of thoroughbred racehorses (many of which established great reputations at the State Fair racetrack) until the property could be resold in 1906 to John S. Armstrong. Like much of Highland Park's development, Trezevant's dream of a Turtle Creek Parkway was postponed for over twenty years, until George Kessler included it in his master plan for Dallas.

John S. Armstrong, the son of an Ohio River steamboat captain, had come to Dallas in 1884 to enter the wholesale grocery business with T. L. Marsalis. He was also a partner with Marsalis in the original development of Oak Cliff, but in 1887 the partnership was dissolved, leaving the Oak Cliff real estate interests to Marsalis and the grocery business to Armstrong. Armstrong later acquired interests in the City National Bank and the Dallas Dressed Beef and Packing Company; in 1906 he sold a portion of the packing business to Swift and Company and used the proceeds to buy Highland Park from Exall and the Philadelphians.

The first real wave of residential migration north from the city into Highland Park began along Turtle Creek on old Cedar Springs Road. J. T. Trezevant, who had become president of the Security Mortgage and Trust Company, built the first of the palatial homes in 1907 at the northwest corner of Cedar Springs and Dickason streets (221); he was followed in 1908 by Edward Tenison (222)

220. JACKSON HOUSE, 1910
Albert Jackson constructed a very formal, Colonial Revival home in 1905 on Oak Lawn at the corner of Gillespie which was demolished in 1928. *Dallas Historical Society Archives*

221. TREZEVANT HOUSE, 1910
Colonel John Trezevant, founder of Trezevant and Cochran Insurance Company and president of the Security Mortgage and Trust Company, led the wave of mansion building along Turtle Creek in 1907 when he hired J. Edward Overbeck to fashion a large, Mission style residence at the northwest corner of Cedar Springs Road and Dickason Street. The home survives today as the Cipango Club. *Dallas Historical Society Archives*

and Sheppard W. King, Jr. (223). Armstrong died in 1908, but his vision of the finest residential city in the South — advertised as "beyond the city's smoke and dust" — gradually became a reality under the direction of his sons-in-law, Hugh Prather and Edgar Flippen. In 1910 the latter built a replica of Mount Vernon on Preston Road near Armstrong Parkway (226) to serve both as his home and as part of Highland Park's promotion. A second shrewd bit of promotion was engineered by Armstrong's wife, Alice, who donated 100 acres of land to the Methodist Episcopal Church South for the establishment of Southern Methodist University in 1911, just prior to Highland Park's emergence (1913) as an independent municipality upon Dallas' refusal of its petition for incorporation.

The original platting of the Highland Park acreage was performed in 1907 by William David Cook, the celebrated landscape architect who laid out Beverly Hills, California. Later topographical and landscape planning was done by George Kessler, who finally actualized Trezevant's dream of a Turtle Creek Parkway from Reverchon Park, along the creek to Oak Lawn Park, through the grounds of the old Dallas Golf and Country Club to Exall's Lake.

Kessler, a Kansas City landscape architect considered by many to have been a near-genius of design, laid out Turtle Creek Parkway as part of his master plan for Dallas which was commissioned by the city government in 1910 for $10,000.[65] Before this time, Dallas had neither felt the need for city planning nor been aware of its benefits. The city had always prided itself on its speculators and developers who controlled large tracts of real estate. These men determined patterns of streets and streetcar lines, and where parks and shopping areas, if any, should be located. By 1910, with the population approaching 100,000, Dallas' leaders gradually began to believe that such unstructured, unregulated growth negated the city's attractiveness when compared to cities like Kansas City, St. Louis, and Atlanta, which were adopting very progressive master plans. They realized that staying a step ahead of the competition had historically been the only way Dallas had survived; with no natural trading advantages like a seaport or commercially usable river,

222. TENISON HOUSE, c. 1910
In 1908, C.D. Hill designed a huge, rambling mansion on a hill overlooking Turtle Creek for Edward Tenison, president of the powerful City National Bank. A beautiful hybrid of the Prairie and the Spanish Colonial Revival styles, it was destroyed in 1947 to build the Gulf Insurance Company Building.
Dallas Historical Society Archives

only innovation, boosterism, and sheer conniving had enabled the city to propel itself to a position of prominence in the South and Southwest.

With an eye toward maintaining land values, the local economy, and trade, the city Park Board hired George Kessler to develop a city plan for Dallas on the strength of his successful designs for Kansas City in 1892, the 1904 Louisiana Purchase Exposition in St. Louis, Cincinnati in 1905, Indianapolis in 1910, and various other cities including Memphis, Salt Lake City, and Denver.

Kessler devised a comprehensive plan for the entire city, based on the premise that Dallas' problems stemmed from its origin as a typical frontier railroad-terminal town which had grown according to the dictates of land speculators who gave no consideration to either continuous thoroughfares or room for the expansion of downtown commerce. Kessler detailed nine areas for improvement. First, he suggested that the Trinity River channel between Dallas and Oak Cliff be straightened and that levees be built for protection against the disastrous floods (like the one in 1908) that regularly swept through the city. This proposal, which was carried out between 1927 and 1933, also contained a provision for a town lake and city harbor which is still being hotly debated today.

Second, he proposed a belt railroad that would loop the city and relieve the downtown congestion of tracks. His third recommendation was for the abolishment of the half dozen small, independent railroad stations in favor of a central Union Depot (realized in 1916) to serve all the lines entering the city. Fourth, he suggested a central freight terminal; and fifth, a civic center composed of several public buildings to house the city's governmental and arts programs (a proposal not acted upon until the late 1970s). Sixth, he recommended the elimination of all railroad grade crossings in the city, including removal of the T&P tracks on Pacific (accomplished in 1923).

Seventh, he diagrammed specific changes to be made in street patterns — especially downtown — including straightening, lengthening, widening, or abolishing many of them. Eighth, he included several general suggestions for cleaning up and beautifying the city, including ridding it of telephone poles and the web of electrified lines used by the streetcars.

223. KING MANSION, 1910
Sheppard W. King, Jr., president of the cotton
brokerage house of King, Collie and Company, built
his first palatial, Mission Revival home in 1908 at
the northwest corner of Cedar Springs and Gillespie.
In 1923, King grew tired of the house, had it
demolished and spent two years touring Europe while
a new mansion was constructed on the property.
Dallas Historical Society Archives

224. DALLAS UNIVERSITY, 1910
In 1905, the Vincentian Fathers founded an institute
of advanced learning known as Holy Trinity College,
commissioning H.A. Overbeck to build a suitably
academic building on the northeast corner of Oak
Lawn and Gilbert Street. Overbeck produced, in
1906, a symmetrically ordered and sternly composed
structure which contained elements of the Georgian
Colonial Revival (of which the Wren Building in
Williamsburg was a strong influence) and of the
Second Renaissance Revival, both of which were
motivated by the desire to restore classical order to
architecture. In 1910, the college was renamed
Dallas University which it remained until that
institution's bankruptcy in the early 1940s. In 1942,
the structure was used as Jesuit High School until it
was demolished in 1963. *Dallas Historical
Society Archives*

225. DALLAS GOLF AND COUNTRY CLUB, c. 1911
The Dallas Golf and Country Club was founded in
1896 along Turtle Creek across Lemmon Avenue
from Oak Lawn Park. In 1911, the club was moved
to its present location in Highland Park, the old
property was sold at a phenomenal profit, and C.D.
Hill was hired to construct a new clubhouse along
the creek. The Elizabethan-inspired structure burned
to the ground in 1955. *Dallas Historical Society
Archives*

Highland Park was, without question, the most far-sighted and well-planned real estate development in Dallas' history and has, since its conception in 1907, had a profound impact on the city's subsequent northern growth and expansion. In 1910, Edgar L. Flippen, president of the Flippen-Prather Real Estate Company, established Highland Park as an elite, ultra-fashionable subdivision by constructing a replica of Mount Vernon between Preston Road and Turtle Creek, north of Armstrong Parkway. The house, designed and constructed by C.D. Hill, still survives but has been remodeled so often it is now unrecognizable. *Dallas Historical Society Archives*

The home of Orville Thorpe, state manager of the Kansas City Life Insurnce Company, is typical of the stately residences built in Highland Park. The house, designed by Thompson and Fooshee, was completed about 1915 on Lakeside Drive. *Dallas Historical Society Archives*

And ninth, Kessler outlined a system of parks, all connected and coordinated by an elaborate network of parkways and boulevards.[66]

From the advantage of hindsight, Kessler's plan contrasted dramatically with the previous random growth of the city, as exemplified by North Dallas. Several factors, including the railroads, real estate speculators, and topography, caused Dallas' expansion northward to be the most complicated and least linearly structured of any of the city's suburbs. Real estate promotions as close as three blocks from the courthouse and as far away as three miles were often executed simultaneously, resulting in a series of small communities which all united under the banner of North Dallas after the city extended its corporation lines in 1890.

The arrival of the T&P Railroad in 1873, though a definite enhancement to the city's business life, depressed land values north of its right-of-way and generated the ethnically diverse but economically deprived Barrio area. The advent of the socially prestigious areas of Munger Place and Highland Park in the early 1900s and the increasing deterioration of The Cedars, the South Boulevard-Park Row area, the near East Dallas community, and the Ross Avenue and Thomas-Colby Street districts resulted in a migration of the wealthier classes from the central city. These more affluent people, aided in their mass flight by the mobility of the personal automobile, left the inner city to urban blight and decay as they moved to the outlying areas. In the north, Turtle Creek created a natural barrier between the new residential areas beyond it and the increasing commercialization of Ross and McKinney avenues, the warehouse district, and the black and Latin quarters.

Yet Kessler's bold and seemingly futuristic proposals staggered the city fathers with what they considered impossible scope and cost, and although some of the proposals have been implemented through the years, many of Kessler's ideas are just gathering dust, waiting to organize the disconnected patchwork that many areas of Dallas stubbornly remain.

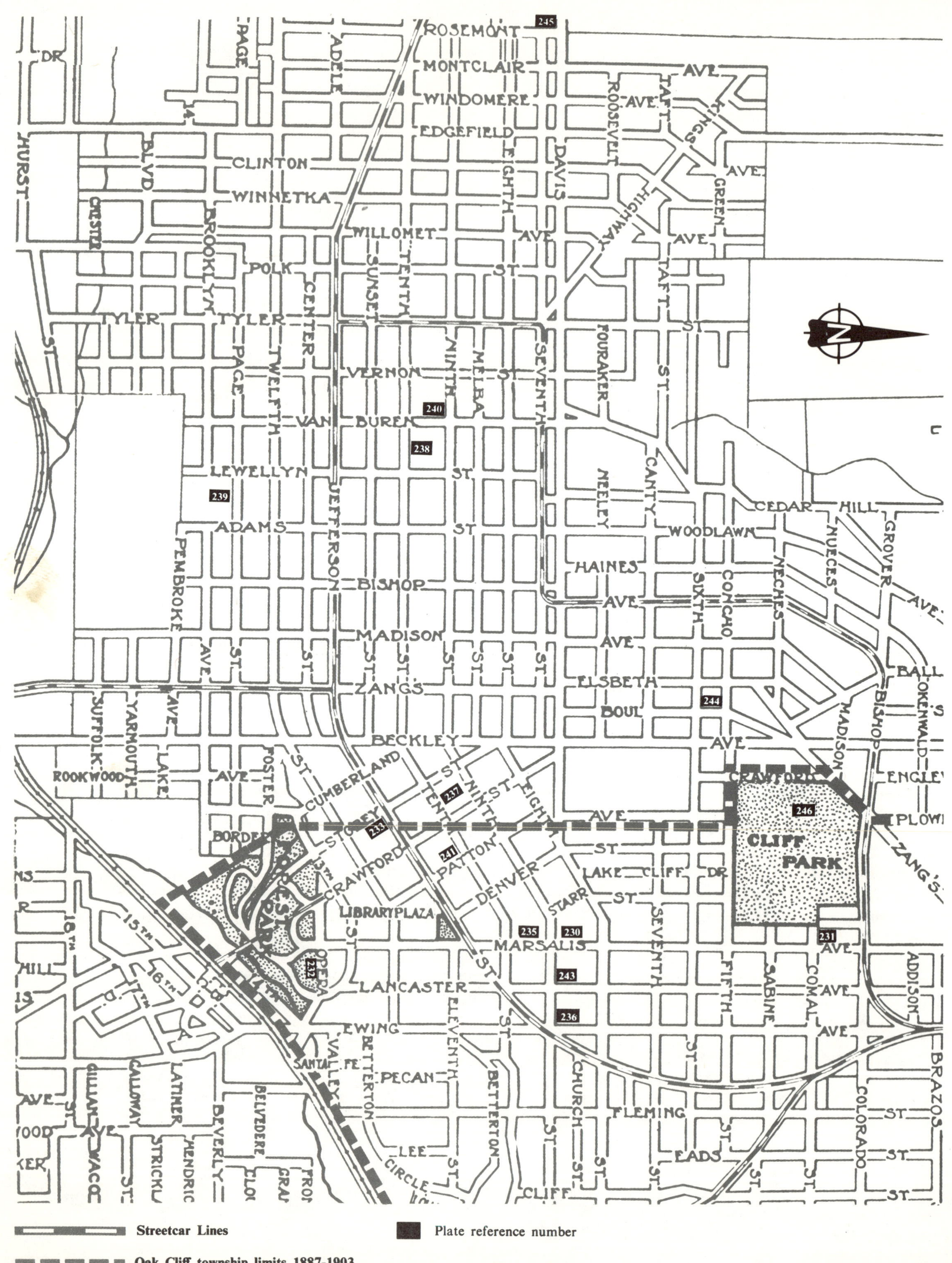

ROSEMONT
MONTCLAIR
WINDOMERE
EDGEFIELD
CLINTON
WINNETKA
WILLOMET
POLK
TYLER
VERNON
VAN BUREN
LEWELLYN
ADAMS
BISHOP
MADISON
ZANGS
BECKLEY
CUMBERLAND
CRAWFORD
LIBRARY PLAZA
MARSALIS
LANCASTER
EWING
PECAN
LEE
FLEMING
EADS
HAINES
ELSBETH
BOUL
WOODLAWN
CEDAR HILL
CLIFF PARK
CRAWFORD
DENVER
PATTON
LAKE CLIFF DR
STARR
HURST
DR
PAGE
ADELE
CHESTER
BLVD
BROOKLYN
CENTER
TWELFTH
PAGE
PEMBROKE
JEFFERSON
SUNSET
TENTH
NINTH
METRA
EIGHTH
SEVENTH
DAVIS
HIGHWAY
ROOSEVELT
TAFT
KINGS
GREEN
FOURAKER
NEELEY
CANTY
SIXTH
CONCHO
NECHES
NUECES
GROVER
BALL
OKENWALD
MADISON
BISHOP
ENGLE
PLOW
ZANG'S
AVE
FIFTH
SABINE
COMAL
ADDISON
COLORADO
BRAZOS
CHURCH
SEVENTH
BETTERTON
ELEVENTH
SANTA FE
VALLEY
BEVERLY
BELVEDERE
LATHER
GALLOWAY
GILLIAM
HENDRIC
STRICKL
WACO
FOSTER
STOREY
TENTH
NINTH
EIGHTH
OPERA
BORDEN
ROOKWOOD
SUFFOLK
YARMOUTH
LAKE
AVE
15TH
16TH
17TH
19TH
HILL
SABINE
CIRCLE
CLIFF
245
240
238
239
244
237
233
241
235
230
243
236
232
246
231
N
TYLER

Streetcar Lines
Plate reference number
Oak Cliff township limits 1887-1903

7 OAK CLIFF

Because of its isolated position across the river, Oak Cliff has always had a unique relationship with Dallas. It has at various times been characterized as the scrappy, independent maverick town fighting for its prosperity and freedom in the face of Dallas' decadence; as Dallas' "Brooklyn," a sleepy little bedroom community; or as Dallas' poor relation, the burdensome stepchild. An element of truth lies in each of these perspectives.

The earliest colonization of the area occurred in the outlying regions rather than next to the river where downtown Oak Cliff was later built. Attracted by the good water and fertile soil along Five Mile and Ten Mile creeks, the first settlers began to arrive just a year or two after John Neely Bryan made his camp across the Trinity in 1841. One of the first families to settle inside the present corporate limits in the spring of 1844 was that of Samuel Browning, the son-in-law of William Smalling Peters, head of the Peters Colony Company of Louisville, Kentucky. In early January, 1845, the William H. Hord family arrived in a covered wagon from Tennessee and made camp on Cedar Creek about where the Marsalis Park and Zoo are now. Mrs. Hord's brother, John M. Crockett, Dallas' second mayor and later lieutenant governor of Texas, moved to the little settlement in 1848 and the area was soon christened Hord's Ridge.

By the time the United States annexed Texas in 1845, Hord's Ridge had become a busy farm community of eighty to ninety people. Its grist mill, set up in 1846 by Aaron Overton at his home on Five Mile Creek, was one of the first in the county. The mill was powered by mules or horses and its production capacity of over 100 bushels a day made it the most important industry in the area, attracting grain farmers from hundreds of miles around.

The area that was to become Oak Cliff grew fairly rapidly in the late 1840s and early 1850s, filling with the refugees from the California gold fields and the Mexican War, or just land-hungry men eager to build an empire out of the rich blacklands. One of these opportunists was William Brown Miller who arrived from Kentucky in 1847. By 1868 he owned over 7,500 acres of prime southwest Dallas County land, making him one of the largest landholders, stock and cotton raisers and slave owners in North Texas. Miller's first log cabin was built on a hill commanding the south bank of the Trinity River with a magnificent view of Dallas, and had the first glass windows in the area installed in it. In 1855, Miller began construction of his antebellum mansion called Millermore (229), which he finished in 1862 on the site of the original log cabin.

In 1850, Hord's Ridge missed becoming the seat of the newly created Dallas County by only fifteen votes in a zealously contested referendum which also included Dallas and Cedar Springs. This loss cost Oak Cliff the best chance it had of becoming the primary urban center for the Three Forks region, and from that point, its role as a satellite of Dallas began to be defined.

This crucial defeat at the polls slowed the momentum of Hord's Ridge and thwarted growth for the next thirty-five years. Also, during the wet seasons the wide floodplain of the Trinity created an impassable barrier of mud and discouraged travel across the river if no urgent need existed; but the area did experience some expansion.

228. LOOKING TOWARD DALLAS FROM
OAK CLIFF, c. 1895
Dallas Historical Society Archives

The members of the ill-fated French colony of La Reunion settled in the area in 1855 but within three years bad crops, a plague of grasshoppers, and the sudden, vicious blue northers discouraged enough of them to call it a failure. The area around La Reunion is now the West Dallas industrial complex, which became known as Cement City about 1901.

During the Civil War, Maxime Guillot established an ammunition and pistol factory for the Confederate government near Lancaster, and several more families built homes, a new mill, a few log churches and a couple of stores near Cedar Hill; but for the most part, attention to the southwest section of the county was drawn not by any noteworthy, industrious growth but rather by the eccentricity and notoriety of some of its citizens.

By September, 1873, the Texas & Pacific Railroad had pushed as far as Eagle Ford before it went temporarily bankrupt during the financial panic of that year, making that area near Oak Cliff a makeshift rail terminus and the most wide open town in the state. It abounded with railroad construction gangs, cattle drovers bringing their herds through town for shipment to market, gamblers, prostitutes and all manner of hustlers in general. Around 1878, Sam Bass and Arkansas Johnson held up the T&P near Eagle Ford, giving the local citizens some longed-for entertainment.

The real birth of Oak Cliff occurred in 1887 when Thomas L. Marsalis and John S. Armstrong, partners in the Dallas Land and Loan Company, purchased 2,000 acres of prime property (including the 640-acre Hord homestead), renamed the area for the massive oaks that crowned the chalk hills, and transformed Hord's Ridge from an isolated backwood farming community into one of the most progressive and desirable residential suburbs of Dallas.

Marsalis' parents were Dutch Quakers who immigrated to Pennsylvania from Holland in the 1840s and later moved to Mississippi where Thomas was born in 1852. In 1871, at

212

229. MILLERMORE, c. 1960

Millermore, the antebellum plantation home of William Brown Miller, was one of the few rare Greek Revival mansions completed in Dallas County. Millermore was originally built in 1855-62 on a bluff near what is now Bonnie View Drive and Illinois Avenue. The home was moved to Old City Park for restoration in 1968. *Dallas Historical Society Archives*

the age of nineteen, he came to Texas and began working as a stockboy in a wholesale grocery house in Corsicana. By 1872, Marsalis felt ready to strike out on his own, and rode the Houston & Texas Central Railroad to the end of the line at Dallas and established a wholesale grocery business. According to his own accounts he was doing $750,000 worth of business by 1877; $1,500,000 by 1882; in 1884 he took John S. Armstrong as a partner and by the time they opened Oak Cliff in 1887, their four stores were ringing up sales of over $20 million a year.[67]

The partnership between Armstrong and Marsalis lasted only a few months after their Oak Cliff promotion began, and reportedly was broken off because of the initial success of the venture. Before noon on November 1, 1887, $23,000 worth of lots were sold in the newly opened "Marsalis Addition" and on the following day, ninety-one lots were sold for $38,113. The Daily Herald called it, "a great beginning of what will be the grandest suburban town in the South."[68] Marsalis reacted to the huge sale of lots by holding some off the market in the hope that the decreased supply would force the prices up and increase their profits. Armstrong disagreed with this policy and the partnership dissolved, Armstrong taking the wholesale grocery half and Marsalis the real estate.

After the break in late 1887, Oak Cliff became solely Marsalis' project. Personally absorbing the $500,000 initial land purchase cost and the $100,000 street improvement cost, everything came under his control and was directed toward the promotion and sale of lots, an endeavor which he assumed with as much characteristic zeal and flair as he later did establishing the town as a "health resort." The high volume of lots sold in 1887-88 guaranteed that by 1889 a sizable town would begin to grow because the deed restrictions to the property stated that improvements must begin within a year of purchase.

230. MARSALIS MANSION, 1895
Thomas L. Marsalis, the man who almost single-handedly promoted and developed Oak Cliff through his control of the Dallas Land and Loan Company, the Dallas and Oak Cliff Railway, and the Oak Cliff Water Supply Company, built this $45,000 palatial residence c. 1889 at the southwest corner of Grand (now Marsalis Avenue) at Colorado Boulevard. The house was unoccupied between 1892 and 1903, partly because his wife refused to move to Oak Cliff and partly because of financial problems caused by the depression of 1893. The structure was sold in 1904 to Dr. J. H. Reuss who reopened it as the Marsalis Sanitarium, a clinic for gynecological disorders. The building burned to the ground in 1915. *Courtesy of Dallas Public Library.*

231. DARGAN HOUSE, c. 1905 *(above right)*
The home of James T. Dargan, one of the more elegant designs of the Dallas architectural firm of Stewart and Fuller, was constructed in 1888 at the northwest corner of Marsalis and Ninth streets. The house was located next door to the first Catholic church to be established within the corporate limits of Oak Cliff, the Church of the Blessed Sacrament, founded by Bishop E.J. Dunne in 1901. In 1902, the house was sold to the Sisters of St. Mary of Namur who used it as the Our Lady of Good Counsel Academy until its demolition in 1968. *Courtesy of Sister M. Adelaide Mars*

232. THE SUMMER OPERA PAVILION IN OAK CLIFF PARK, c. 1889
Dallas Historical Society Archives

233. OAK CLIFF COLLEGE, 1895
The Oak Cliff College for Young Ladies, a mammoth example of the Victorian Stick style of architecture located at the southwest corner of Jefferson and Crawford streets, was originally The Park Hotel. Constructed in 1889 by Thomas Marsalis as part of his resort spa promotion of Oak Cliff, the hotel was converted into the girls school in 1892. In 1907, the college was sold at auction for $6,507 to T. Scott Miller, Wirt Davis, and Leslie Stemmons who reconverted the great building into the Hotel Cliff; eight years later they completely remodeled it and renamed it the Forest Inn, which it remained until its destruction in 1945. *Courtesy of Dallas Public Library*

216

One of the more elegant and spacious of Oak Cliff's early homes was built by James T. Dargan (231), a part-owner with Marsalis in the Dallas and Oak Cliff Railway Company, a partner in the Dargan and Trezevant General Insurance Company, and a vice-president of the Security Mortgage and Trust Company of Dallas. To prod construction efforts and to set a good example for the new property owners, Marsalis also built himself a mammoth Victorian chateau (230), surrounded by several acres of grounds about 1889 near Lake Cliff, which was the social center of town for many years.

The Marsalis house was a remarkable building, reflective of the diverse abilities and energy of the remarkable man who built it — a man who regularly worked from fifteen to eighteen hours a day and drove himself with a fierce determination to accomplish tasks that normally would have required the energies of several men.

With the conspicuous exception of Jefferson Street, the original layout of the streets in Oak Cliff was a rather strict and unimaginative north/south — east/west grid which completely ignored the river valley, the natural topography and the orientation of Dallas' street patterns.[69] Within this grid pattern, the original township extended to Colorado Boulevard on the north, to just beyond Miller Street (now Cliff) on the east, to Thirteenth Street on the south and was bounded on the west by a north/south line between Spring Lake (later called Lake Cliff) and Marsalis Park.

Marsalis' first step in developing Oak Cliff was to provide reliable rapid transit service over the Trinity River which would effectively alleviate the area's traditional problem of isolation due to flooding. His solution, modeled after New York City's elevated metropolitan rail system, was a steam-powered railway that ran from the Dallas County Courthouse square down Jefferson Street and crossed the river on a rail viaduct. Touted as "the first elevated railway in the South," the Dallas to Oak Cliff "dummy" line actually ran at ground level and the only elevated portion was the shaky trestle which spanned the river channel. After the line reached Oak Cliff, it branched into two sections, one leading west toward Lake Cliff and the other following Jefferson Boulevard to its terminus at the center of Oak Cliff's downtown, the intersection of Tenth and Jefferson, with stops made at small wooden stations built on every other street. The use of Jefferson Boulevard as the railroad's right-of-way accounts for its curvilinear configuration in the face of an otherwise rigid street plan; the steam traction engines were not powerful enough to climb the river bluff directly, but had to curve gently along its face in order to negotiate the incline more gradually. This rail line, which cost over $250,000 to build and employed nearly 200 men, 100 teams of mules, and a monthly payroll of $18,000 at the height of its construction, was financed by a group of investors: Jeptha H. Simpson of St. Louis, Leon Blum of Galveston, Lieutenant Governor J. R. Hindman of Kentucky, Marsalis, Thomas Field, J. T. Dargan, and several other Dallas capitalists.

To induce people to make the trip from Dallas, Marsalis set aside 180 acres of the old Hord property as Oak Cliff Park (now called Marsalis Park and Zoo), then almost gave away rides on the steam railway into the new township. By 1889, the park was fully landscaped, including the construction of a dam across Cedar Creek to create a two-mile-long lake. Marsalis also constructed a three-story dance pavilion with a cedar plank floor and a summer opera house (232), all of which helped to promote the new development as a health spa and vacation resort in the manner of Atlantic City.

Marsalis recognized from the beginning that he would have to create a major attraction in Oak Cliff in order to make his real estate development successful and decided to use the spa and recreation type promotion which had worked so well in other parts of the country. Toward this end he built, in 1889, at a cost of over $150,000, the monumental, four-story resort facility known as The Park Hotel (233), a magnificent wooden structure just two blocks from Oak Cliff Park. Modeled after the famous Hotel del Coronado in San Diego, The Park featured "life-restoring mineral baths" fed by several

234. LOOKING NORTH ON EWING AVENUE AT THE CORNER OF E. SEVENTH STREET, 1895 *(left)*
These homes were built between 1890 and 1895 and were demolished in the 1940s for commercial usage. *Courtesy of Dallas Public Library*

235. COWART HALL, c. 1900 *(below left)*
Cowart Hall functioned as both a private girls school and the residence of Miss Lora Cowart, principal (seated, far left). Built about 1890 on Marsalis Avenue near Tenth Street, the school was torn down in the 1940s and is now an auto garage. *Dallas Historical Society Archives*

236. DIETZEL HOUSE, 1895 *(right)*
Oscar Dietzel, editor and publisher of the *Texas Post,* built his enormous, four-story residence c. 1889 at the corner of Ewing and Ninth streets. It was leveled in the early 1960s and remains a vacant lot. *Courtesy of Dallas Public Library*

237. RESIDENCE OF WILLIAM LANG, c. 1890 *(below)*
The solid, respectable home of Colonel William W. Lang, president of the Texas Paper Mills Company, was built c. 1890 on E. Tenth near the corner of Crawford Street and remained standing until the mid-1950s. Notice the advanced technology of the curved corner windows. *Courtesy of Old City Park, a Museum of Cultural History, Dallas, Texas*

artesian wells drilled on the property. The hotel's promotional literature cited the virtues of Oak Cliff's "cool and healthful breezes away from the dust and heat of the city" and pointed out that "to the south and southwest for hundreds of miles stretch level and unobstructed prairies over whose bosom these breezes sweep from the Gulf without infections from unsalubrious conditions."[70]

By 1890, Marsalis' little Oak Cliff subdivision had grown into a city, incorporating itself in September of that year, with a population of nearly 2,500 and several hundred new homes either finished or under construction. The Dallas Land and Loan Company had opened several smaller additions west of the original township in 1888, 1889, and 1890 progressively pushing the town's limits westward between Pembroke and Eighth streets as far as Willomet Street. North Ewing Avenue (234) developed as the most elite and prestigious street in town and many large two- and three-story homes, some costing as much as $50,000, were built there by such people as Judge George Aldredge, Mayor Hugh F. Ewing, and Judge Robert Cowart, whose daughter Lora opened Cowart Hall, a private girls' school on Grand Avenue, about 1891 (235). Serving the community were four grocery stores, one feed and grain store, two meat markets, two physicians, one hardware store, and three miles of transit line feeding into downtown Dallas.[71] There were a few fledgling businesses and industries such as the Oak Cliff Artesian Well Company, which supplied the town's water independent of Dallas' mains, Dr. Edward G. Patton's medicine laboratories, the Oak Cliff Ice and Refrigeration Company, the Oak Cliff Planing Mill, and Colonel William Lang's Texas Paper Mills Company (237).

The only businesses which offered any sizable employment to Oak Cliff's citizens were the planing mill and paper mill, making the newly incorporated town extremely dependent upon Dallas for many goods and services and for much of its employment. This is dramatically illustrated by the fact that all of Marsalis' enterprises, the Dallas Land and Loan Company, the Dallas-Oak Cliff Railway, the Oak Cliff Water Supply, Electric Light and Power Company, and the Oak Cliff Hotel Company, had their headquarters in Dallas even though the focus of their business was across the river. In short, Oak Cliff had firmly established itself as a bedroom community satellite, albeit a very desirable and exclusive one, of Dallas.

The year 1893 witnessed two important events in the evolution of Oak Cliff: the completion of the first public school, the Oak Cliff Central School (241), and the complete collapse of the fortunes of Thomas Marsalis. By 1892, Marsalis had invested well over $1 million in his Oak Cliff venture, having become totally dependent on the profits from that property after the dissolution of the partnership with Armstrong. The Panic of 1893 almost completely stifled growth not only in Oak Cliff but all over Dallas, where the total population declined by nearly 5,000 between 1892 and 1894. Completely bankrupt, Marsalis was forced to sell his business interest in the Dallas and Oak Cliff Railway to Henry Scott of St. Louis, the Oak Cliff Water Supply and Electric Light and Power Company to J. T. Dargan, and The Park Hotel to a group of investors who converted it into a college. He left for New York to begin a new career, but died a poor man just a few years later.

The depression of 1893 created a severe slack in the demand for Dallas resorts and The Park Hotel was converted that year to the Oak Cliff College for Young Ladies. The college's 1893 catalogue states that it "was

240. GARDINER HOUSE, 1895 *(facing page, above)*
The residence of Joshua A. Gardiner, manager of the Commercial Club Cigar factory, was built c. 1895 at the corner of W. Ninth and Van Buren streets. It was destroyed by fire about 1910. *Courtesy of Dallas Public Library*

241. CENTRAL HIGH SCHOOL, 1895 *(left)*
The Oak Cliff Central High School, a design of James Flanders, was built at the southwest corner of E. Tenth Street at Patton in 1893. It was demolished in 1927 for residential construction. *Courtesy of Dallas Public Library*

242. PROPOSED OAK CLIFF FEMALE INSTITUTE, c. 1892
A vision of the future that never materialized, the Oak Cliff Female Institute remained only one of Marsalis' many dreams which were shattered by the depression of 1893. *Dallas Historical Society Archives*

243. ZANG'S CRYSTAL HILL, c. 1907
Zang's Crystal Hill Addition was John F. Zang's attempt to develop an exclusive, affluent housing subdivision in Oak Cliff. Begun in 1905, the area did not sell well and was gradually parceled out to other developers after World War I. *Courtesy of Old City Park, a Museum of Cultural History, Dallas, Texas*

chartered for the accomplishment of young ladies and for the purpose of teaching the arts, social culture, parliamentary law, self-government, essay writing, reading, singing in public, grace and beauty of carriage and proper physical development." The catalogue concluded with the assertion that "there is no question but that it is the best college in the Southwest and the people of Dallas have yet but a faint conception of its magnitude, perfect equipment, elegance and convenience."

Originally, Marsalis had never planned for the hotel to be converted into a college. He recognized the promotional advantage of having an educational institution in the town but reserved that role for the Oak Cliff Female Institute (242). Planning for the Institute had begun as early as 1889 with a charter application, site selection and architect's renderings, and as late as 1892, Marsalis was insisting that it would still open very shortly on the south side of Eighth Street between Marsalis and Lancaster avenues. But the building and the Institute remained only a projected vision, wiped away by the economic misfortunes of 1893.

A third educational institution did arise in Oak Cliff in those early years. The Patton Seminary was a private institution established in 1895 by Dr. Edward G. Patton, an inventive druggist who concocted and manufactured a patented medicine known as Patton's Chill Tonic, from which he became quite wealthy. Dr. Patton built his school at the northwest corner of Lancaster at Ninth Street, where it was taken over by the Southern Baptist Convention in 1905 to become Texas Baptist University.

Aside from education, little happened in Oak Cliff between 1893 and 1900. The population grew from about 1,000 to 3,624 after Batholomew Blankenship's Dallas and Oak Cliff Real Estate Company took over the holdings of the Dallas Land and Loan Company and resubdivided the large, spacious lots into smaller ones on which more modest frame houses could be built. This decision marked the end of Oak Cliff's elite status, and the beginning of its reorientation as a middle- to working-class area. The trend would continue, during the area's second major boom (1900-14), with the intrusion of large numbers of less permanently attractive and desirable bungalow-type tract houses. Often poorly constructed, these houses would quickly weather and deteriorate and helped to create the depressed conditions of the area in the 1960s and 1970s. One of the few projects of benefit in this era was the electrification in 1894 of the Dallas to Oak Cliff Railway.

In 1903, Oak Cliff was annexed to the city of Dallas. Dallas and Dallas County had actively campaigned to merge the cities since 1900, but the proposal had repeatedly been defeated at the polls by Oak Cliff voters. This spirit of independence was finally undermined by the town's growing financial troubles and in the spring of 1903, the annexation referendum passed by eighteen votes. The annexation question created a bitter division within Oak Cliff as well as between the town and the city of Dallas, from which it still suffers.

Oak Cliff again began to prosper after the annexation, its population more than doubling to 8,179 by 1910. This new growth was largely in the prosperous middle class, which brought badly needed professional services, such as banks and clinics, and new mercantile businesses which settled primarily along the streetcar line on Jefferson Street. The influx of people stimulated the westward growth of new housing developments and subdivisions.

Among the first of these was the Flanders Heights Addition, begun in 1884 by the architect James Flanders while Marsalis was still trying to buy the Hord farm. Flanders miscalculated, placing his development too far west (near the intersection of the Fort Worth Pike and Sylvan Avenue) and it foundered. The area was renamed Western Heights in 1901 and repromoted in 1902 just as the Dallas to Fort Worth Interurban was finished. This transport facilitated further expansion west and spawned new towns like Midway (now Arlington) in that still-primitive outback area. In 1903, one of the largest and most important of Oak Cliff's later developments, the Miller-Stemmons Addition, was opened, located west of Lake Cliff and bounded by Cedar Hill, Eighth, Colorado/Greenbriar and Zang boulevards. This was augmented in 1905 by Zang's Crystal Hill Addition (243) bounded by Beckley, Davis, Elsbeth, and Nueces streets. J. F. Zang,

244. ROSEMONT, 1910
Rosemont, the residence of Roman S. Waldron, was one of the first homes built in the Winnetka Heights section of Oak Cliff. Waldron, an independent real estate broker, constructed the home c. 1906 at the southwest corner of Rosemont and Davis streets. It was razed in 1957 to build an apartment complex. *Dallas Historical Society Archives*

the area's developer, wrote in the plat filed at the county archives, "I reserve the right to remove silica sands from Fifth Street between Elsbeth and Beckley;" sand which he believed would be valuable in the making of glass (though none was ever made) and for which he named his addition.

The last major subdivision of Oak Cliff was Winnetka Heights, platted in 1908 by Miller-Stemmons, and occupied very early by Roman S. Waldron, who built a large, Greek Revival-inspired home called Rosemont there about 1906 (244).

In line with Dallas' customary approach to the promotion of new subdivisions, Charles A. Mangold and J. F. Zang acquired the property around Lake Cliff and transformed it into the enormously popular Lake Cliff Amusement Park (245). The man-made lake had been created in the early 1890s by the Llewellyn Club and sold with the surrounding property in 1899 to Dr. Robert Spann, who converted the old Llewellyn clubhouse into Spann Park and Sanitarium. In 1906, Mangold and Zang purchased 50.3 acres of this property from Spann, built a floating pool and bath-house in the lake, and around the shore constructed carnival devices, dancing pavilions, a roller-skating rink, a bowling alley and a ride called shoot-the-shoots (similar to the present log ride at Six Flags in Arlington). Fireworks were set off over the water on holidays, and thousands of people assembled on Sunday afternoons to watch "balloon ascensions" and thrill at a man or woman descending by parachute, sometimes performing feats on an aerial trapeze as they floated down.[72] At one time, Lake Cliff had three theaters in operation. One featured light operas, and a second, smaller one showed a novelty item called motion pictures. The third, the Lake Cliff Casino, produced stock company plays including performances by the famed Orpheum Vaudeville Circuit featuring Al Jolson and Tom Moore. However, financial difficulties arose within a few years and in 1913, Lake Cliff Park was purchased by the city of Dallas for $55,000. By the early 1940s all of the buildings and amusements had been torn down to make way for residential construction, with the exception of the Llewellyn clubhouse, moved by Mangold in 1909 to 232 East Sixth Street, where it still stands.

Mangold, an entrepreneur of German descent who arrived in Dallas from Cincinnati in 1885, made his fortune selling whiskey through his wholesale firm of Swope and Mangold. He was zealously dedicated to the civic and cultural betterment of Dallas and Oak Cliff and organized or helped to found several projects, including the Dallas park system; the Grand Order of the Kaliphs, which staged a series of balls, festivals, and parades during the annual State Fair; the 1904 Saengerfest; and horse racing at the fairgrounds. Mangold was also the first to propose a high-level, all-weather viaduct between Dallas and Oak Cliff to prevent a repetition of the disaster which struck the city in 1908. The Trinity River flood of that year was the most destructive in history, severing Oak Cliff from Dallas for over a week. The swirling waters were knee-deep in downtown Dallas as far east as Akard Street and property damage in the millions was reported, including the destruction of the Forest Avenue Bridge and the T&P trestle. Construction of the Oak Cliff-Dallas Bridge (now known as the Houston Street Viaduct) was started in October, 1910, by the Kansas City architectural firm of Hedrick and Cochrane and completed in February, 1912. At that time, the structure, built by Dallas County at a cost of over $675,000, was the longest (5,840 feet) reinforced concrete bridge in the world.[73]

In the early 1920s, Oak Cliff began to experience a surge of new growth, not only in terms of population but also in commercial, industrial, and retail expansion. Two important residential developments were organized in the 1920s, the exclusive and very affluent Kessler Park Addition and its economic antithesis, the low-income area of Trinity Heights. In the 1930s and 1940s, Oak Cliff's pastoral beauty, combined with the post-World War II economic boom, contributed to the continuation of the area's prosperity; a prosperity which reached its peak in the late 1950s.

Prior to 1887, Hord's Ridge was satisfied to be a quiet farming community and to leave

the confusion of gathering industrial power and commercial wealth to the growing city across the river. After Marsalis began his promotion of the area, Oak Cliff had the potential to surpass Dallas as a very elite and desirable residential community. During this period, the river actually enhanced Oak Cliff's attractiveness by allowing the wealthy to maintain their class distinctions away from the turmoil and egalitarianism of Dallas. After the depression of 1893, Marsalis' vision of an exclusive suburban neighborhood of large, prestigious homes began to dissolve and the river became a barrier to progress.

Between 1900 and the 1970s, Oak Cliff experienced alternating periods of economic prosperity and depression, governed not only by national trends but also by many factors in Dallas' social, political, and economic fabric on which Oak Cliff was still dependent. Although the community's tie to Dallas remains very strong, Oak Cliff has largely retained the fierce independence instilled at its founding by Thomas Marsalis; it is the only fully incorporated Dallas suburb still regarded as a city within a city.

245. LAKE CLIFF, c. 1906 *(left)*
The Lake Cliff Amusement Park, opened in 1906 by Charles Mangold, was an oasis of pleasure during the hot, dry Texas summers. Its attractions included (from left to right) the Casino, a floating pool, the Skyride, the Lake Cliff Restaurant and Club, a movie theater, a dancing pavilion and an opera house (behind the trees to the right). *Dallas Historical Society Archives*

246. LAKE CLIFF, c. 1906
The Sullivanesque arched entry to Lake Cliff Amusement Park, through which the opera house can be seen. *Dallas Historical Society Archives*

247. BAGDAD, c. 1930

The Bagdad Supper Club was Dallas' ultrafashionable nightclub during its sporadic existence. Between 1929 and 1945, the club was open only intermittently as it passed through several bankruptcies and sales. Located ten miles west of Dallas at the intersection of U.S. 80 and Bagdad Street in Grand Prairie, the nightspot's glory days ended in 1952 when the building burned to the ground. *Dallas Historical Society Archives*

248. BAGDAD, c. 1930

Built in 1928, reputedly with Chicago money, the lavish Middle Eastern motif of the Bagdad Supper Club was highlighted by a $10,000 silk ceiling canopy imported from Istanbul.
Dallas Historical Society Archives

8 THE CITY AS CELEBRATION

Dallas' State Fair has historically been the city's single most important instrument in maintaining its position as the commercial and cultural center of North Texas. From its earliest days, when the tiny community first nurtured the collective hope that it might one day develop a commercial scope equal to St. Louis or Kansas City, controlling or influencing trade throughout the entire Southwest, the "Dallas Fair" — as it was invariably known to the thousands who migrated there every October from outlying farms and ranches — became the most popular (if not the most financially solvent) manifestation of this empire of trade. As the Fair grew from a neighborly little four-day frontier get-together into a nationwide exposition with a seasonal attendance in the millions, its function and purpose remained constant: to promote the city of Dallas.

County and local fairs in America have always basically served as expressions of boosterism. Dallas' city boosters — its real estate speculators, developers, merchants, and businessmen — realized the importance of the occasion in attracting people to settle in the community, or at least to come to town to trade. An expanding population benefited everyone and fairgoers could be expected to spend a great deal of money in the local hotels, boardinghouses, restaurants, livery stables, stores, saloons, and gambling halls. The Fair was the one enterprise in which the whole community stood to profit at least as greatly as any particular individual, and a civic and business philosophy of almost true benevolence and city pride coalesced around it, in which the competitive profit motivations usually associated with a few wealthy and influential businessmen were instead held in common by the entire community against the advancement of other area towns. The old rallying cry of "whatever is good for business is good for the city," which dominated the thinking behind much of Dallas' spatial growth and expansion was subordinated to a genuine public-spiritedness and sense of civic responsibility in the dealings of the Dallas Fair.

This spirit was exhibited many times over the Fair's history when seemingly imminent financial disaster was averted only through the outright philanthrophy or the dogged stubbornness of a handful of business leaders like W. H. Gaston and J. B. Wilson. In such crises these men devoted their time, energies, and money with no expectation of direct compensation, hoping only that the fair would survive, continue to draw visitors, and contribute to the economy of the city as a whole, thus insuring their personal enterprises a healthy environment in which to grow.

Aside from the obvious benefits to local business, another important aspect of the fair was its function as an instrument of social interaction. Like hundreds of other state and county fairs throughout the South and Midwest, the Dallas Fair served as the catalyst for not only the creation of new friendships and business contacts, but the reaffirmation of old ones as well. The tradition of exhibiting the products of home craftsmanship — quilts, canned fruits, artwork, hand-tooled leather goods, etc. — worked hand in hand with the organized display of horses, cattle, sheep, goats, swine, and poultry to create bonds of friendly rivalry with the important outlying areas of North Texas. This social aspect of the fair was very important in the dissemination of new ideas and products; it was the nineteenth-century equivalent of the modern museum or shopping center. The classic example of this principle occurred at the De Kalb County Fair of 1873 when Jacob Haish, Isaac Ellwood, and Joseph Glidden, out with their families at the fair for pleasure, companionship, and the usual interest in seeing goods on display, chanced upon a curious example of fencing made by a local farmer named Henry Rose. Rose's invention, "The Wooden Strip with Metallic Points," sparked the imagination of the three casual fairgoers into the manufacture of barbed wire, the device which revolutionized the face of the American West.

Dallas' first fair, held in 1859, was a competitive response to the small fairs held in the local towns of Marshall, Sherman, and Waxahachie in 1858. The Dallas County Agricultural and Mechanical Association, through its president, Amos McCommas, chose its site at what would become the intersection of the Texas & Pacific and the Houston & Texas Central railroad lines, where the East Dallas Union Depot would later be built. The first fair was a great success, filling the little town with a four-day attendance of over 2,000 visitors. The facilities were quite primitive and humble, but several immediate benefits were realized. First, the organizers did not lose money (which they fully expected to do), and the fact that they broke even financially on the first try probably was a powerful inducement for the promoters to sustain the fair in the face of terrific adversity in later years.

Secondly, the fair gave the agricultural machinery business in the city a tremendous boost, which served to make Dallas a leading center for implement distribution and sales and also to establish a pattern by which the fair continued to serve primarily as a showcase for the implement dealers and manufacturers. The fair's agrarian orientation, which today still characterizes a major portion of the grounds and activities, was reflected by the exhibits of plows, domestic manufactures, flour samples, needlework, quilts, shawls, and other handcrafts, and by the social activities such as the horsemanship trials, square dances, and buggy driving tournaments. Basically, the first fair gave the farmers and ranchers an excuse and a place to gather, to buy and sell cattle, to exchange new ideas and agricultural techniques, and to see and order newly patented farm machinery.[74]

Because the first fair was such a success, a second followed at the same site in 1860, drawing a five-day attendance of 10,700 — far beyond the expectations of even the most optimistic boosters. But the disruptions of the Civil War and the desolate days afterward forced a halt to succeeding fairs until 1868, when the Dallas County Agricultural and Mechanial Association tried to reinstate the fair as an annual event. Because of the generally depressed economy, both the 1868 and 1869 fairs lost money and the Association ceased its sponsorship.

Yet the city could not afford to lose its influential link with the distant farms and towns of North Texas which had begun to identify Dallas as the urban and economic center of the area, so in 1870 the North Texas Agricultural, Mechanical and Blood Stock Association incorporated, with Captain W. H. Gaston as its president, and made plans to hold a fair in 1871. That fair was postponed by Dallas' decision to donate the 1859 fairgrounds to the H&TC and T&P railroads for use as a depot site, but by 1872 Gaston had relocated the fair in East Dallas in a grove of trees just off Moon Lake (now the grounds of Baylor Hospital). The 1872 fair was a disappointment, drawing very few people. The move to the new grounds had rushed and disorganized preparations to such an extent that the major attractions were

249. STATE FAIR, c. 1886
The Dallas State Fair and Exposition Association, the forerunner of the modern State Fair of Texas, opened the first permanent Dallas fair in 1886 on the site of the present fairgrounds. This photograph illustrates the exposition's dominant concern—promoting the city's business interests. *Courtesy of the State Fair of Texas*

250. RACETRACK, 1898
The State Fair racetrack and grandstand, built in 1887, were removed only a few years later when the 1902 Texas Legislature dealt a death blow to public horse racing by outlawing track gambling. *Courtesy of Dallas Public Library*

JOS. W. MOON BUGGY

251. EXPOSITION BUILDINGS, 1895 *(facing page, above)*
The main Exposition Buildings at the fairgrounds, built in 1887, were designed by James Flanders in subdued imitation of the Philadelphia Centennial Exposition of 1876. The wooden structures burned completely in 1902. *Courtesy of Dallas Public Library*

252. CONFEDERATE REUNION, 1902 *(facing page, below)*
The Confederate Reunion of 1902 drew over 25,000 visitors to Dallas in April to witness the last major celebration of the memory of the Confederacy. Over 7,000 Southern veterans, many on crutches or carrying sabers and muskets, joined in uniformed parades, speeches, and tearful embraces between old comrades at arms. These survivors of Gettysburg, Shiloh, and the Wilderness Campaigns camped at the State Fairgrounds where this rare photograph was made. *Courtesy of Dallas Public Library*

253. ENTRANCE TO FAIR PARK, 1910 *(above)*
James Flanders' 1904 entrance gate housed the Administration Offices of the State Fair of Texas. *Dallas Historical Society Archives*

254. VIEW IN FAIR PARK, 1910
"Progress," a sculptured monument to the promise of the age of technology which disappeared mysteriously just before the 1936 Centennial. *Dallas Historical Society Archives*

limited to exhibits of corn and cotton samples, and Uncle Billy Miller's pedigree bull. Furthermore, the fair was overshadowed by the public barbecue and festivities held upon the arrival of the railroads only a few months earlier. The 1873 fair, despite elaborate improvements and preparations, was also a failure, due in large part to the financial panic of that year. The Dallas economy was not too severely affected, mainly because the crash interrupted construction of the T&P Railroad, making the city a temporary railroad terminus; but the depression numbed the rest of North Texas, leaving few products for exhibit at the fair or people prosperous enough to attend it. No fair was held in 1874 or 1875, in part because of the lingering effects of the panic, but also because Dallas did not really need the economic boost as a result of its sudden railroad prosperity.

By 1876, however, the T&P had reached Fort Worth, making that cowtown rival to the west the railhead, and Dallas' merchants revived the fair in an effort to sustain their dominance over the region.

The 1876 fair was extraordinary in that its entire focus was shifted away from agriculture to "the promotion of the industrial interests."[76] This was a direct result of the new transportation and distribution possibilities open to the manufacturers and industrialists after the arrival of the railroads in 1872 and 1873. The change in focus also precipitated several innovations in the fair's planning and production. With an eye toward national scope, the 1876 fair was scheduled to follow those in St. Louis and Kansas City so that Dallas could be included in the major exhibitors' circuit. Also, a track for horse racing was built, with barrooms and billiard halls underneath the grandstands. This carnival atmosphere was so successful, drawing 30,000 people in six days, that it inspired a repeat performance in 1877 which attracted several prominent northern businessmen to investigate the local opportunities for capital investment.[76]

For the next eight years Dallas' economy boomed, prompted by the opening of a number of profitable trade channels with St. Louis, Chicago and the Gulf ports through the new rail connections. Apparently, Dallas was doing so well that the merchants, bankers, and real estate speculators did not feel the need to spend time or money on a fair, and it was not until 1886 that the next one was held.

In that year, a split divided the monied interests that had traditionally backed the fair. Under the leadership of Captain W. H. Gaston, the Dallas State Fair and Exposition Association was chartered in January, 1886, and its officers decided to purchase the eighty-acre site in East Dallas where the present Fairgrounds are situated.[77] Gaston himself purchased the land for $16,000 and deeded it to the association in return for 140 shares of stock, all of which he later donated to the fair. A small group of wealthy farm implement dealers opposed the site and their spokesman, C. A. Keating, loudly protested that "the ground selected for the fair is the worst kind of hog wallow" and that the "black waxy" soil was unsuitable for the demonstration of their equipment. With the backing of the Farmers Alliance and the Knights of Labor, Keating obtained a section of John Cole's farm in North Dallas (now the site of the North Dallas High School). His group opened the Texas State Fair for six days on October 25, while the Dallas Exposition opened on October 26 and continued through November 6.

The rivalry between the fairs was essentially a struggle between the power brokers of the retail and banking business and the vested interests of the agricultural implement industry and the North Dallas Improvement Company. The directors of the Dallas Exposition — Gaston, Alex Sanger, Bartholomew Blankenship, T. L. Marsalis, W. J. Keller, and J. B. Simpson — either lived or had sizable business investments in South and East Dallas; the officers of the Texas State Fair — Keating, O. P. Bowser, F. M. Cockrell, A. J. Porter, and J. A. Hughes — were heavily involved in North Dallas real estate speculation or related ventures.

Amazingly, both of the 1886 fairs were marginally successful and drew between them almost 38,000 people a day. But it was readily apparent that the arrangement could not

255. GENERAL EXHIBITS BUILDINGS, 1910
After the 1887 wooden exhibition halls burned,
James Flanders used the same site in 1905-06 to
build the General Exhibits buildings. In 1936, the
stone entrance piers were removed and the General
Exhibits Buildings were incorporated into the Texas
Centennial as the Varied Industries Buildings. They
survive today on the north side of the reflecting pool
as the World Exhibits Buildings. *Dallas Historical
Society Archives*

256. A DAY AT THE FAIR, c. 1915 *(facing page, above)*
Dallas Historical Society Archives

257. COLISEUM, c. 1915 *(facing page, below)*
Facade of the State Fair of Texas Coliseum (left)
built in 1910 by James Flanders. The building was
later converted from an open auditorium into office
space and studios for Peter Wolf and Associates.
Dallas Historical Society Archives

258. COLISEUM INTERIOR, c. 1915
The 8,000-seat Coliseum was the focal center of
the early State Fair. It was the site of President
Woodrow Wilson's address to the city in 1911, of
the 1916 exhibition match by world heavyweight
champion Jess Willard, and saw one of the first
American appearances of General Alvaro Obregon,
President-elect of Mexico, in 1920. *Dallas Historical
Society Archives*

continue and a compromise was effected. Both charters were canceled and a new company was organized, consolidating the old names to form the Texas State Fair and Dallas Exposition, and settling upon the East Dallas site as its fairground.

Improvements were begun immediately in anticipation of the 1887 fair and within months, after an expenditure of over $100,000, the "hog-wallow" site was transformed into a beautiful, landscaped park with drives and shaded walks. Thirty-eight additional acres were purchased, a race track was built at a cost of over $10,000 (250), several small machinery halls were erected, an artesian well was drilled, and James Flanders was hired to design and build the Exposition Buildings (251). The largest, a mammoth, five-story hall was built entirely of wood and was structurally supported by dozens of half-circle, 750-foot clear-span arches. Flanders spent almost $25,000 on the Exhibition Hall and later noted with wry smugness that, "such an apparition on the bald prairie attracted crowds of the curious from far and near."[78]

This united association finally succeeded in organizing a stable fair which managed to present some kind of public exhibition on an annual basis, but for the next seventeen years the fair wavered between financial gain and seasonal calamity. Lean years followed good ones, debts piled up, and the directors constantly faced a myriad of crises from which evolved a recurring ritual of fund raising.

In 1890, the newly constructed livestock building caught fire and had to be replaced. As it neared completion in 1892, the racing stables burned to the ground on the only rainless day of the season (the roads were all but impassible the other eleven). In order to keep the fair afloat, President Jules Schneider contracted with the Manchester Trust Company of England to assume the notes. The fair of 1893 showed a small profit but more miraculously, the fair of 1894, staged in the face of the worst depression in the country's history, proved to be one of the biggest and most profitable ever. About 1897, the fair was once again in its customary financial difficulty and Captain Gaston negotiated an issuance of bonds from the Holland Trust Company of New York to relieve the fair's indebtedness. Two years later, the Manchester Trust Company's $72,000 bonds were called due and ruination was averted only when J. B. Wilson bought the bonds and rechartered the organization under the name of the Texas State Fair.

W. H. Gaston assumed the presidency that year and guided the fair through several successful seasons, marred only by $150,000 in damage suits filed when the grandstands collapsed during a performance by the Chicago Fire Company.

The Fair appeared to be headed for oblivion in 1902 when the Exposition Buildings burned and the Texas Legislature destroyed horse racing by outlawing track gambling, the Fair's primary source of revenue. A group of speculators offered the directors $125,000 for the Fairgrounds with the idea of turning it into a residential subdivision, but the Fair's directors refused to admit defeat and struck a bargain with the city in 1904. In exchange for the money to pay off its outstanding debt, they deeded the Fairgrounds to the city as a park, with the understanding that the State

259. THE PIKE, 1908
On Coney Island in 1884, La Marcus Adna Thompson revolutionized the outdoor carnival with the installation of the world's first rollercoaster, "The Switchback Railway." At Chicago's Columbian Exposition of 1893, the concept of a centralized "midway" was created when George W. Ferris introduced his engineering marvel, the "Ferris Wheel." But the State Fair of Texas steadfastly refused to stoop to the level of installing carnival devices until the popularity of the amusement area known as "The Pike" at the Louisiana Purchase Exposition of 1904 convinced the Texas Fair's directors that such an area would be highly profitable. In 1905, Dallas installed its first amusement row, also called "The Pike," with rides such as a double track "Tickler" rollercoaster (background) and a water slide called "Shoot the Chutes" (foreground), both of which had been developed at Coney Island in the 1890s. The Pike, originally located near the front gate where the Music Hall now stands, was dismantled and moved to the present Midway site before the 1936 Centennial. *Dallas Historical Society Archives*

260. FAIR PARK MIDWAY, c. 1915
Courtesy of Texas State Historical Association

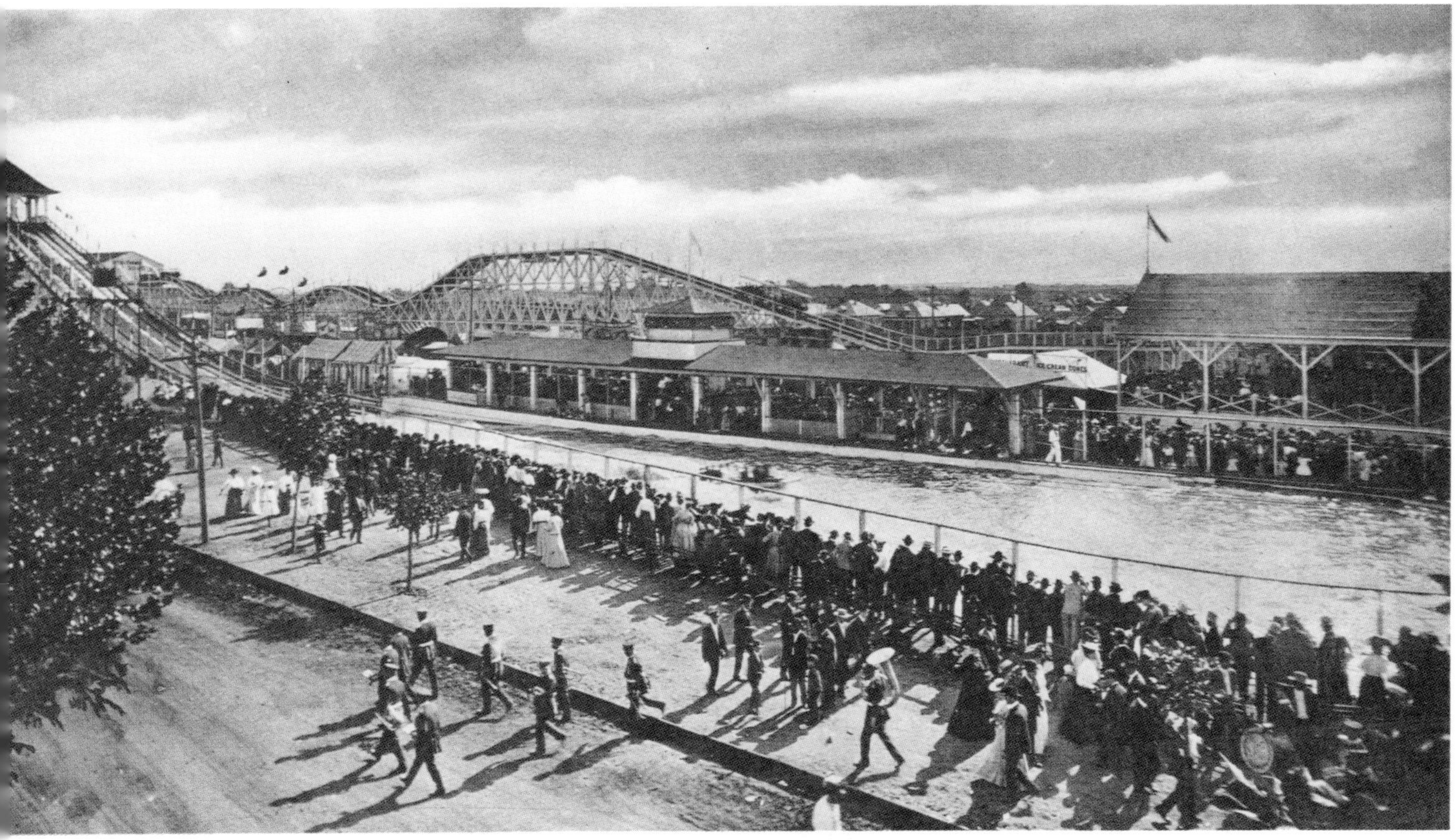

SCENIC RAILWAY SCENIC TUNNEL
AMUSEMENT ROW,
FAIR PARK.

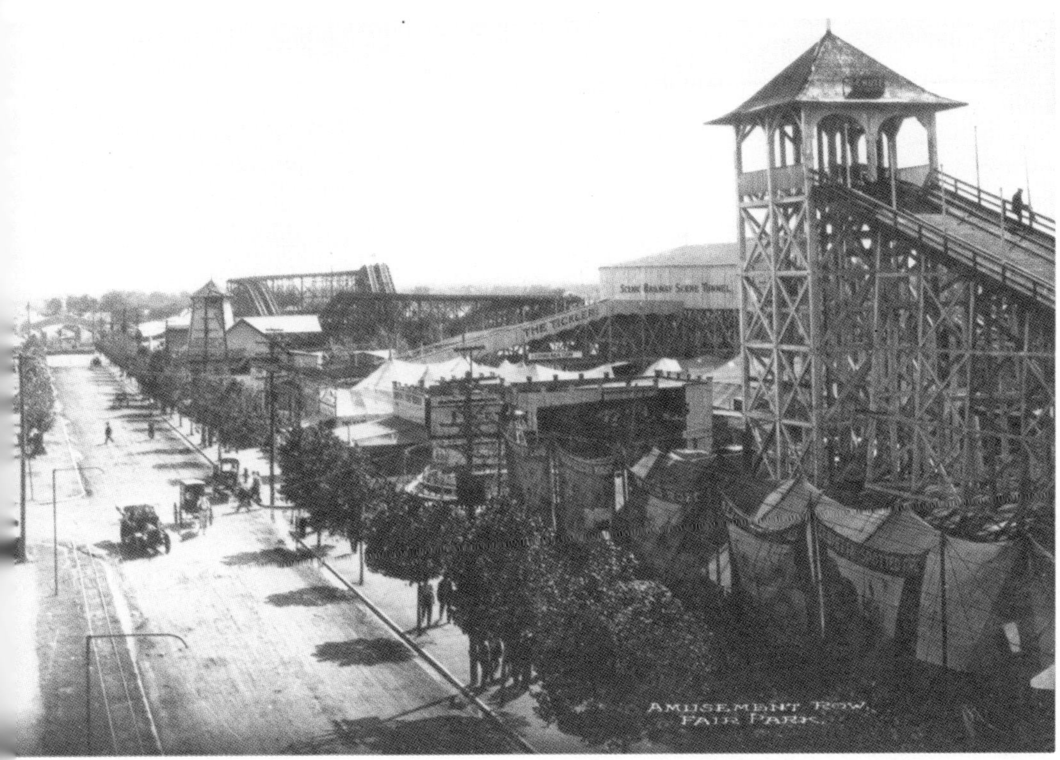

261. **TEXTILE AND FINE ARTS BUILDING**, c. 1910
The Textile and Fine Arts Building served for many years as the permanent museum of the Dallas Art Association. Designed in 1908 by the architectural firm of Hubbell and Greene in the manner of the mercantile classicism of Chicago's "White City" Columbian Exposition of 1893, the Art Building specifically duplicated the central crystal dome and flanking twin domed pavilions of William LeBaron Jenney's Horticulture Hall. After a hailstorm in 1928 demolished the dome's glass and destroyed parts of the collection, the building was converted into a service facility and finally leveled in 1956. *Dallas Historical Society Archives*

Fair board would run the annual exhibition and allow the city a percentage.

That year, the city incorporated the grounds and hired George Kessler to replan and landscape the park. J. E. Flanders was again retained to build a new entrance gate and Administration Building (254), and the horse track was converted into a banked automobile racing track on which Barney Oldfield drove to victory before a roaring crowd in 1905.

With the city now underwriting the venture, many improvements were made in the Fair's facilities. In 1906, Flanders finished the General Exhibits Buildings (255) along Kessler's tree-lined Esplanade. These exhibition halls, along with the Coliseum which Flanders finished in 1910 (257), were stuccoed over, revamped, and incorporated into the Texas Centennial Exposition in 1936. In 1908, Dallas' first, full-time public museum, the Textile and Fine Arts Building (261), was built at the Fairgrounds next to the Coliseum.

The surge of civic interest in the Fairgrounds grew steadily and the construction of new buildings was continued by many diverse organizations, climaxing in a frenzy of activity for the 1936 Texas Centennial.

In 1909, The Dallas *News* erected a scale replica of the Alamo in the extreme southeast corner of the park and in 1922 a huge Automobile and Machinery Hall was built on the south side of the reflecting pool at a cost of $28,000. The last major, non-Centennial-inspired construction projects included the Cotton Bowl in 1930, a livestock pavilion, and the cavernous Auditorium built by Lang and Witchell in 1925 (262), which served in 1936 as the General Motors Pavilion (263).

Dallas' presentation of the 1936 Texas Centennial Exposition was yet another example of the city's outstanding leadership during a time of crisis and despair. The whole country was deep in the grasp of a crushing depression and Dallas desperately needed an economic boost. Led by the bull-headed persistence and expert salesmanship of R. L. Thornton, Sr., Dallas outbid San Antonio, Austin, and Houston — cities with much greater claims to the bulk of Texas history — as prospective sites for this world's fair by offering the State Centennial Committee more front money, more land, and more civic support for the celebration. The Fair's $25 million cost was a vital business stimulus and roused the city into an economic ferver.

The Texas Centennial was not only a celebration of Texas Independence, but also of Western culture in the same manner and spirit as Paris' Exposition Universelle of 1889 which saw the erection of Gustave Eiffel's 1,000-foot tower, St. Louis' Louisiana Purchase Exposition of 1904, and Chicago's Century of Progress in 1933 where the then-new International style of architecture was displayed. Traditionally, world's fairs are the testing grounds for new ideas in design, but Dallas had little interest in architectural innovation and was satisfied to simply reflect the style which had originated at the Exposition des Arts Décoratifs in Paris in 1925.

The Fairgrounds were expanded to 180 acres for the occasion and most of the structures which compose the present park were built under the direction of George L. Dahl and Paul Cret, a consulting architect from Philadelphia. The Art Deco motif of the Texas Centennial buildings was characteristically modern in its disposition of large, unadorned and unbroken masses, geometric crispness, and bold color. In many ways it was a fortunate choice of styles, aesthetically pleasing in the contrast of its stark, planar monumentality against the expansive flatness of the North Texas plain and the unrelieved brilliance of the Southwestern sun. It also seemingly embodied the particular "consciousness" of Dallas at that time, thrusting itself forcefully and creatively into public focus; it succeeded admirably in its objective of elevating Dallas' traditional boosterism to a world stage.

262. AUDITORIUM, c. 1925
"Dedicated to the Good, the True and the Beautiful," Lang and Witchell's graceful Spanish Colonial Revival Auditorium functionally replaced the Coliseum when completed in 1925. *Dallas Historical Society Archives*

263. TEXAS CENTENNIAL, 1936
The Auditorium housed the General Motors exhibit during the 1936 Centennial and the 1937 Pan American Exposition, and now serves as the State Fair Music Hall. *Dallas Historical Society Archives*

NOTES

Introductory Essay

1. *Handbook of Texas,* Vol. I "Caddo Indians"

2. Rex Strickland, "Moscoso's Journey Through Texas," *Southwestern Historical Quarterly,* XLVI (1942-43)

3. *Handbook of Texas,* Vol I, ibid.

4. Carlos E. Castaneda, *Our Catholic Heritage,* I

5. Noel M. Loomis and Abraham P. Nasatir, *Pedro Vial and the Road to Santa Fe,* 38-39 (citing Herbert E. Bolton, *Athanase de Mezieres,* I, 30-31.)

6. Ibid, 36

7. Ibid, 37 (citing Le Page du Pratz, *Histoire de la Louisiane,* II, 273-78.)

8. Herbert E. Bolton, *Texas in the Middle Eighteenth Century,* Berkeley (1915).

9. *Who's Who in American History,* Historical Volume 1607-1896 (1967)

10. Justin F. Kimball, *Our City-Dallas,* 2-3, Dallas (1927).

11. Seymour V. Connor, *The Peters Colony of Texas,* 22-23, 53, 164 (Austin, 1954).

Chapter 1

1. John Henry Brown, *History of Dallas County, Texas: From 1837 to 1887* (Dallas: Milligan, Cornett and Farnham, Printers, 1887), pp. 13-14.

2. From the transcription of the Billingsley family papers: "From Missouri to Texas," transcribed from the original diary by the Dallas Historical Society, January, 1936.

3. Herbert Gambrell, "Dallas, Texas," *The Handbook of Texas,* ed. Walter Prescott Webb (Austin: Texas State Historical Association, 1952), 1:456.

4. William J. and Margaret F. Hammond, *La Reunion, A French Settlement in Texas* (Dallas: Royal Publishing Co., 1958), p. 101.

5. *Ibid.*

6. Jim Atkinson, "The Caruth Saga," *D Magazine* (September, 1975), p. 81.

7. A.C. Greene, *Dallas: The Deciding Years* (Austin: Encino Press, 1973), p. 16.

8. John William Rogers, *The Lusty Texans of Dallas* (New York: E.P. Dutton and Co., 1951), p. 91.

9. *The Texas Almanac for 1873* (Galveston: W&D Richardson and Co., 1873), p. 60.

10. From the personal letters of Henry C. Coit, Dallas Historical Society Archives (A3577), Dallas, Texas.

Chapter 2

11. Philip Lindsley, *A History of Greater Dallas and Vicinity* (Chicago: Lewis Publishing Co., 1909), 1:73.

12. John Stricklin Spratt, *The Road to Spindletop* (Austin: University of Texas Press, 1970), p. 256.

13. L. Tuffly Ellis, "The Revolutionizing of the Texas Cotton Trade, 1865-1885," *The Southwestern Historical Quarterly* 73 (April, 1970):478.

14. *Ibid.,* p. 503.

15. *Ibid.,* p. 487.

16. *Ibid.,* pp. 507-8.

17. Greene, *Deciding Years,* p. 18.

18. Rogers, *Lusty Texans,* p. 143.

19. *History 1850—July 4, 1976* (Dallas: Northpark United Presbyterian Church, 1976), p. 11.

20. Gambrell, *Handbook of Texas,* p. 461.

21. W.S. Adair, "Interview with James E. Flanders," *Dallas Morning News,* (November 15, 1925).

22. *Morrison and Fourmy's General Directory of the City of Dallas, 1891-92* (Galveston: Morrison and Fourmy, Publishers, 1891), p. 2.

23. *Directory of the City of Dallas for the Year 1875* (arranged and prepared by F.E. Butterfield and P.M. Rundlett), pp. 48-50.

24. Lawrence Goodwyn, *Democratic Promise, The Populist Movement in America* (New York: Oxford University Press, 1976), p. 18.

25. *Fourth Annual Report of the Railroad Commission of Texas* (Austin: Railroad Commission of Texas, 1895), p. 18.

26. Goodwyn, *Democratic Promise*, p. 75.

27. *Ibid.*, p. 547.

28. William Faulkner, *Absalom, Absalom!* (New York: Random House, 1936), p. 9.

Chapter 3

29. William Faulkner, "The Courthouse (A Name for the City)," *The Portable Faulkner*, ed. Malcolm Cowley (New York: Viking Press, 1967), p. 22.

30. *Railroad Commission Report for 1895*, p. 19.

31. "Murphy and Bolanz' Official Map of Dallas and Suburbs, 1891," Dallas Historical Society Archives (A3951), Dallas, Texas.

32. Thomas E. Tallmadge, *Architecture in Old Chicago* (Chicago: University of Chicago Press, 1975), p. 74.

33. Louis H. Sullivan, "The Tall Office Building Artistically Considered," *Kindergarten Chats*, ed. Isabella Athey (New York: Wittenborn, Schultz, Inc., 1947), p. 213.

34. Otto C. Lightner, *The History of Business Depressions* (New York: B. Franklin, 1970), pp. 186-93.

35. Gambrell, *Handbook of Texas*, p. 457.

36. Ben M. Barrows, *A People Called Cumberland Presbyterians* (Memphis: Frontier Press, 1972), p. 87.

37. *History 1850—July 4, 1876*, pp. 8-9.

38. Alfred D. Chandler, Jr. and Stephen Salsbury, *Pierre S. du Pont and the Making of The Modern Corporation* (New York: Harper and Row, 1971), p. 41.

39. Research notes, Sam Acheson papers (original source unidentified), Dallas Historical Society Archives, Dallas, Texas.

40. Marcus Whiffen, *American Architecture Since 1780* (Cambridge: MIT Press, 1969), p. 167.

41. "Dallas Architecture," *The Western Architect*, 20 (July, 1914):81.

Chapter 4

42. *Dallas City Directory, 1873*, p. 9.

43 Autobiographical letter of Alfred H. Benners, "My Life in Dallas, Texas—1875 to 1885," Dallas Historical Society Archives (A3891), Dallas, Texas.

44. Charles Burmeister papers, 1877, Barker Texas History Center, University of Texas Archives, Austin, Texas.

45. Edward Eakins' firm, called Crutcher Brothers and Eakins Real Estate and Land Agents, was responsible for subdividing and promoting much of the property between Pocahontas Street and Mill Creek along South Harwood Street, a middle class area known as Eakins Addition, as well as the blue collar Santa Fe Addition about 1900 which was located east of Ervay Street, south of the Santa Fe tracks, north of Grand Avenue, and west of Latimer Street.

46. Whiffen, *American Architecture*, p. 124.

47. Harry Jebsen, Jr., Robert M. Newton, and Patricia R. Hogan, "Centennial History of Parks" (unpublished report for Dallas Park Board, prepared by the Department of Park Administration, Landscape Architecture and Horticulture, and the Department of History, Texas Tech University, Lubbock, Texas), p. 13.

Chapter 5

48. Born in 1840 and raised to farm life, Gaston left home in 1861 to enlist in the Confederate Army. He served in General J.B. Hood's Texas Brigade as the "Boy Captain"—commanding officer of Company H at age 21—and distinguished himself in some of the bloodiest fighting of the Civil War: at Eltham's Landing, the Seven Days' Siege of Richmond, the Second Battle of Bull Run, and the Battle of Sharpsburg.

49. Cole Younger, who gained some notoriety as one of Quantrill's Raiders in Missouri before the Civil War and as an outlaw afterwards, spent part of 1874 hiding out in Texas, raising (or rustling) cattle on a small ranch near the town of Scyene (now Mesquite). During this period, two years before his capture in the Northfield, Minnesota Bank robbery, Younger was courting Belle Starr (who was also living in Scyene with her mother) and utilizing this East Dallas pastureland for his herds before shipping them to Kansas City out of Dallas' railhead.

50. Judge William Clark's grandfather had been president of the first constitutional convention of Kentucky in 1792 and was later the first United States Judge for that state. His father was circuit judge for the state of Mississippi and a colonel in the 46th Mississippi Regiment of the Army of the Confederacy when he was killed on the battlefield at Altoona, Georgia in 1864. A graduate of the Cumberland University School of Law at Lebanon, Tennessee, William Clark immigrated in 1885 to Dallas, where he established the firm of Clark and Clark and was elected the youngest president of the Texas Bar in 1897. His son, Tom Clark was born in the house on Ross Avenue in 1899, became Attorney General of the United States in 1945, and was sworn in as Associate Justice of the Supreme

246

Court in 1949. Justice Clark resigned from the bench when his son Ramsey was appointed Attorney General by Lyndon Johnson in 1967.

51. "Dallas Social Affairs," *Dallas Morning News* (1914 clipping), Dallas Historical Society Archives, Dallas, Texas.

52. "Murphy and Bolanz' Map of Dallas," 1891.

53. Ted Dealey, *Diaper Days of Dallas* (Nashville: Abingdon Press, 1966), p. 84.

54. Powhatan W. James, *Fifty Years of Baylor University Hospital* (Dallas: Baylor University, 1953), p. 34.

55. "Munger Place" (promotional booklet printed for use by C. H. and Robert Munger), Dallas Historical Society Archives, Dallas, Texas, p. 1.

56. *Ibid.*, p. 4.

Chapter 6

57. Dallas County Deed Records, Volume BB, p. 152.

58. Melvin J. Banks, *A Century of Faith* (Dallas: New Hope Baptist Church, 1973), p. 11.

59. Ralph W. Widener, Jr., *William Henry Gaston: A Builder of Dallas* (Dallas: Historical Publishing Co., 1971), p. 8.

60. Lindsley, *Greater Dallas*, p. 189.

61. Whiffin, *American Architecture*, p. 120.

62. A check of S. G. Reed's *A History of the Texas Railroads* does not list the Sunset & Southern Pacific, the Houston & Central Arkansas or the Houston Central & Northern Railroads as ever having been chartered or built. The list came from the biography of George Dilley in the 1892 *Memorial and Biographical History of Dallas County,* which was most likely written by Dilley himself. The discrepancy probably lies in the fact that these specific lines were only sections of much larger railroad companies and Dilley gave them his own peculiar designations, the usage of which was later abandoned.

63. Sam Acheson, "Dallas Yesterday: Philadelphia and Turtle Creek," *Dallas Morning News* (November 6, 1967).

64. *Ibid.*

65. From the George Kessler papers, Missouri Historical Society, St. Louis, Missouri.

Chapter 7

66. Jebson, Newton and Hogan, *Centennial History of Parks,* pp. 263-66.

67. *Memorial and Biographical History of Dallas County, Texas* (Chicago: Lewis Publishing Co., 1892; reprinted, Walsworth Publishing Co., 1976), p. 148.

68. "Dallas Guide and History" (an unpublished manuscript prepared for the American Guide Series; written and compiled by the Dallas Unit of the Texas Writers' Project of the Work Progress Administration, 1940) p. 10. Texas History Collection, Dallas Public Library.

69. Jay Henry and Jack Luby "From Status to Stasis, An Historical Examination of Oak Cliff, 1887-1975" (graduate project, School of Architecture and Environmental Design, University of Texas at Arlington, 1975), p. 20.

70. *Catalogue of the Oak Cliff College for Young Ladies* (Battle Creek: Ellis Publishing Co., 1893), Dallas Historical Society Archives, Dallas, Texas.

71. Henry and Luby, "Status to Stasis," p. 21.

72. Rogers, *Lusty Texans,* p. 209.

73. Don Dreesen, "History of Oak Cliff," *Dispatch Journal* (March 6-June 22, 1939).

Chapter 8

74. Jebson, Newton and Hogan, *Centennial History of Parks,* p. 134.

75. *Ibid.*, p. 140.

76. *Ibid.*, p. 141.

77. There is some dissension among Dallas historians as to the exact site of the 1886 Dallas State Fair and Exposition. Sam Acheson, on page 239 of *Dallas Yesterday,* states that "some forty acres in the then separate town of East Dallas, near where Main Street reached the Texas & Pacific tracks, were selected as its site;" Frank M. Cockrell, in his privately printed *History of Early Dallas,* indicates on page 94 that the 1886 Fair was merely a reorganization of the Fair Association of 1872 which "continued to be held in the same location in East Dallas" (meaning the present Baylor Hospital grounds). However, J. T. Trezevant, who was for many years a director of the State Fair and served in 1896 as its president, wrote on page 4 of his *A History of the State Fair of Texas 1886-1904,* that "after weeks of inspection the directors finally decided the best location was the back portion of the present Fair Grounds, on 80 acres owned by several people." Mr. Trezevant's version is, in the opinion of this writer, probably the most accurate.

78. W. S. Adair, Dallas *News* (November 15, 1925).

BIBLIOGRAPHY

In the search for information about Dallas, a great many sources were utilized including not only archival documents, manuscripts, pamphlets, and maps, but also personal interviews. This bibliography is not intended, however, to include either general architectural references or to be an exhaustive list of all of the holdings in the various depositories in Dallas and other cities, but rather only a list of Dallas-related materials used directly by the author.

PRIMARY SOURCES AND RARE BOOKS

(A) City of Dallas, Department of Public Works: Foley, Ray. *Flood Control and Reclamation Project Study.* City and County of Dallas Levee Improvement District Board of Supervisors, 1931.
(B) Dallas County Records Office: Deed Records for the County of Dallas.
(C) Dallas Historical Society Archives, Dallas:

Diaries, Letters, and Journals

Sam Acheson Papers. (unaccessioned).

Letters of Alfred H. Benners. "My Life in Dallas, Texas—1875 to 1885." (A3891).

Billingsley Family Papers. "From Missouri to Texas." (A3637). Transcribed from the original diary by the Dallas Historical Society, 1936.

Personal letters of Henry C. Coit. (A3577).

George Bannerman Dealey Collection. (A6667).

Papers of C. B. Gillespie. (A3537).

Mackay Diaries, 1874-79. (A342).

McCoy Family Papers. (A1082).

Journal of Edward Parkinson, 1843. (A4243).

Maps

Bird's-eye View of the City of Dallas, Texas by H. Brosius, 1872. (A3347).

Dallas Railway Company's Key and Guide to Dallas, 1925. (A1043 OS).

Gillespie and Cullum's Map of Oak Lawn, c. 1895. (A3537 OS).

Gollner's Map of the City of Dallas, Texas, 1876. (unaccessioned).

John G. Worley & Company's City Directory Map of Dallas, Texas, 1903. (A40178 OS).

Jones and Murphy's Map of the City of Dallas, 1882. (A6661 OS).

Koch and Fowler's Streetmap of Dallas, 1915. (A44134 OS).

Map of La Reunion, 1858. (A3748 OS).

Map of Oak Cliff, 1889. (A347).

Murphy and Bolanz' Official Map of the City of Dallas, 1887. (A4462).

Murphy and Bolanz' Official Map of the City of Dallas, 1891. (A3951 OS).

Myers and Noyes Business District of Dallas, 1926. (A6081 OS).

Webster and Wood's Caruth Addition, c. 1890. (A5386).

Books, Pamphlets, and Reports

Art Works of Dallas. Chicago: The Gravure Ilustration Co., 1910.

Church, Clifton. *Dallas, Texas Through a Camera.* Chicago: Henry O. Shepard Co., 1898.

The City of Dallas and the State of Texas. St. Louis: George W. Englehardt & Co., 1890.

Cockrell, Frank M. *History of Early Dallas.* Chicago, 1944.

Cockrell, Monroe F. *Sarah Horton Cockrell in Early Dallas.* Evanston, Illinois, 1961.

Dallas, Where Men Are Looking Forward. Dallas: Chamber of Commerce and Manufacturers Association, 1919.

Directory of the City of Dallas for the Year 1875. St. Louis: F. E. Butterfield and P. M. Rundlett, 1875.

Dreesen, Don. *A History of Oak Cliff*. Reprint of a series of articles originally published in the Oak Cliff *Dispatch Journal* (March 6-June 22, 1939).

Greater Dallas Illustrated. The American Illustrating Co., 1908.

Harris, Henry Camp, Sr. *Dallas: Acorn Planters of Yesteryear 1867-1924*. Dallas: Dallas History Books, 1924.

Kessler, George E. *A City Plan for Dallas: Report of Park Board*. Dallas, 1911.

Lawson and Edmondson's Dallas City Directory. 1873-74. Springfield, Mo.: 1873.

Morrison and Fourmy's General Directory of the City of Dallas. 1880-1896. Galveston: Morrison and Fourmy, Publishers.

Morrison, Andrew. *The Industries of Dallas*. St. Louis: Metropolitan Publishing Co., 1887.

Munger Place. Dallas. (A promotional booklet printed by C. H. and Robert Munger), c. 1910.

The Natural Resources and Economic Conditions of the State of Texas. The Merchants Exchange of New York, 1901.

1905 Dallas As It Is. Dallas: Samuel Jones Printing Co., 1905.

Polk's Greater Dallas City Directory. 1959-1978. Dallas: R. L. Polk & Co.

Texas Almanac for 1873. Galveston: W&D Richardson and Co., 1873.

Trezevant, J. T. *A History of the State Fair of Texas, 1886-1904*. Dallas, 1904.

Worley's Directory of the City of Dallas. 1897-1958. Dallas: John F. Worley & Co.

Newspapers

Dallas *Daily Times Herald*.

Dallas *Herald*.

Dallas *Mercury*.

Dallas *Morning News*.

(D) Dallas Public Library Archives, Dallas:

Manuscripts and Pamplets

Art Work of Dallas. Chicago: The Gravure Illustration Co., 1895 and 1925.

Dallas Democrat, Illustrated Annual, Dallas, Texas, 1901 and 1902.

Mangold and Allied Families. New York: privately printed by the American Historical Society, 1937.

Souvenir of Dallas. Columbus, Ohio: Ward Brothers, 1888.
United States Census for the City of Dallas, 1880, 1890, 1900.
United States Census for the County of Dallas, 1850, 1860.

Weichsel, Christian. *Dallas*. 1908.

(E) Missouri Historical Society Archives, St. Louis:

George E. Kessler Papers (not numbered).

(F) University of Texas Archives, Austin:

Papers of Charles Burmeister, 1877. Collection 340.

SECONDARY SOURCES

Acheson, Sam. *Dallas Yesterday*. Edited by Lee Milazzo. Dallas: Southern Methodist University Press, 1977.

__________ . *35,000 Days in Texas: A History of the Dallas News and its Forbears*. New York: The MacMillan Co., 1938.

Adams, Nathan. *The First National in Dallas*. Dallas: First National Bank, 1942.

Alexander, Drury Blakely. *Texas Homes of the Nineteenth Century*. Austin: University of Texas Press, 1966.

Atkinson, Jim. "The Caruth Saga." *D Magazine*, September 1975, p. 81.

Banks, Melvin J. *A Century of Faith, 1873-1973*. Dallas: New Hope Baptist Church, 1973.

Barnstone, Howard. *The Galveston That Was*. New York: The MacMillan Co., 1966.

Barr, Alwyn. *Black Texans: A History of Negroes in Texas 1828-1971*. Austin: Jenkins Publishing Co., 1973.

Blanton, Burt C. *400,000 Miles by Rail*. Berkeley: Howell-North Books, 1972.

Box, John Harold, Wiley, James, and Pratt, James Reece. *The Prairie's Yield*. New York: Reinhold, 1962.

Brown, John Henry. *History of Dallas County, Texas: From 1837 to 1887*. Dallas: Milligan, Cornett & Farnham, Printers, 1887.

Centennial History of St. Matthew's Cathedral. Dallas: The Episcopal Diocese of Dallas, 1975.

Chandler, Alfred D., Jr., and Salsbury, Stephen. *Pierre S. duPont and the Making of the Modern Corporation*. New York: Harper and Row, 1971.

City of Dallas: Its Growth and Resources (Souvenir Edition). Dallas: *Daily Times Herald*, 1892.

Cochran, John H. *Dallas County: A Record of Its Pioneers and Progress*. Dallas: Arthur S. Mathis Service Publishing Co., 1928.

Congregation Shearith Israel Diamond Anniversary 1884-1959. Dallas: Congregation Shearith Israel, 1959.

Connor, Seymour V. *The Peters Colony of Texas: A History and Biographical Sketches of the Early Settlers*. Austin: The Texas State Historical Association, 1959.

"Dallas Architecture." *The Western Architect* 20 (1914):81.

"The Dallas Story." Dallas *Times Herald* 73 (August 28, 1949):218.

Davis, Ellis A. and Grobe, Edwin H., eds. *The Encyclopedia of Texas*. Dallas: Texas Development Bureau, 1924.

Dealey, Ted. *Diaper Days of Dallas*. New York: Abingdon Press, 1955.

Ellis, Tuffly. "The Revolutionizing of the Texas Cotton Trade, 1865-1885." *Southwestern Historical Quarterly* 73 (1970):478.

1863-1963: The First Hundred Years. Dallas: Central Christian Church, 1963.

Foscue, Edwin J. "Transportation Adjustments to Topography in Dallas, Texas." *Field and Laboratory* 4 (1936):60.

Goodwyn, Lawrence. *Democratic Promise, the Populist Moment in America*. New York: Oxford University Press, 1976.

Graff, H. J.; Barton, C.; and Baron, A. R. *Dallas, Texas: A Bibliographical Guide to the Sources of Its Social History to 1930*. Dallas: The University of Texas at Dallas, 1977.

Greene, A. C. *A Place Called Dallas*. Dallas: Dallas County Heritage Society, 1975.

__________. *Dallas: The Deciding Years—A Historical Portrait*. Austin: Encino Press, 1973.

Grove, Larry. *Dallas Public Library: The First 75 Years*. Dallas: Dallas Public Library, 1977.

Hammond, William J. and Hammond, Margaret F. *La Reunion, A French Settlement in Texas*. Dallas: Royal Publishing Co., 1958.

Hilton, George *The Cable Car in America*. Berkeley: Howell-North Books, 1971.

Jackson, George *Sixty Years in Texas*. 2d ed. Dallas: Wilkinson Printing Co., 1908.

James, Powhatan W. *Fifty Years of Baylor University Hospital*. Dallas: Baylor University Hospital, 1953.

Kimball, Justin G. *Our City—Dallas*. Dallas: Kessler Plan Association of Dallas, 1927.

Lindsley, Philip. *A History of Greater Dallas and Vicinity*. Vols. 1 and 2. Chicago: The Lewis Publishing Co., 1909.

Makers of Dallas. Dallas: Dallas Newspaper Artists Association, 1912.

McBeth, Leon. *The First Baptist Church of Dallas: Centennial History 1868-1968*. Grand Rapids: Zondervan Publishing House, 1968.

Memorial and Biographical History of Dallas County, Texas. Chicago: The Lewis Publishing Co., 1892.

Northpark United Presbyterian Church, History 1850-July 4, 1976. Dallas: 1976.

Oak Lawn: 1880-1976, An Historical Study. Arlington, Texas: University of Texas, 1976.

Potts, Charles S. "Railroad Transportation in Texas." *Bulletin of the University of Texas* 7 (1909).

Railroad Commission of Texas. *Annual Report* Vols. 1-8. Austin: Railroad Commission of Texas, 1891-1899.

Reed, S. G. *A History of the Texas Railroads*. Houston: St. Clair Publishing Co., 1941.

Rifkind, Carole. *Main Street: The Face of Urban America*. New York: Harper and Row, 1977.

Rogers, John William. *The Lusty Texans of Dallas*. New York: E. P. Dutton and Co., 1951.

Santerre, George Henry. *Dallas First Hundred Years 1856-1956*. Dallas: Book Craft, 1956.

__________. *White Cliffs of Dallas: The Story of La Reunion The Old French Colony*. Dallas: The Book Craft, 1955.

Schiebel, Walter J. E. *Education in Dallas: Ninety-two Years of History 1874-1966*. Dallas: Dallas Independent School District, 1966.

Spratt, John S. *The Road to Spindletop: Economic Change in Texas, 1875-1901*. Austin: University of Texas Press, 1955.

Texas: *A Guide to the Lone Star State*. American Guide Series. New York: Hastings House, 1940.

Wallis, George A. *Cattle Kings of the Staked Plains*. Dallas: American Guild Press, 1957.

Webb, Walter P., ed. *The Handbook of Texas*. Vols. 1-3. Austin: The Texas State Historical Association, 1952.

Werry, Adolphus. *History of the First Methodist Church, Dallas, Texas 1846-1946*.

Widener, Ralph W., Jr. *William Henry Gaston: A Builder of Dallas*. Dallas: Historical Publishing Co., 1977.

Williams, J. W. "The National Road of the Republic of Texas." *Southwestern Historical Quarterly* 48 (1944):207.

Yoakum, H. (Esq.). *History of Texas from Its First Settlement in 1685 to Its Annexation to the United States in 1846.* Vol. 1. New York: Redfield, 1855.

UNPUBLISHED SOURCES

Alexander, Drury B. "Dallas Historic Landmarks." Report prepared for City of Dallas, Department of Urban Planning, 1974.

Cretien, Charles F. "Early Days in Dallas and Oak Cliff 1856-1920." An unpublished history of La Reunion colony based on Cretien family papers. Dallas, 1963.

"Dallas Guide and History." An unpublished manuscript prepared for the American Guide Series; written and compiled by the Dallas Unit of the Texas Writers' Project of the Works Progress Administration, 1940.

Fisk, Hollye Carson. Project Proposal and Historic Structures Report for A. H. Belo Residence. Prepared for Dallas Bar Association by Burson, Hendricks and Walls, Architects and Planners, 1978.

Henry, Jay and Luby, Jack. "Status to Stasis, An Historical Examination of Oak Cliff, 1887-1975." Vols. 1 and 2. A research project of the School of Architecture and Design, University of Texas at Arlington, 1975.

Jebson, Harry; Newton, Robert M.; and Hogan, Patricia R. "Centennial History of the Dallas, Texas Park System 1876-1976." Unpublished report prepared for City of Dallas, Department of Park Administration, Landscape Architecture and Horticulture; in cooperation with the Department of History, Texas Tech University, 1976.

Rosenburg, Leon Joseph. "A Business History of Sanger Brothers, 1857-1926." An unpublished Ph.D. dissertation, New York University, 1967.

Woodcock, David G. "Some Influences on the Growth of Two Texas Cities." An unpublished research project, School of Architecture, Texas A&M University, 1966.

ACKNOWLEDGMENTS

The idea for this book occurred in the late summer of 1976 as I was doing research for an article on East Dallas which eventually appeared in the January, 1978, issue of *Dallas.* That article served as the catalyst of not only *Dallas Rediscovered,* but also of a major museum exhibition produced by the Dallas Historical Society covering the evolution of several early Dallas neighborhoods.

This publication was made possible through the encouragement and generosity of the Hoblitzelle Foundation, together with the Executive Committee and the staff of the Dallas Historical Society. The membership of the Executive Committee includes Robert M. Olmstead, Mrs. Reuben Adams, Henry C. Coke, Joe M. Dealey, Nelson Phillips, Jr., John R. Scott, William H. Seay, Mrs. Frederick M. Smith II, John M. Stemmons, A. W. Walker, and Robert A. Wilson. I am particularly grateful for the capable assistance and cooperation of the staff of the Dallas Historical Society under the direction of John W. Crain.

Gratitude is also extended to the members of the Special Advisory Board to the overall project for their perceptive suggestions and assistance. They include: Mayor Robert S. Folsom; Sidney Stahl, President, Dallas Park and Recreation Board; Lillian M. Bradshaw, Director, Dallas Public Library; Dr. Harvey Graff, University of Texas at Dallas; Louise W. Kahn; Weiming Lu, Program Manager of Urban Design, City of Dallas; Harry S. Parker III, Director, Dallas Museum of Fine Arts; James R. Pratt; Norman Ross; and Dr. R. Hal Williams, Chairman, Department of History, Southern Methodist University.

In my search for documents and photographs, the following people were most helpful: Lucile Boykin of the Geneology section and Lois Hudgins of the Texas Collection, Dallas Public Library; Dr. L. Tuffly Ellis, Texas State Historical Association; Dr. Chester V. Kielman, Barker Texas History Center; Lee Milazzo, Archivist, Southern Methodist University; Mary Kate Akkolla, Dallas *Times Herald;* Louis F. Gorr and Shirley Pettengill, Dallas County Heritage Society; Raymond R. Floyd, Richardson Historical Society; Ruth Chenoweth, Old Oak Cliff Conservation League; Mary Crain, Historic Preservation League; Gerry Cristol, Temple Emanu-el; William Clark, First Presbyterian Church; Mary Reynolds, Hockaday School; Sister Adelaide Mars, Bishop Dunne High School; Betty Ensminger, Buckner Baptist Benevolences; Pat Fought, St. Paul's Hospital; David Nixon and Jean Baker, State Fair of Texas; J. Hamilton Coleman, Southwest Book Services Inc.; Mrs. Max Clampitt, William Sparkman, Mrs. Thomas Burke, Mrs. Elisabeth Morse, Royal A. Ferris III, Mrs. Samuel Shelburne, William Crawford, Mrs. Julian Capers, Mr. and Mrs. John N. Jackson, Mrs. Claude McGlamery, Musti Roller, Mr. and Mrs. William Temple Spencer, Donald Payton, Mrs. Manning B. Shannon Jr., Ann Roberts, Billie Vincent, Charles E. Coldwell, Burt Blanton, Barrett Sanders, Mrs. Katherine Houghton, Joe Holley, Mrs. Franklin Reeves, Mary Padgitt, Sarah Meriwether, Mrs. Harriet Lang Worsham, Mrs. Johanna Lang Frost, Rawlins Thompson, Mrs. Edward Maher, Morris Friedman, Jack Gordon, Joe Rucker, Mrs. Hazael Beckett, Fred Longmore, Mrs. Margaret Scuggs-Carruth, L. James Wathen, L. B. Houston, Hugh E. Prather, Mrs. J. B. McEntire, Jr., and Al Reynolds.

Some of those who read the early drafts and

contributed much wise counsel and informed criticism during the writing of the text were: Mrs. Max Clampitt, A. C. Greene, Mr. and Mrs. W. L. McDonald Jr., James Pratt, Lonn Taylor, Curator of History to the Dallas Historical Society, and Dr. R. Hal Williams.

I am most appreciative for the experienced judgment and skill of the book's editor, Karen Dewees, who organized and corrected the manuscript with meticulous care; for the superbly imaginative layout and design by Fred and Barbara Whitehead of Austin; and for the finely crafted maps by Charles McMahan of Southwest Book Services. I am also deeply grateful for the patient editorial and organizational assistance of Candace Hagan of the Society staff. I was continually impressed by her insight and by her dedication to details in the revision and typing of each succeeding draft of the manuscript. If *Dallas Rediscovered* is found deserving of praise, it is because of the devoted efforts of all of these people.

INDEX